I've Been Walking

In 2020, like so many of us—especially those who take photographs—I've been walking.

For me, walking and taking photographs have felt especially vital because for much of 2019, I couldn't walk. A year of Injuries, among them serious fractures as well as surgeries kept me out of commission. I lost my health; I also lost creative time. As an artist who arrived at photography late in life, I felt that loss of time acutely.

Now, thanks to intense physical therapies and with deep gratitude, I'm back to myself, able to walk without support and with camera in hand. From the beginning of the Covid-19 pandemic here in Los Angeles—March, 2020 when we were told to stay at home and mostly did—I've been walking, protected by mask and gloves but under the spell of the virus and what it has done to my city.

I've been walking through Los Angeles' streets with heightened intensity, in Downtown's Little Tokyo where I live in one of L.A.'s oldest communally active neighborhoods, now mostly shuttered, and in nearby alleys of vibrant open-air shops that remind me of Mexican markets, now closed. I've walked with tears in my eyes remembering when my father's small market went bankrupt. On all sides, so many aspirations dashed.

At first, I saw mostly desolation, then gradually traces of human presence began to assert themselves—a vase in a shop window reflecting faces in a poster at the Japanese American National Museum; faded photographs in display cases along the outside walls of the abandoned Los Angeles Times building. For the latter, I've been standing in front of those recessed images at different hours of the day, returning over time to choose a detail and photograph what is in front of me and also behind me as reflected in the scratched glass. Past and present fuse in the moment.

I'm not documenting Los Angeles during the pandemic. Nor am I trying to present a comprehensive view of the city. Rather I want these images to be a meeting place of my way of seeing and the world out there.

As always, I am attracted to odd juxtapositions (although I don't know they are odd at the moment I take the photograph); to formal composition that doesn't insist on its formal qualities; to the collapse of foreground and background as well as other conventional spatial distinctions; and always to the ravishment of color. Then there's a quality that I can sense—of something more in the images that I choose to keep, of layers and metaphors that refuse to be reduced to only one meaning.

As in the past, I am interested in what goes unseen. And as always, I choose to use no digital or optical manipulation (not a technological aversion but a practice). At an earlier time in my photography, I had wanted to meld front and back, inside and outside, solid and fluid by means of reflection and a disposable camera, so that everything in the image would blur and interpenetrate. I remain interested in the multi-dimensional possibilities within a single moment, but now that I'm using a different camera—also low tech but more advanced—it's easier for me to make sharper photographs if I want them. And I do. In a world desperately afraid of infection, I feel uncomfortable emphasizing porosity.

There is another difference between the new work in this book and the photographs in my 2016 monograph, *OVERSPILLING WORLD*. That book celebrated abundance. This past year though has witnessed a world drained, of people as we have been used to seeing them in social landscapes of streets and gatherings, and of the vitality that human beings give off. During these months, there have been times when the threat seems to lessen and the world fills up again, all too often at our cost. And then we go back to a world that often feels, and is, empty, lonely as we learn to live in unfamiliar singularity. At times too, in this enforced lessening, I have felt my own mind and eyes to be sharper, fuller.

Complexity remains, and it is that which I want to reveal through my images. In a public presentation that accompanied a 2018 exhibition of my work at the University of Southern California Fisher Museum of Art, border studies scholar Juan De Lara put it well: *Sternburg's photos are methodological interventions because they insist that "ambiguity and complexity prevail.... Her photographs represent what art historian Gavin Grindon and curator Catherine Flood have called "disobedient objects" because they disrupt how we see the world... they represent radical imaginaries for what is possible."*

Disobedient objects: that phrase joins others that have come into my life as gifts. Merleau-Ponty's "living perception" is another such, a beautiful notion that perception Is alive as much as any other aliveness in the world. And now aliveness is given to objects, whether used for protests as in the authors' original meaning or for that flicker of agency by which objects can assert their presence.

In a way that is new to me, these photographs are impersonal in the sense that they feel as though they have been given to me, appearing and accepted without my judgement. Until the very recent images in this book, my choices in both photography and writing were informed by a high degree of subjectivity. I was, even if sometimes unknowingly, looking for something that would become part of the larger schema of a project, turning what I was seeing into what I was seeking. Instead, I've discovered the gift of negative capability – a suspension that is often attributed to writers, now present in myself as a photographer. These photographs are obdurate. They move from thereness to hereness. This individual, (inevitably *I*), restored after a period of disability, is now querying what it is *to be* and, if she is lucky, surprised afterward by its appearance as an image.

In these past months, I've gone to the geographical edges of Los Angeles County, where I walked photographing what I've come to think of as a kind of fullness—an enlargement of the senses that can be found in the midst of emptiness—and of beauty gained through looking at what is revealed between the bare branches of loss. I do not mean to turn the griefs and losses caused by Covid into artistic gain. I do mean that we are enlarged when we become part of the landscape of all of us. I walked near the ocean at Point Fermin at the southern tip of Los Angeles and in the fold of mountains that is Green Valley near the northern edge, threatened by the wildfires of 2020. I've walked with hope and despair in my lens, often together, and sometimes—thank goodness—mingled with delight in discovery.

I've been hearing people say that it is difficult for them to cope with the present uncertainty. My own belief is that we were never promised certainty. Art, however—making it, experiencing it—can clear paths to go forward in uncertain times. There is a line I love in a poem by Antonio Machado: *Traveler, there is no path, you make the path as you walk*. This book is that path.

Janet Sternburg
Los Angeles, 2021

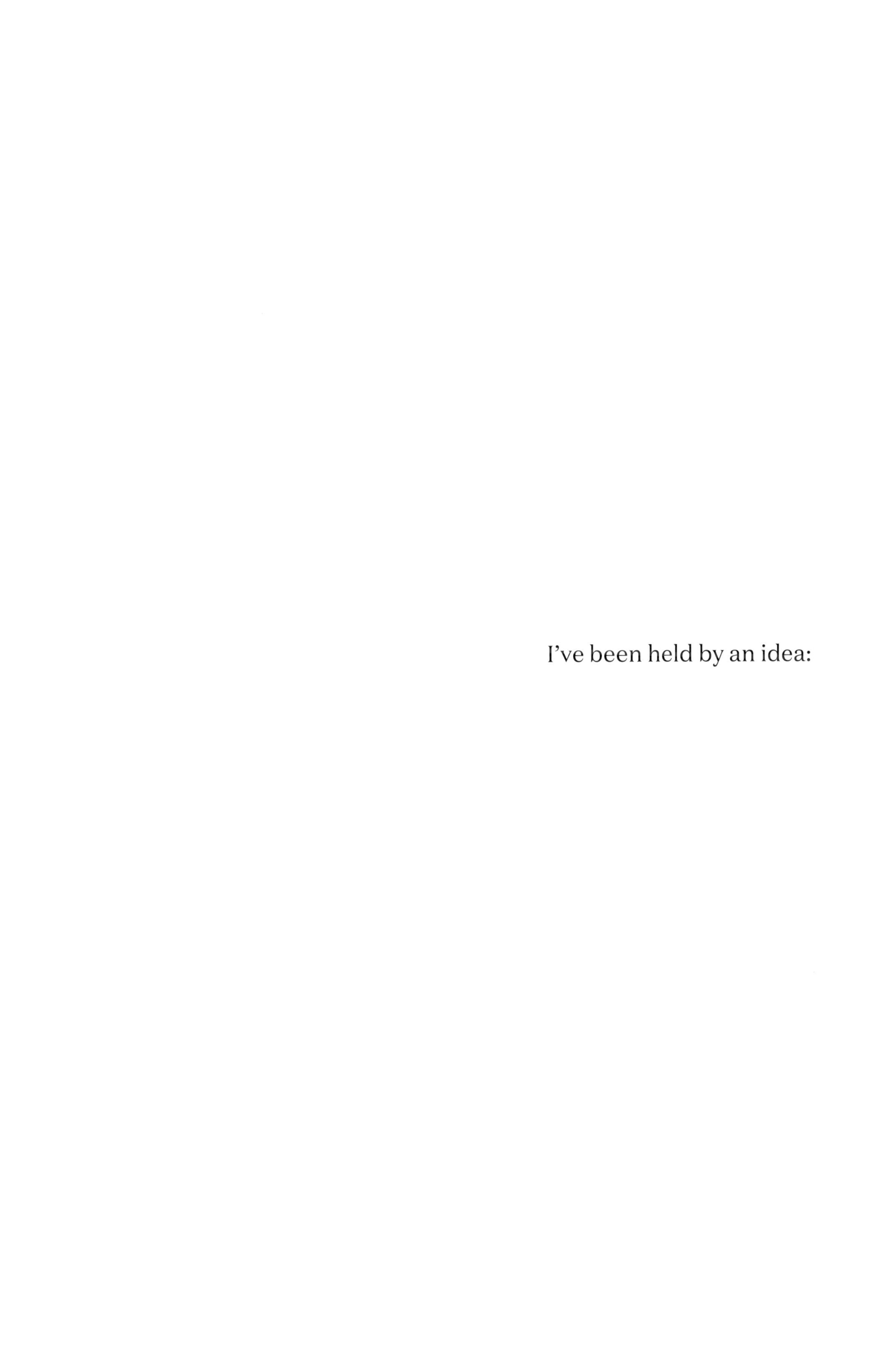

I’ve been held by an idea:

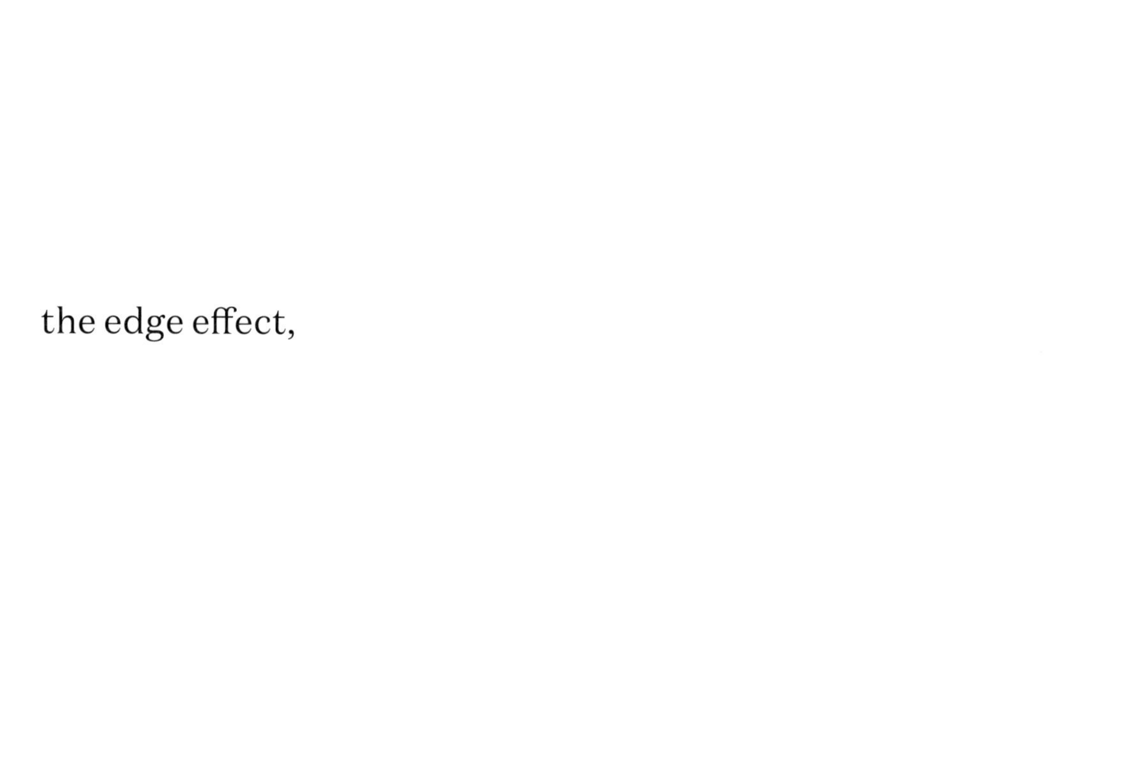

the edge effect,

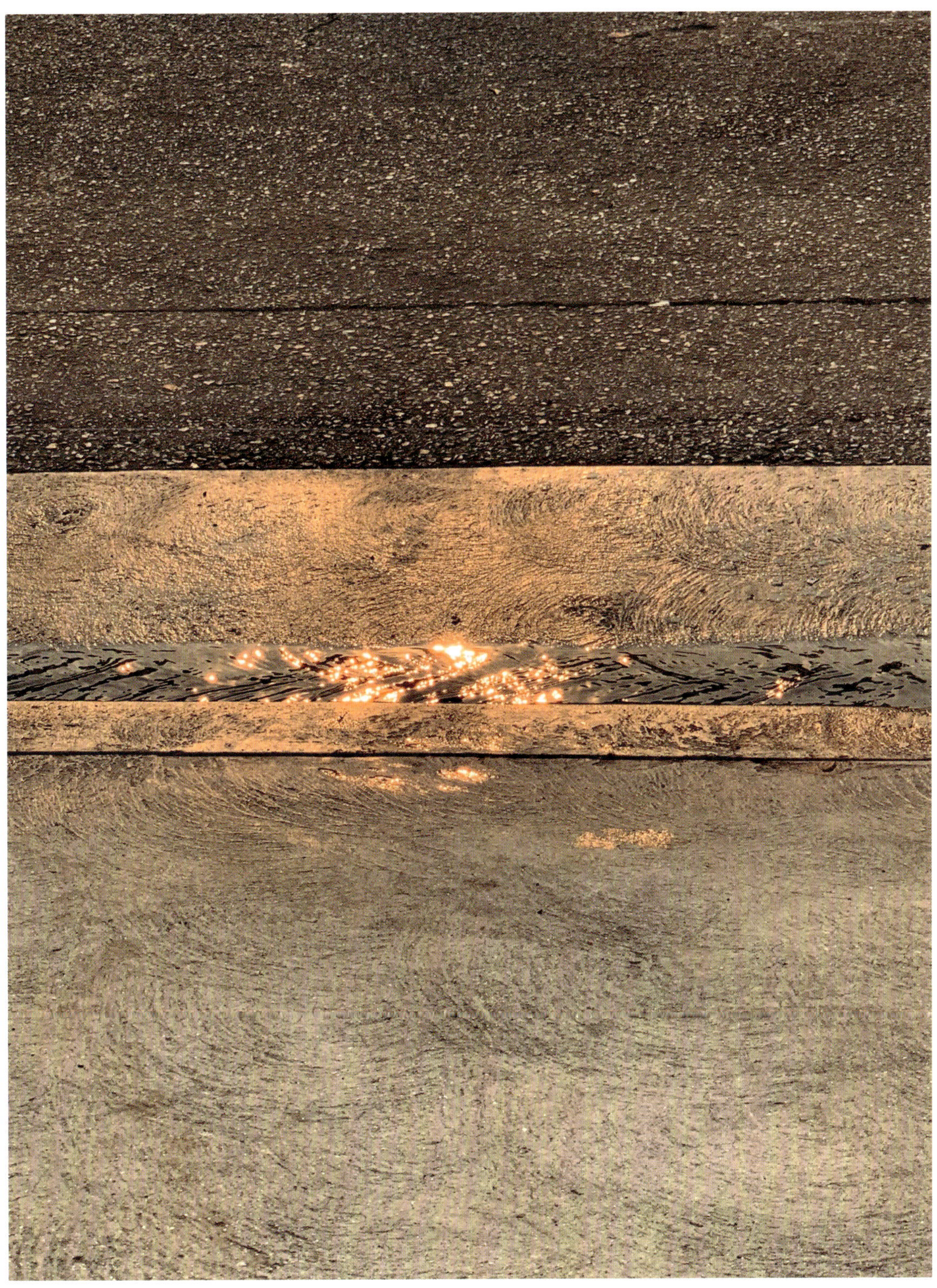

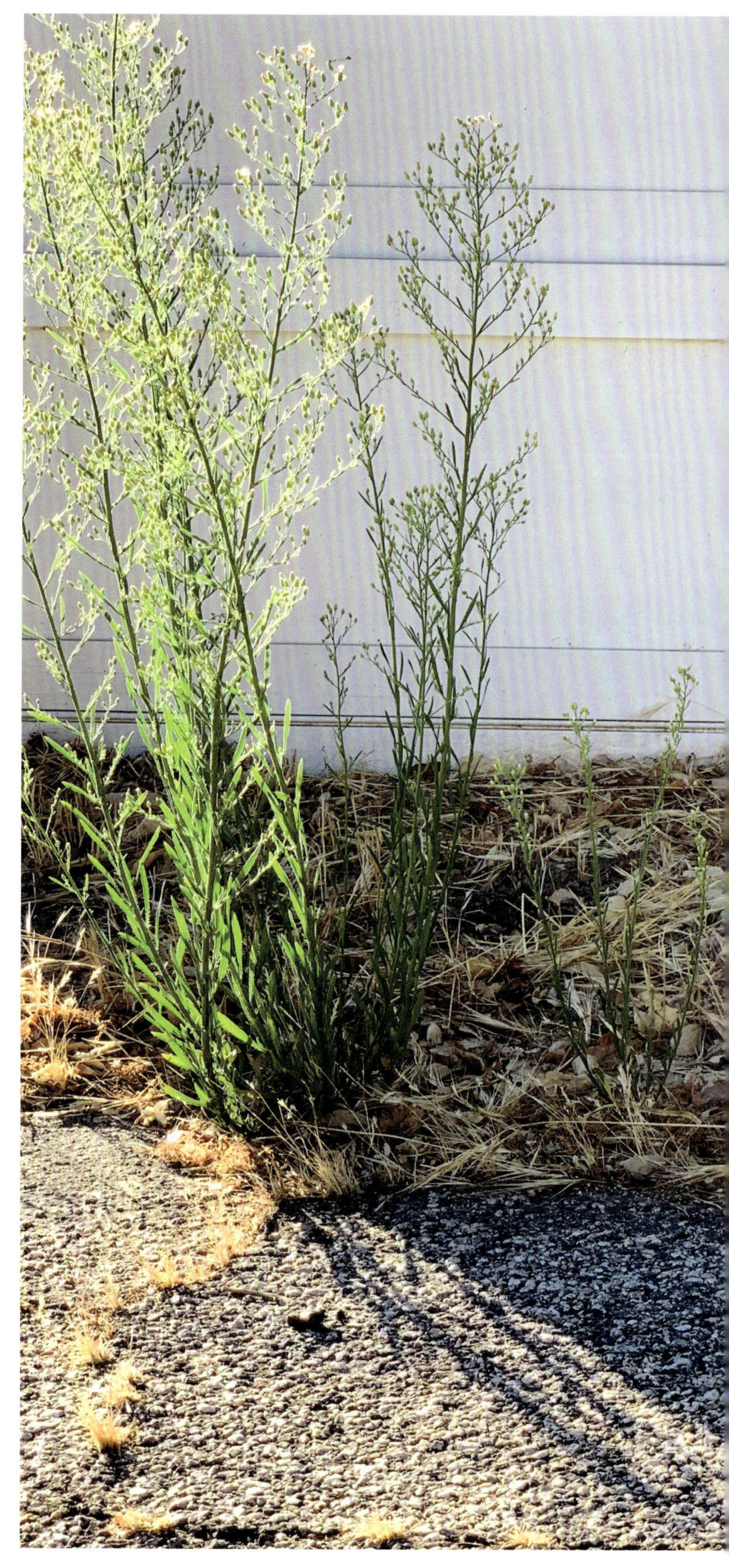

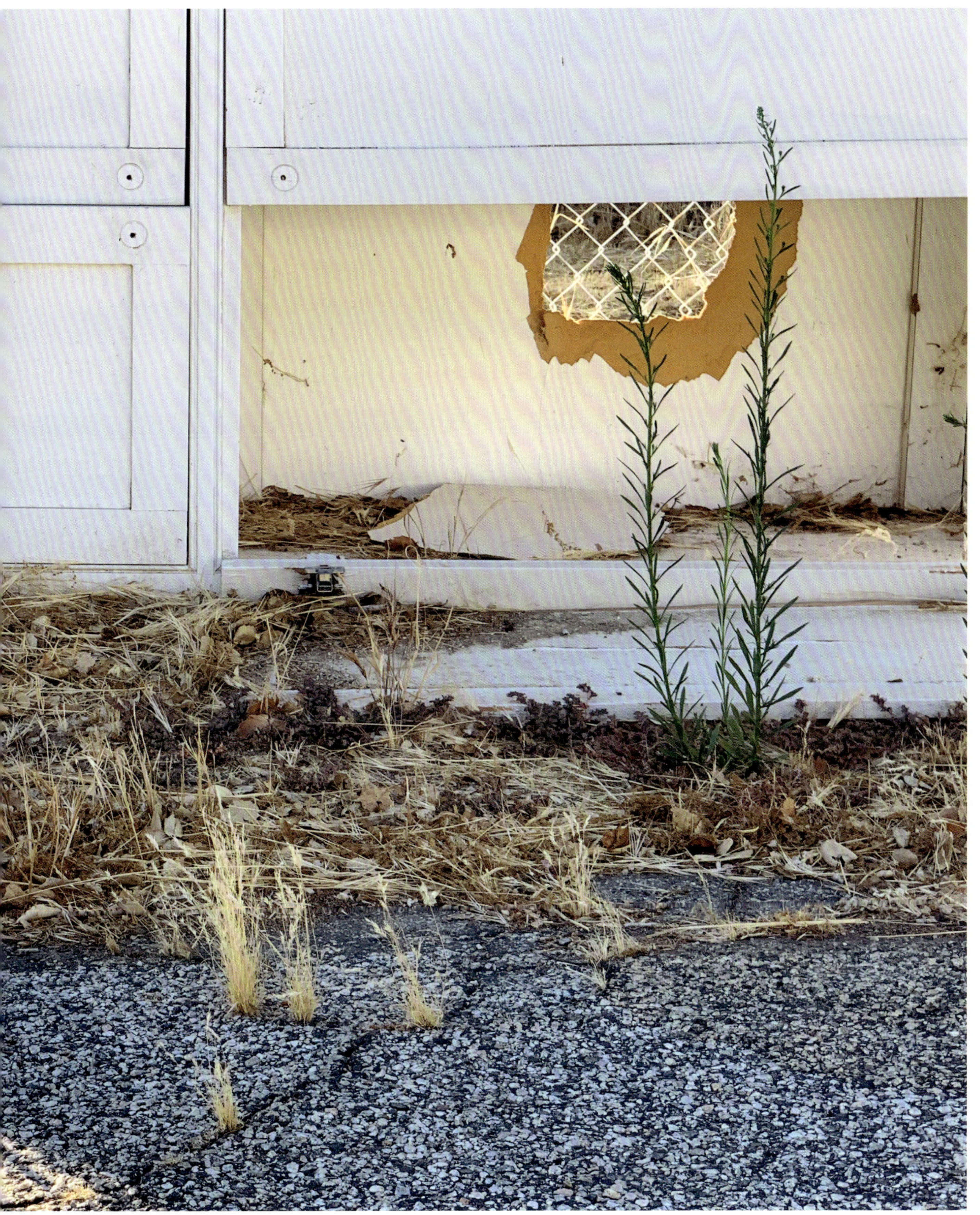

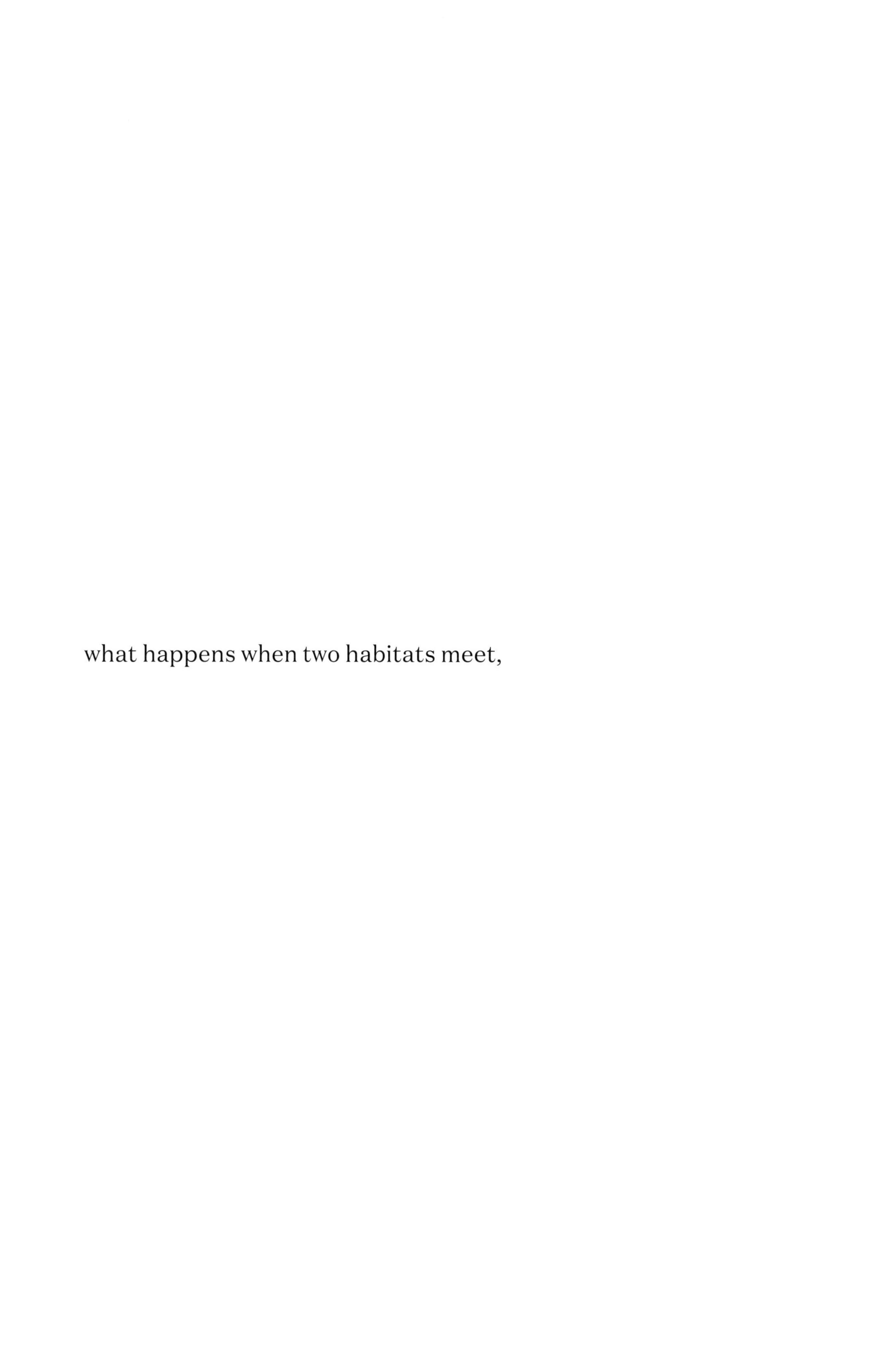

what happens when two habitats meet,

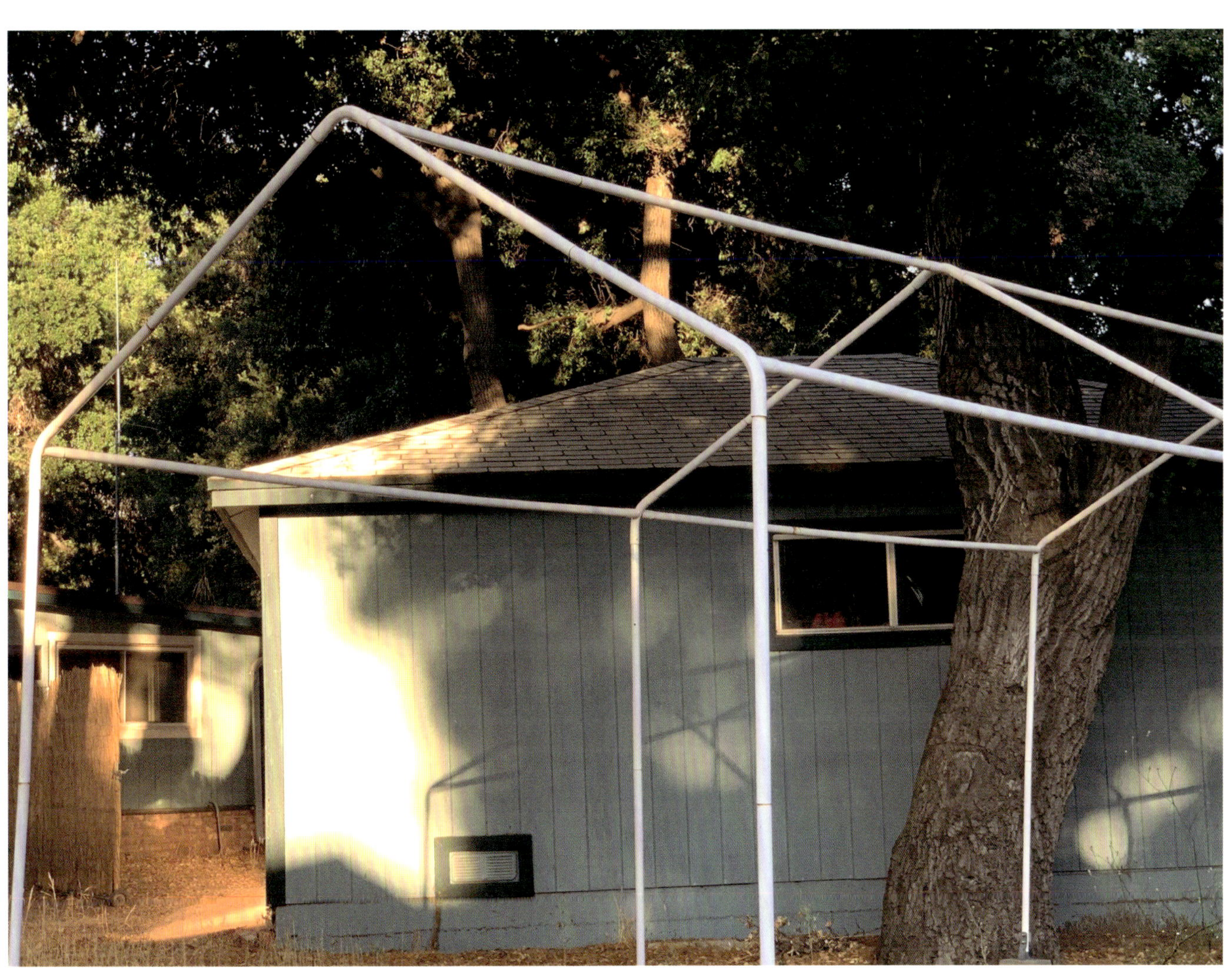

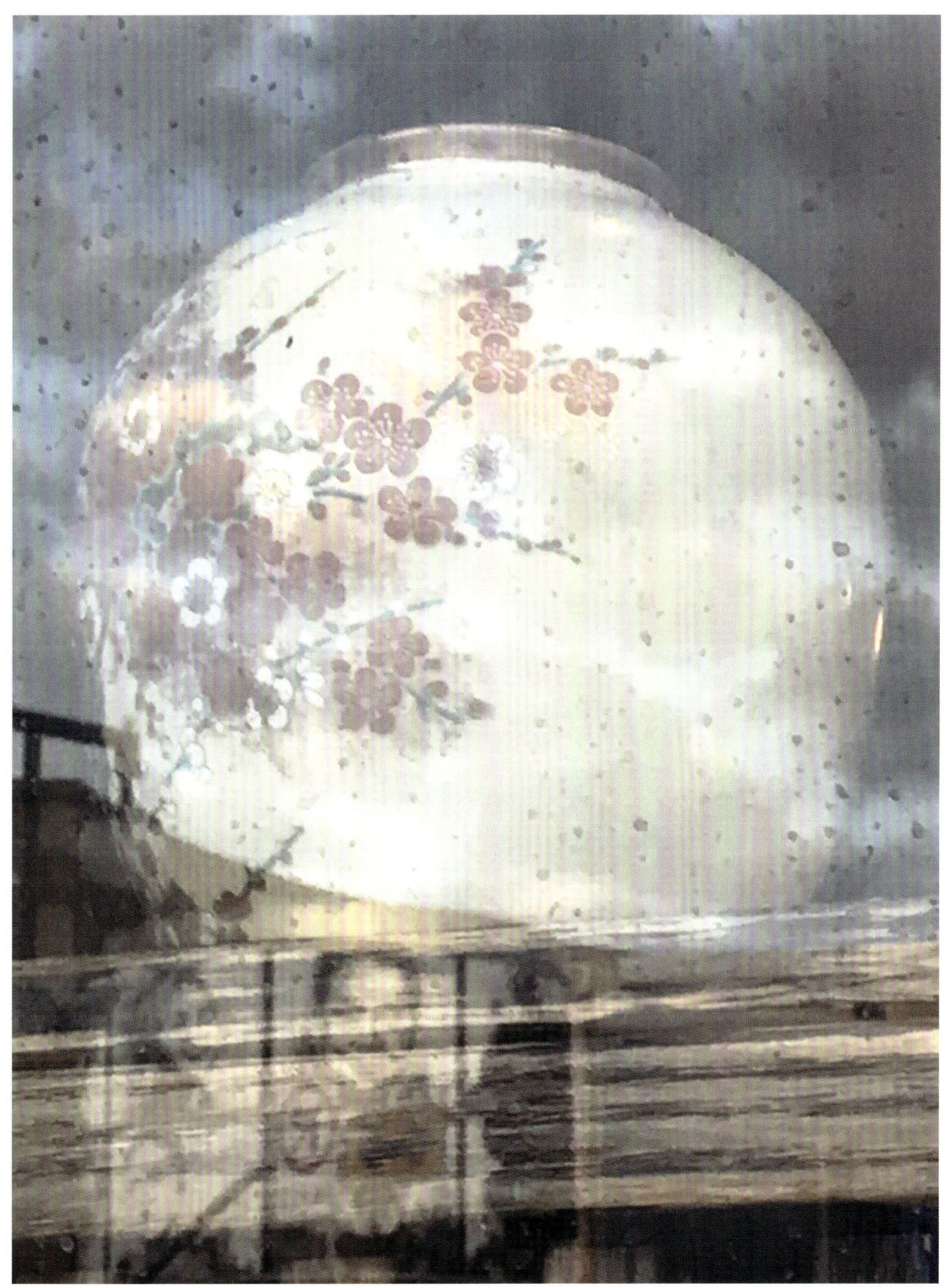

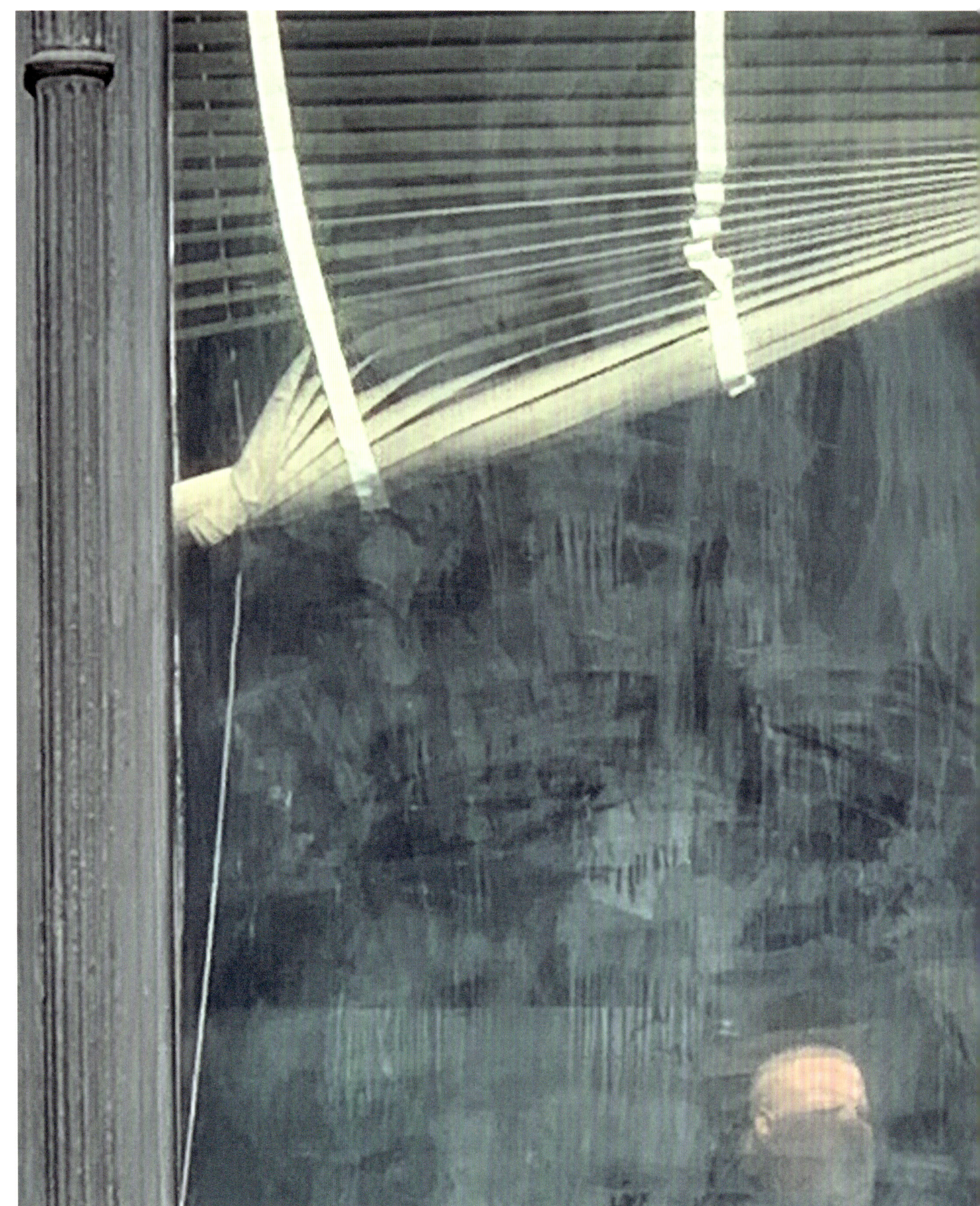

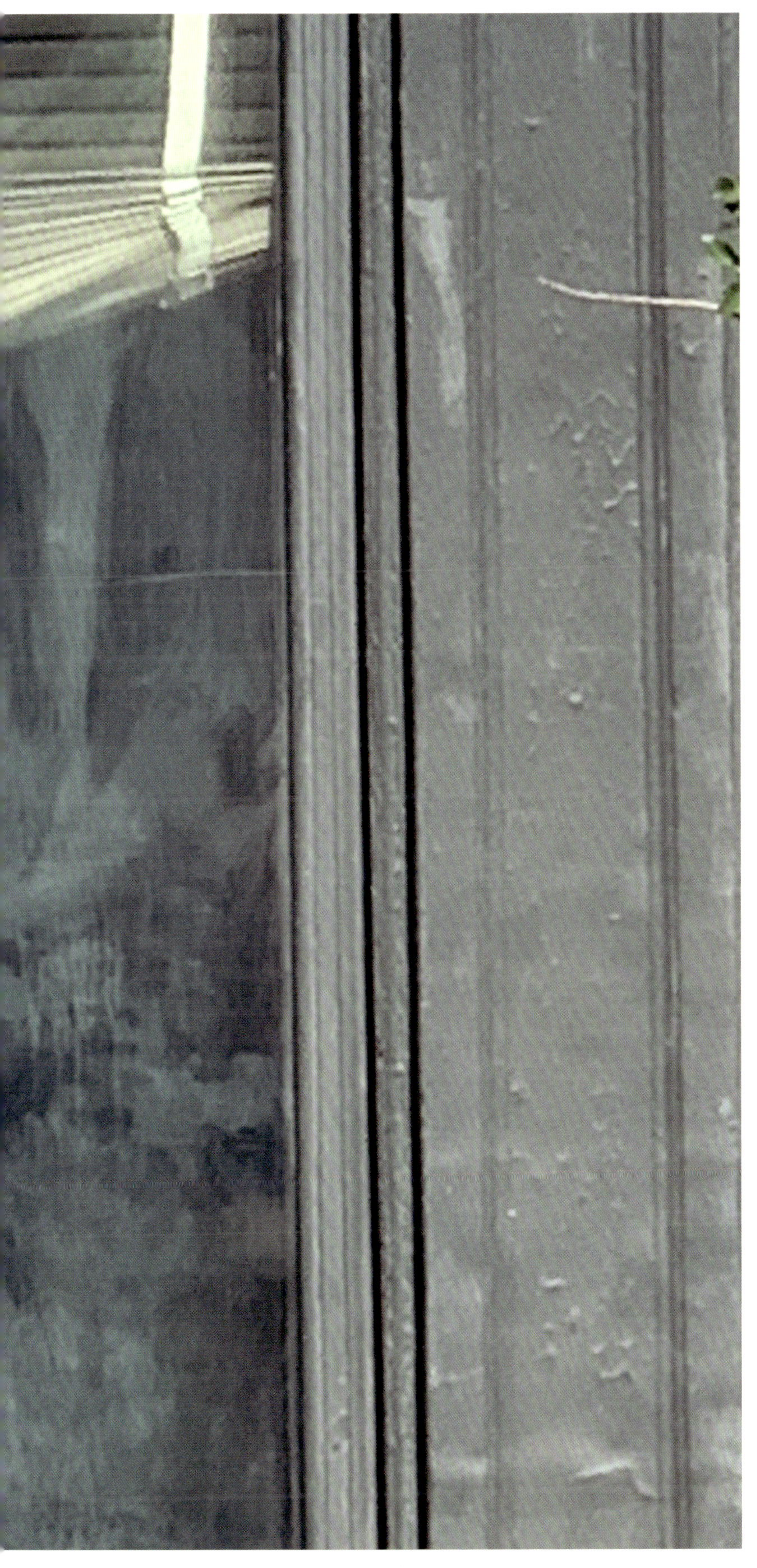

“the threshold

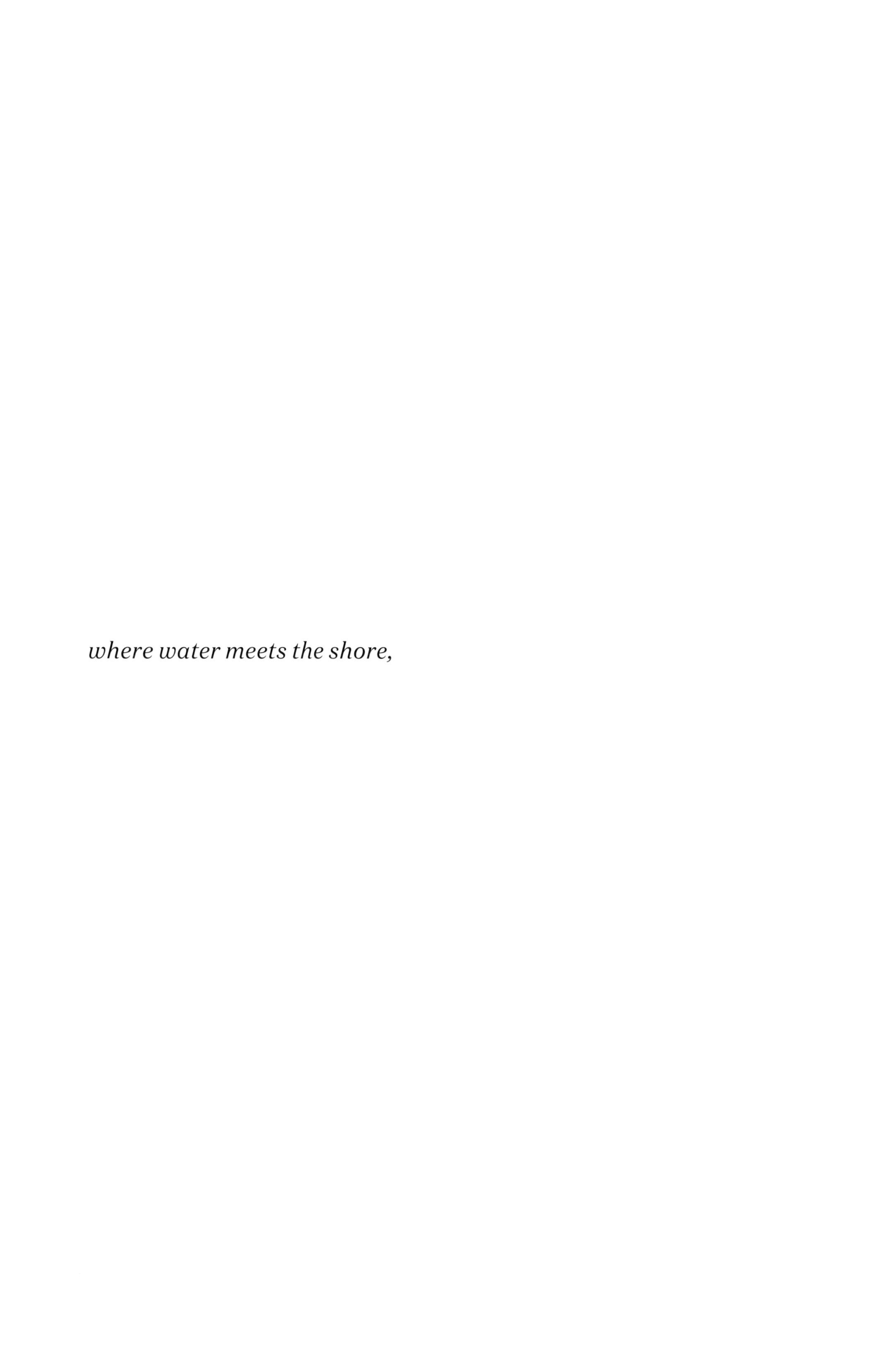

where water meets the shore,

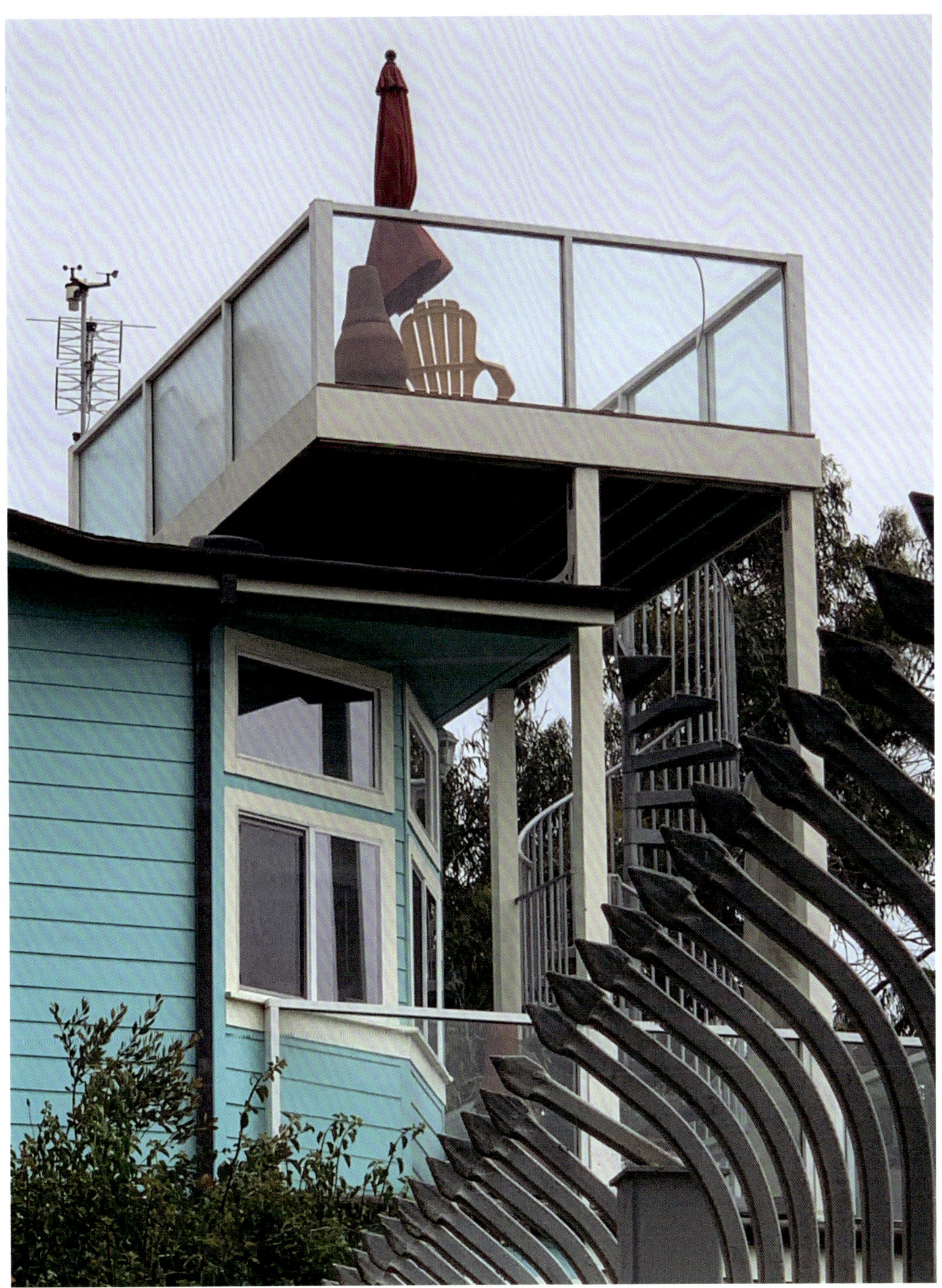

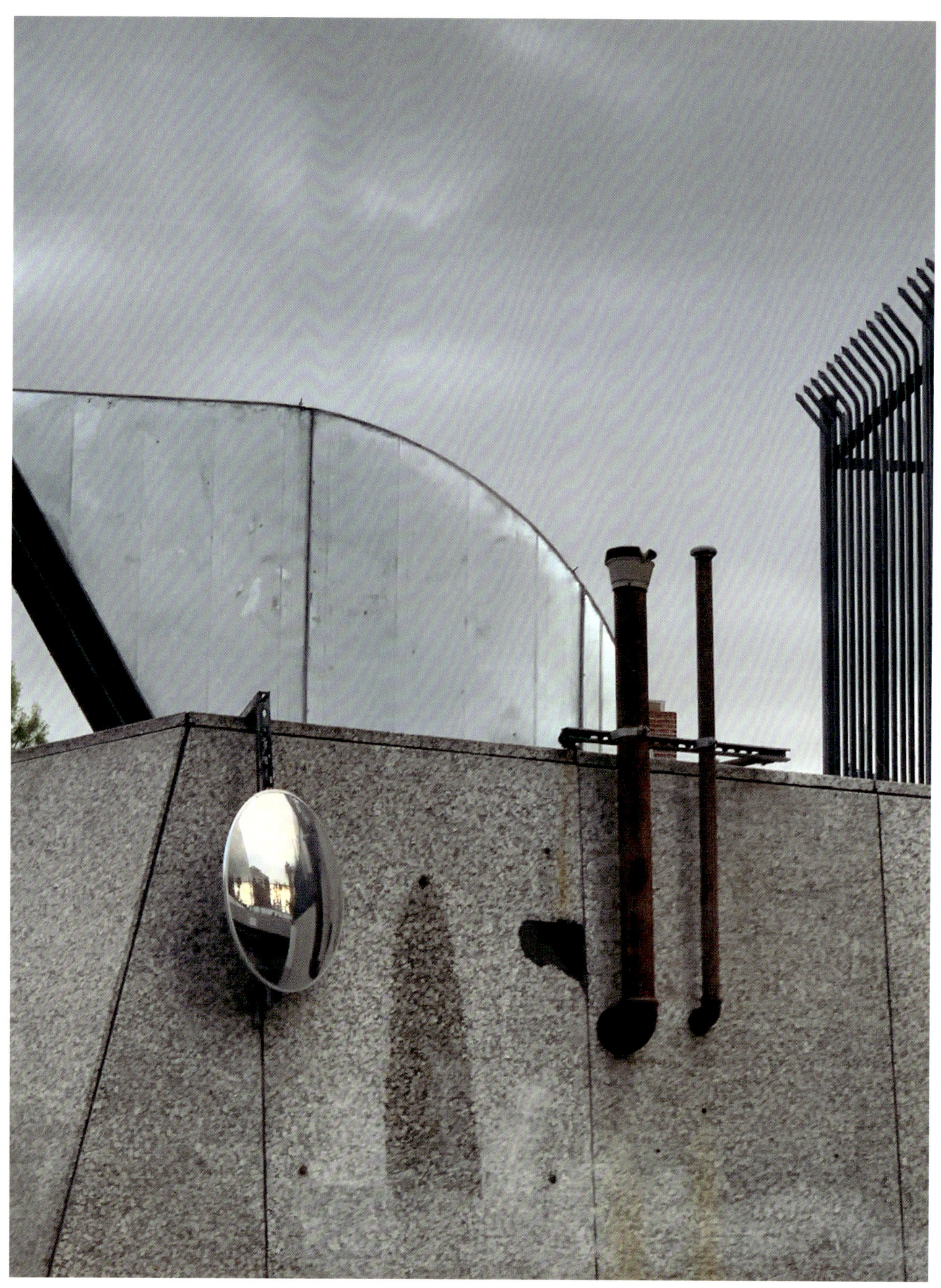

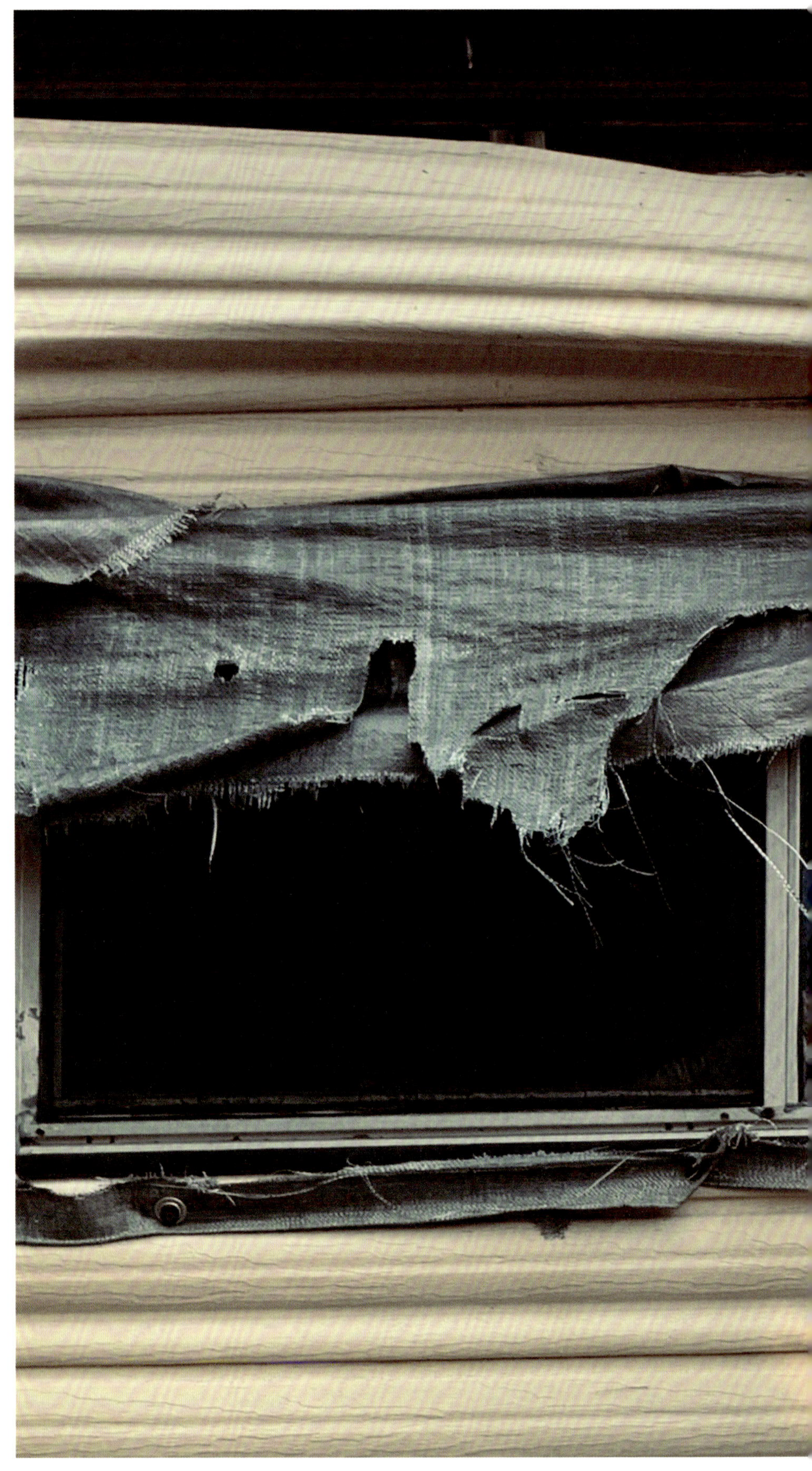

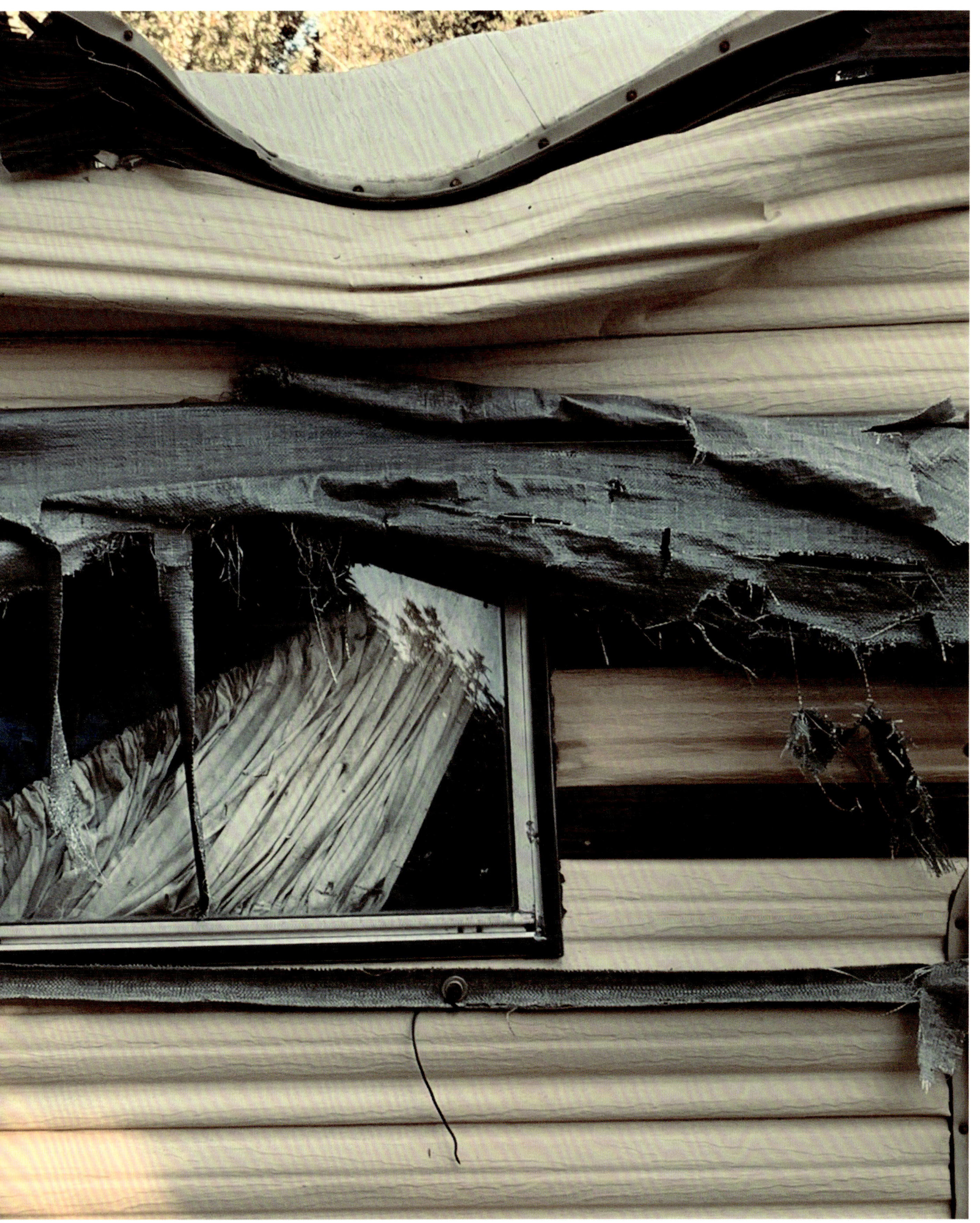

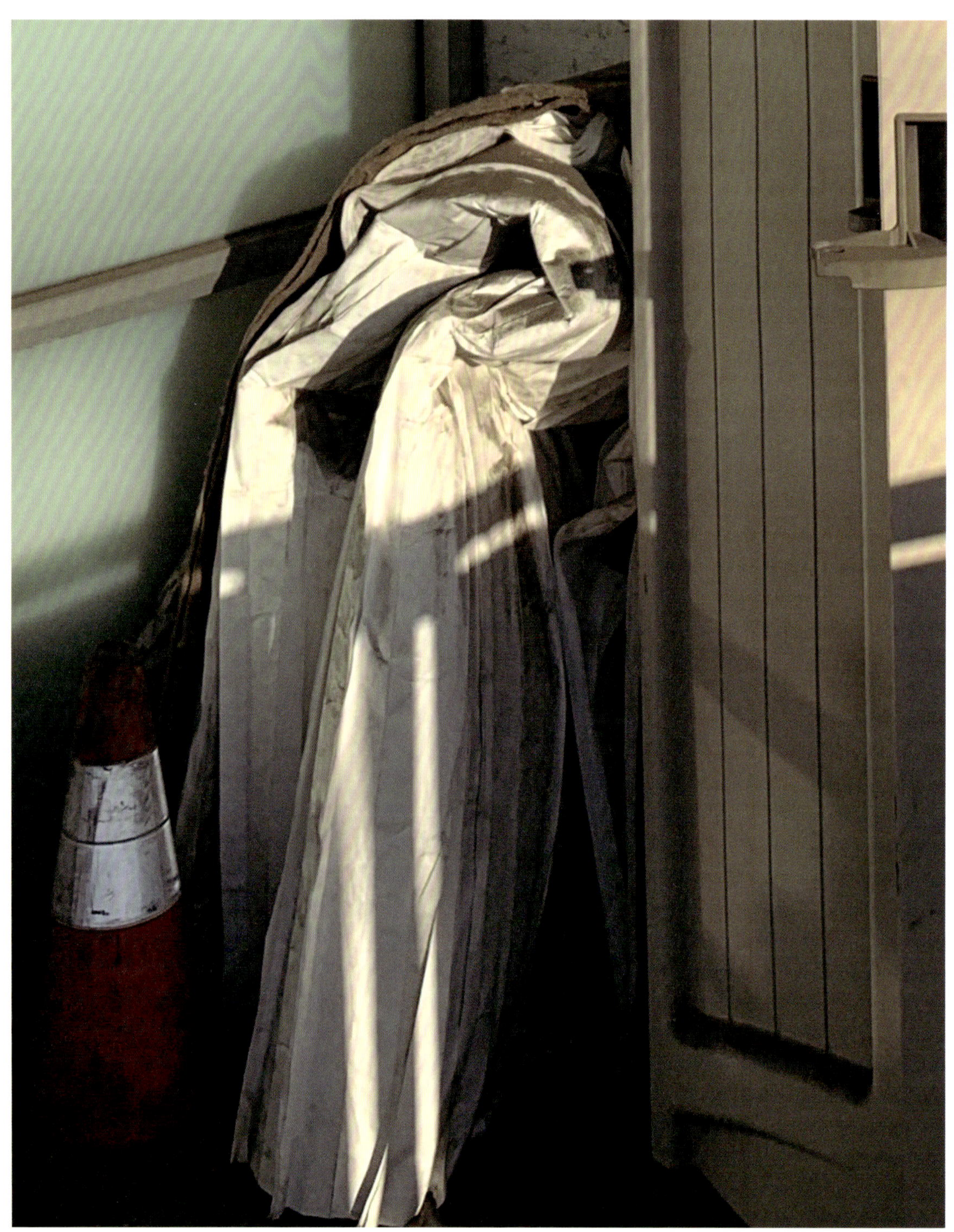

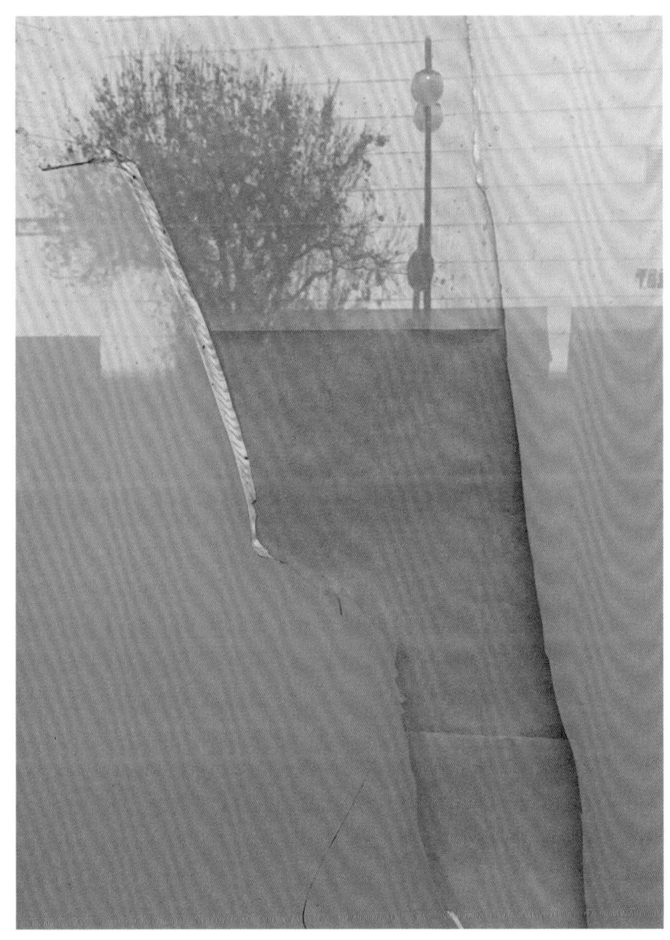

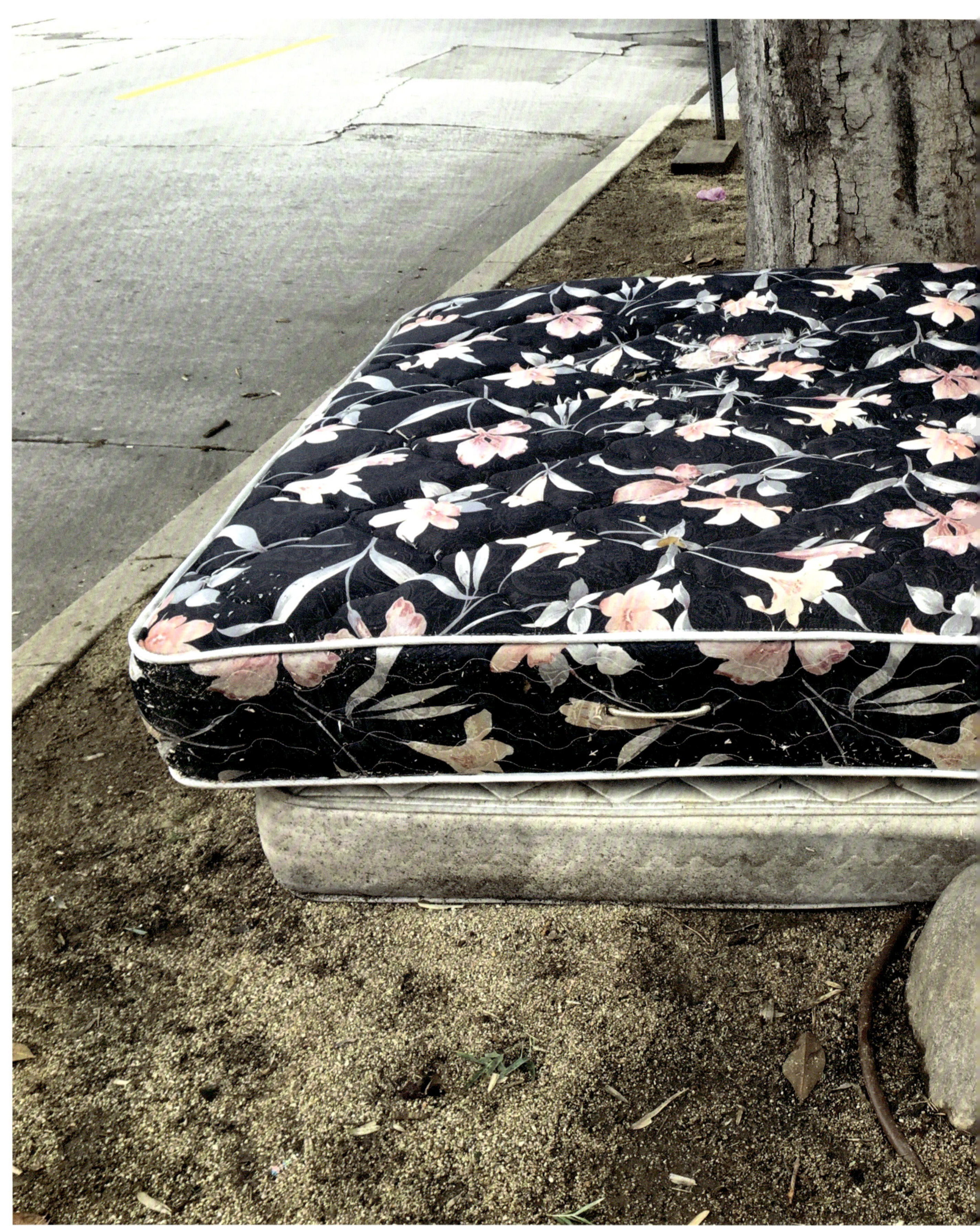

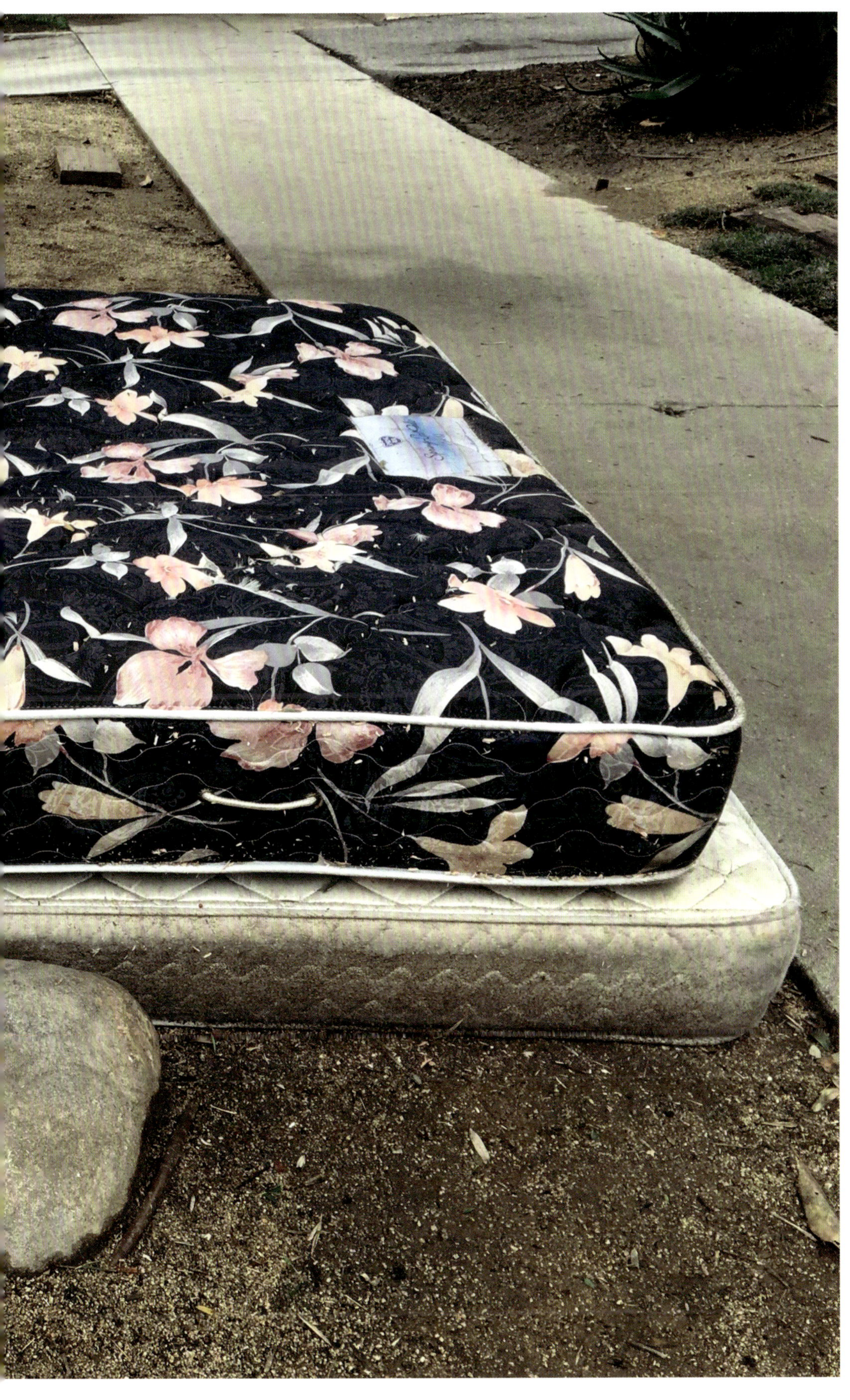

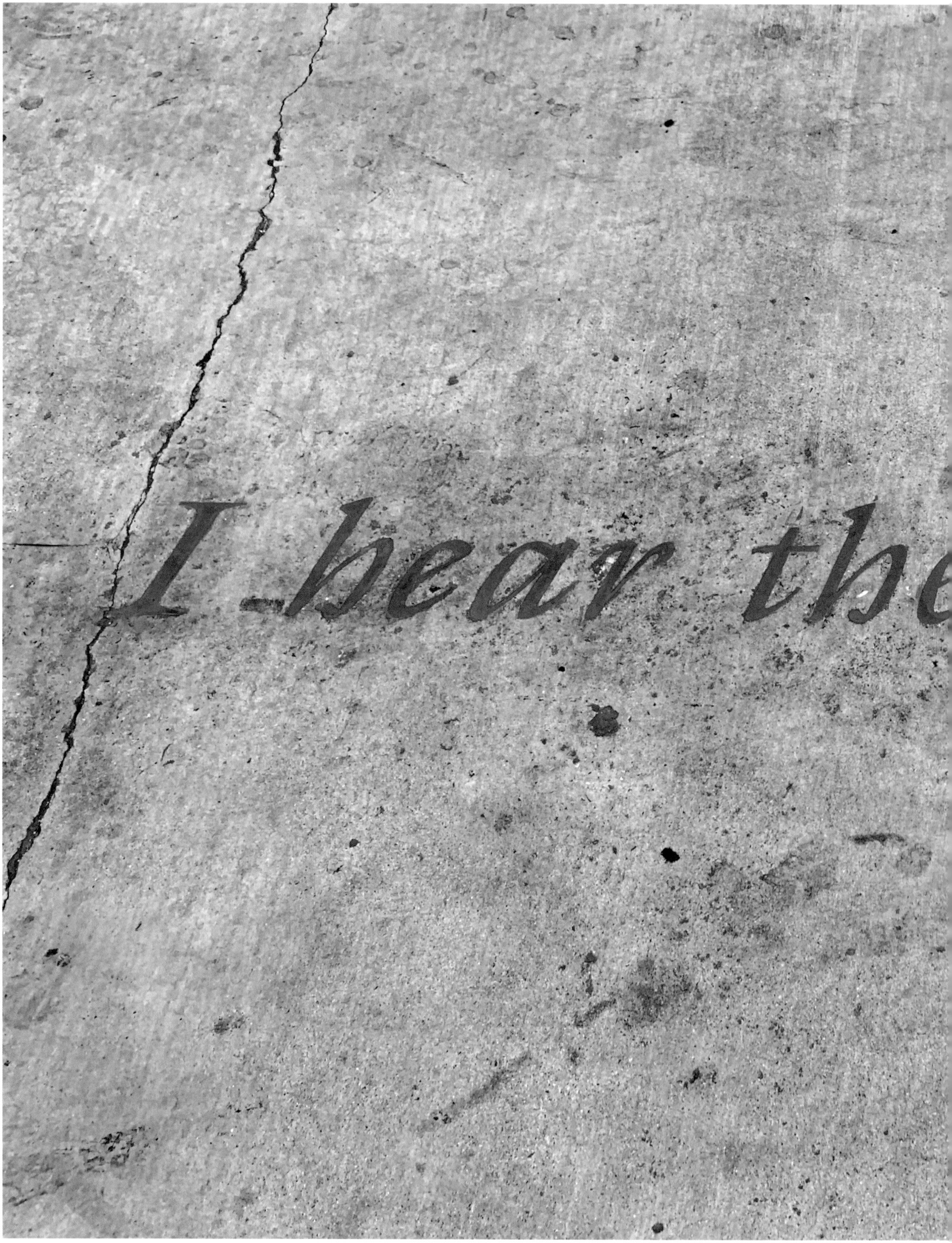

I bear the

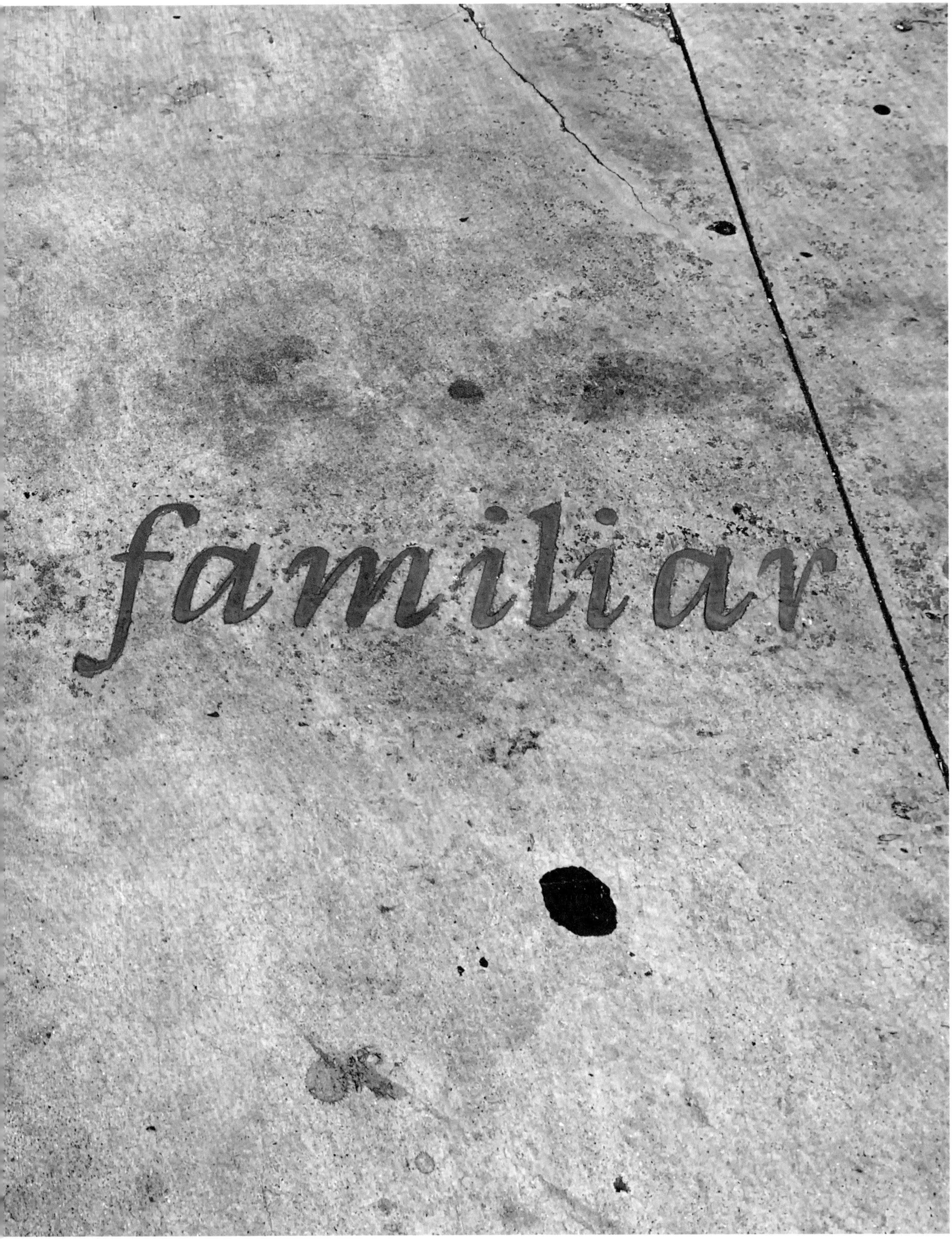

familiar

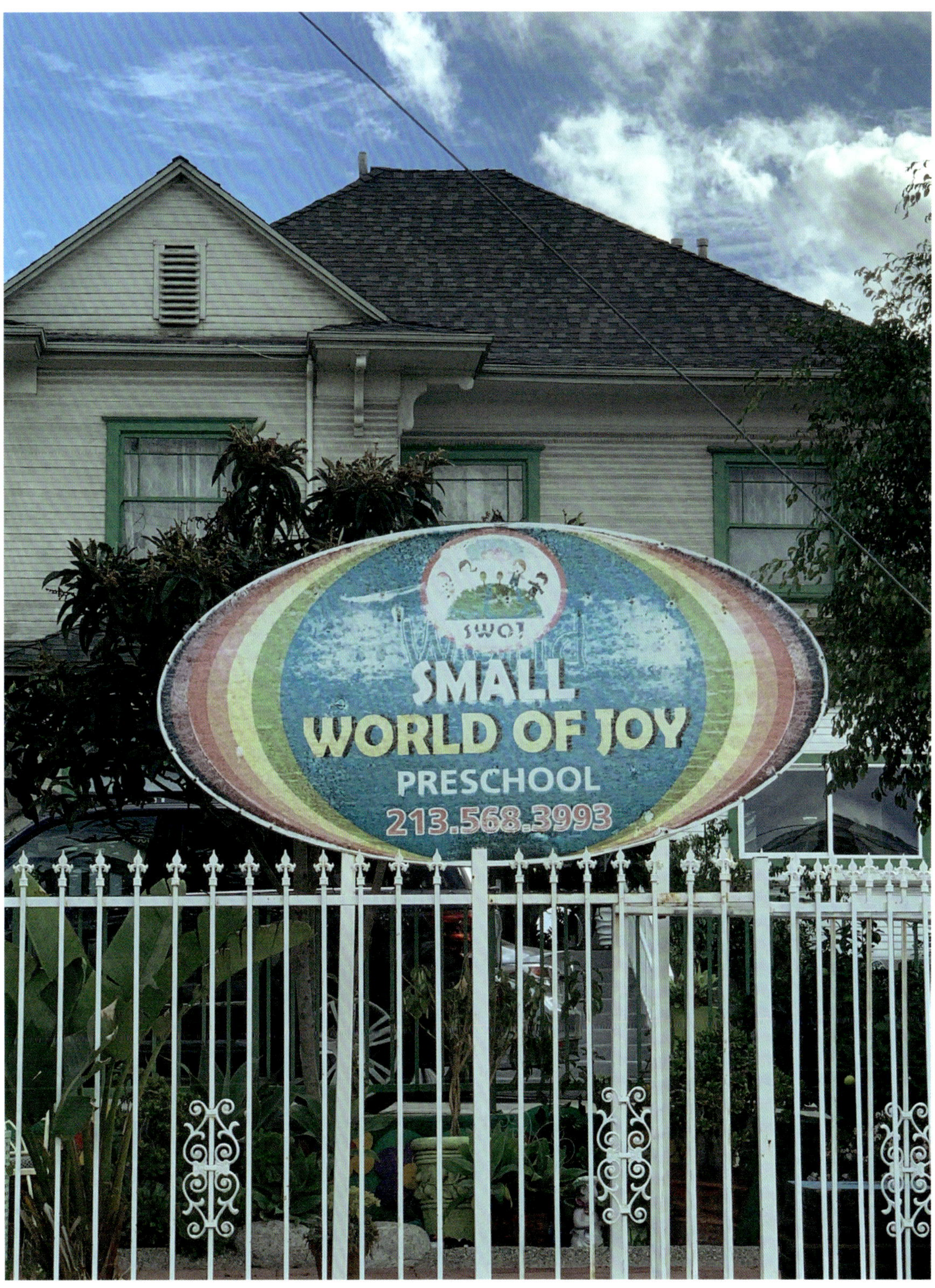
SWOJ
SMALL
WORLD OF JOY
PRESCHOOL
213.568.3993

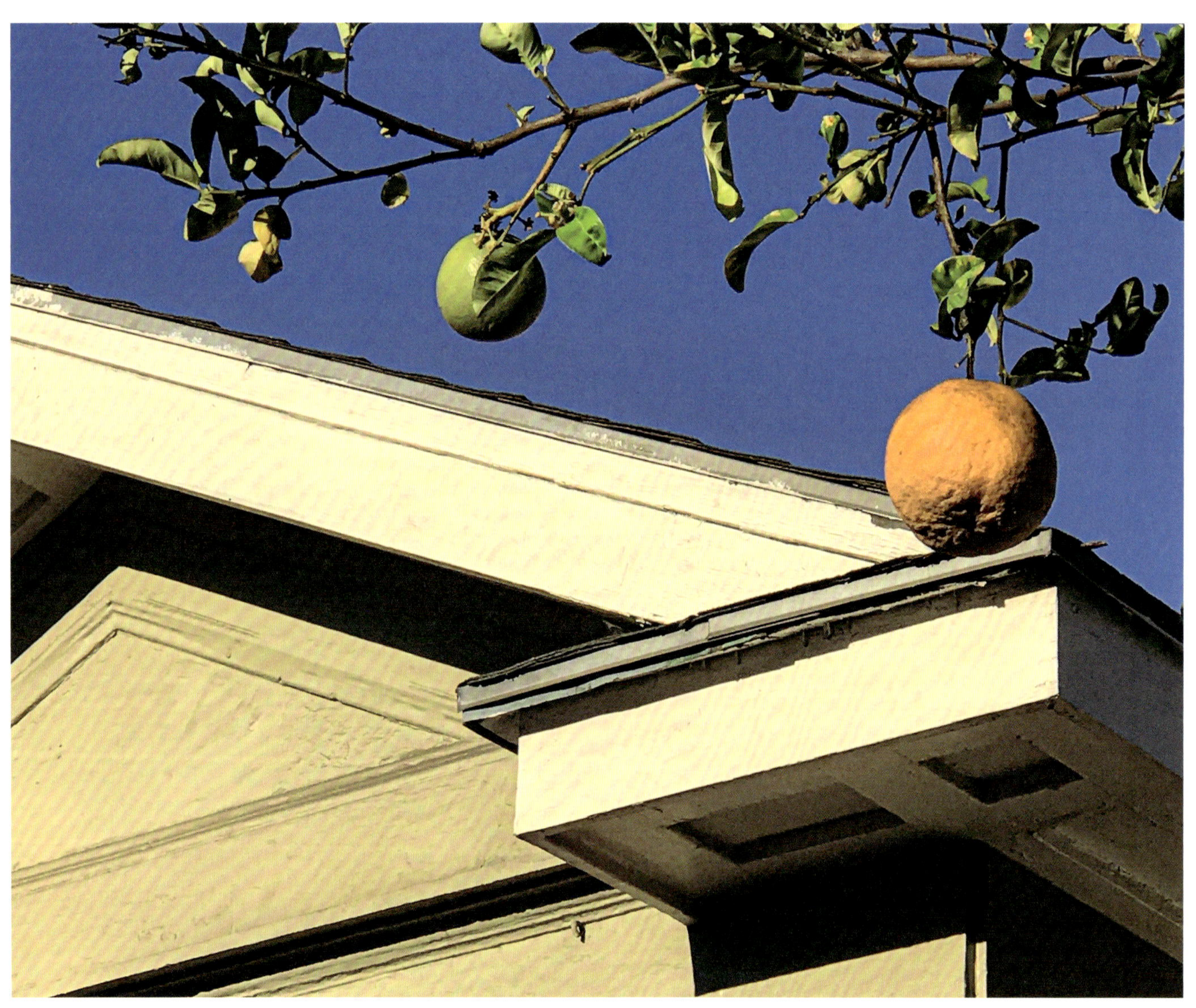

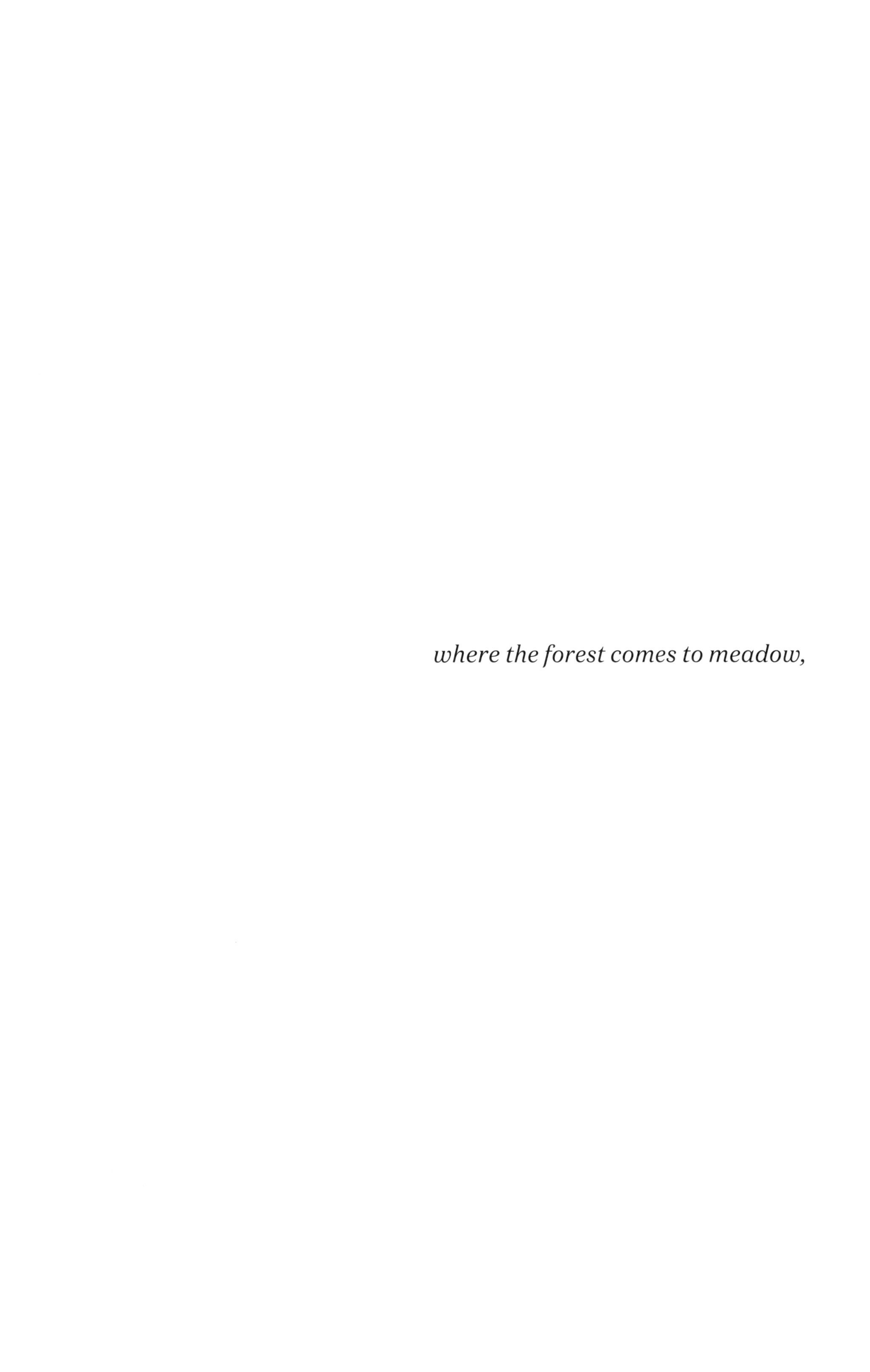

where the forest comes to meadow,

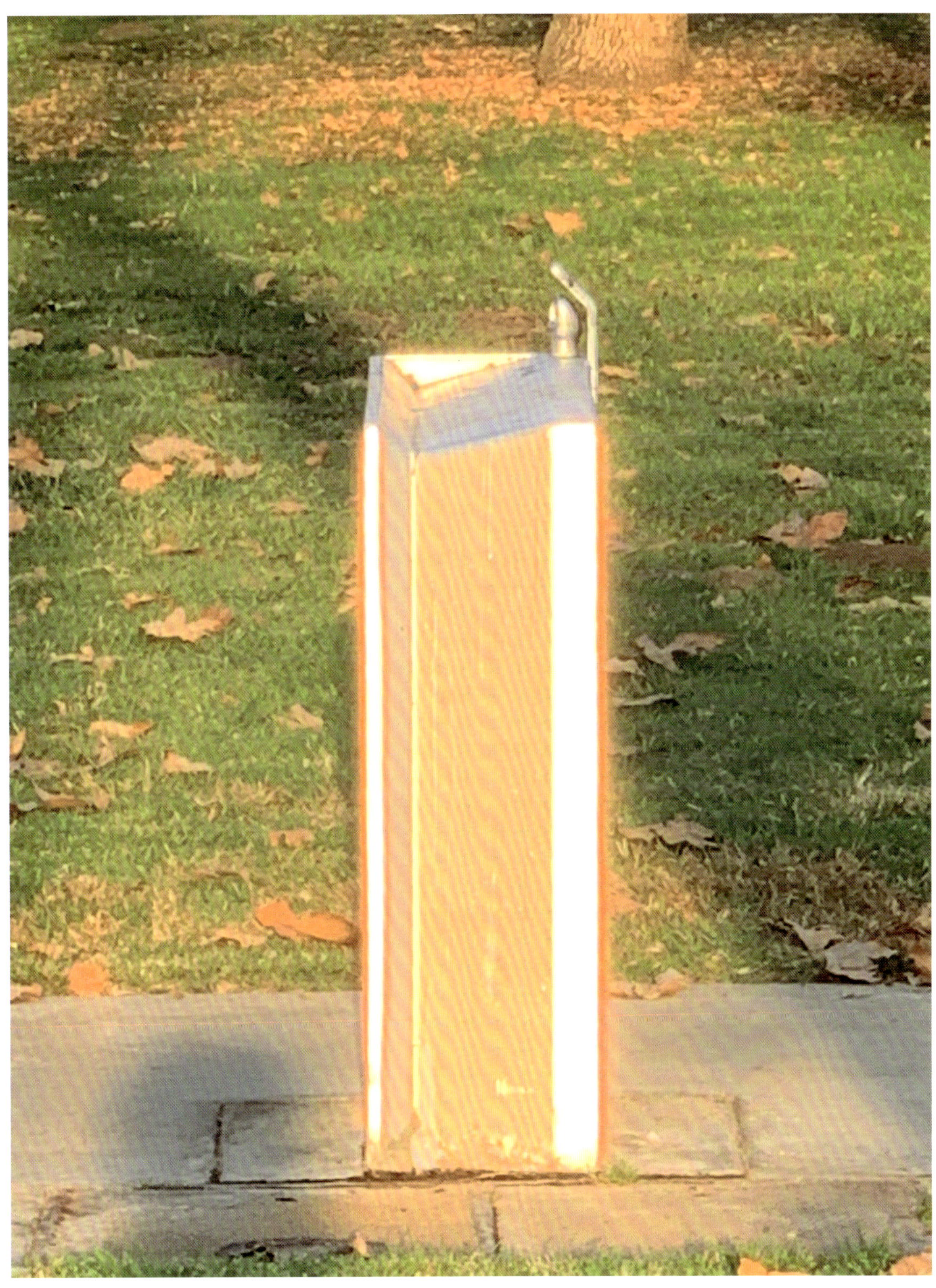

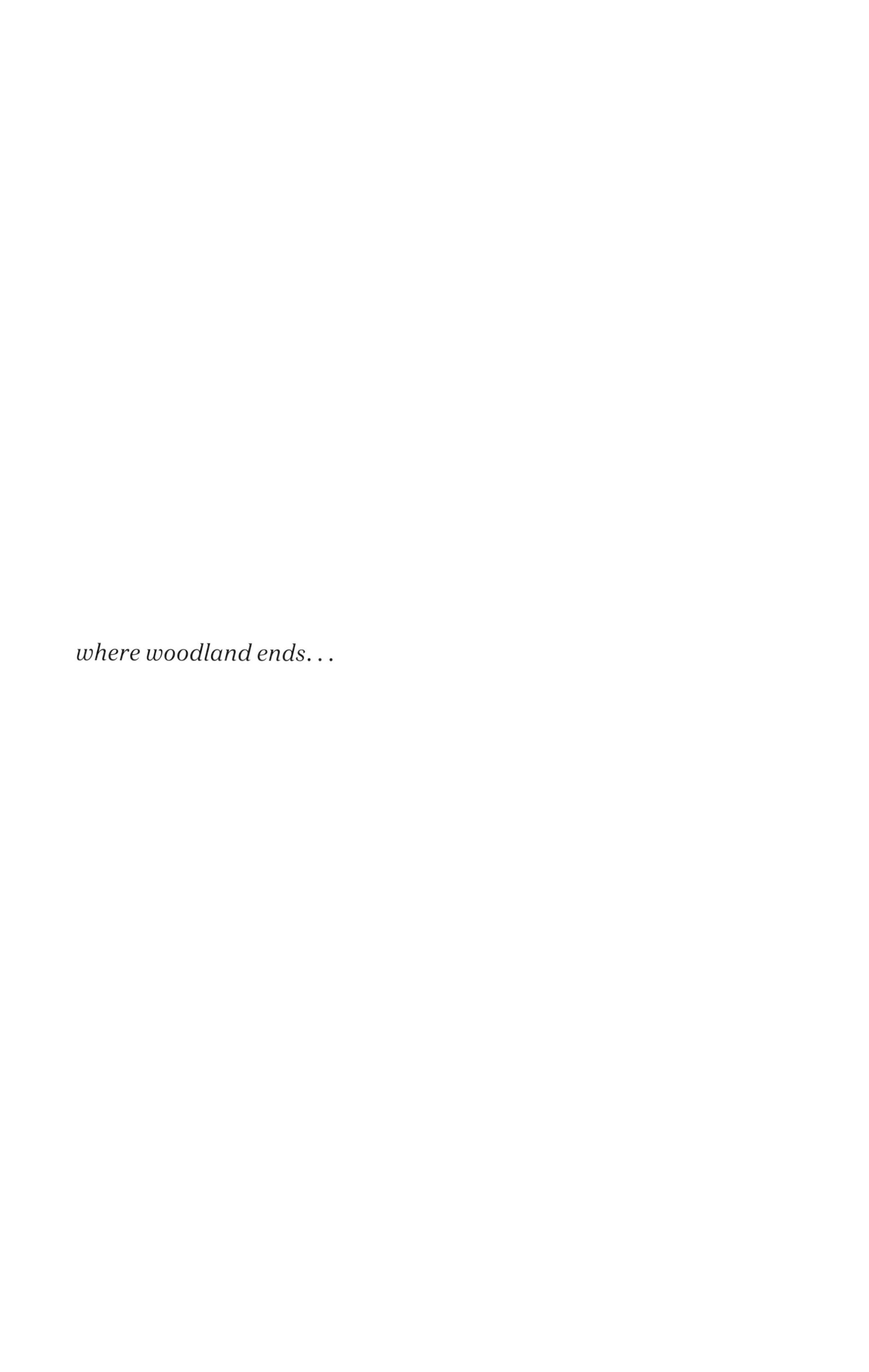

where woodland ends. . .

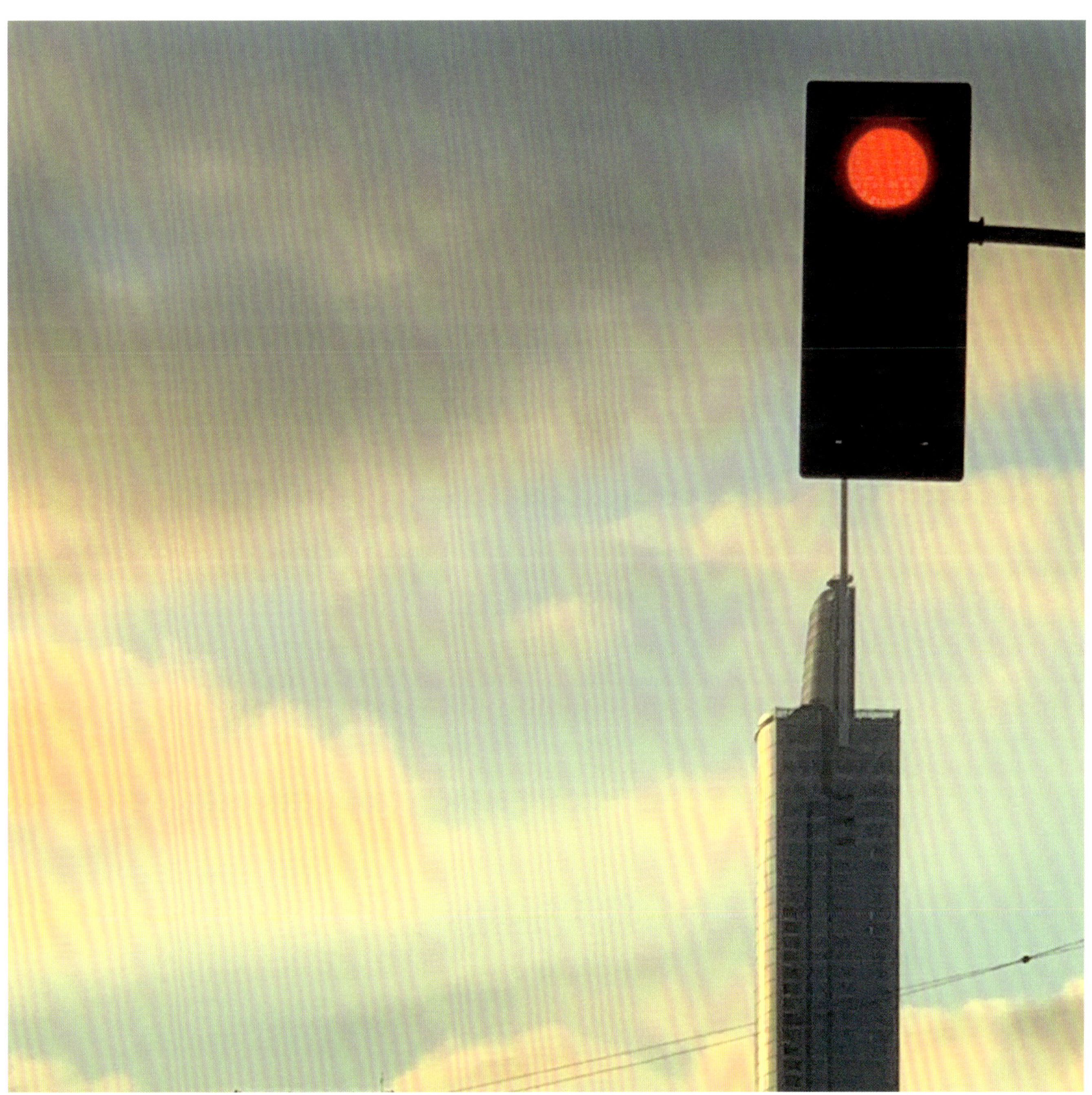

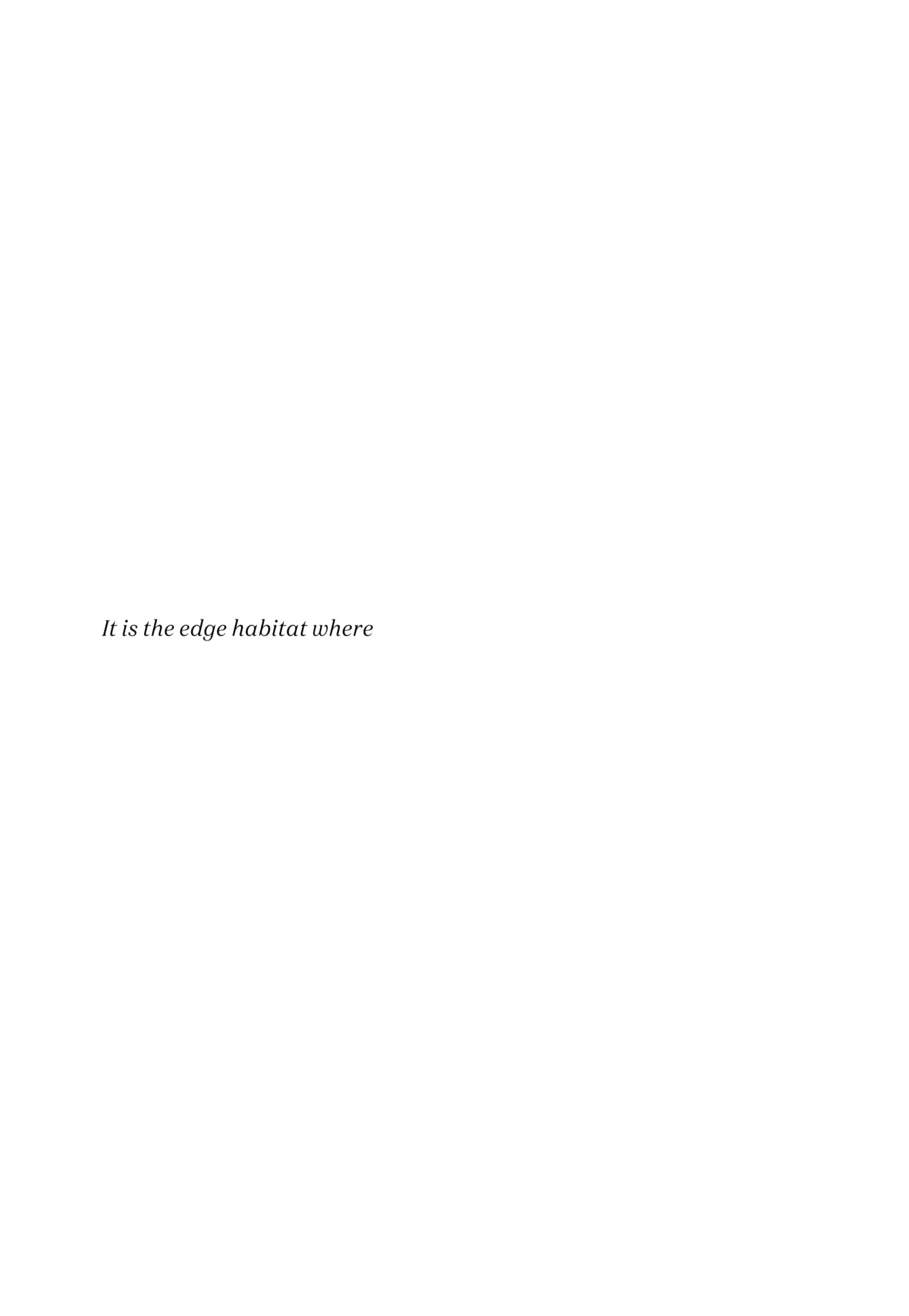

It is the edge habitat where

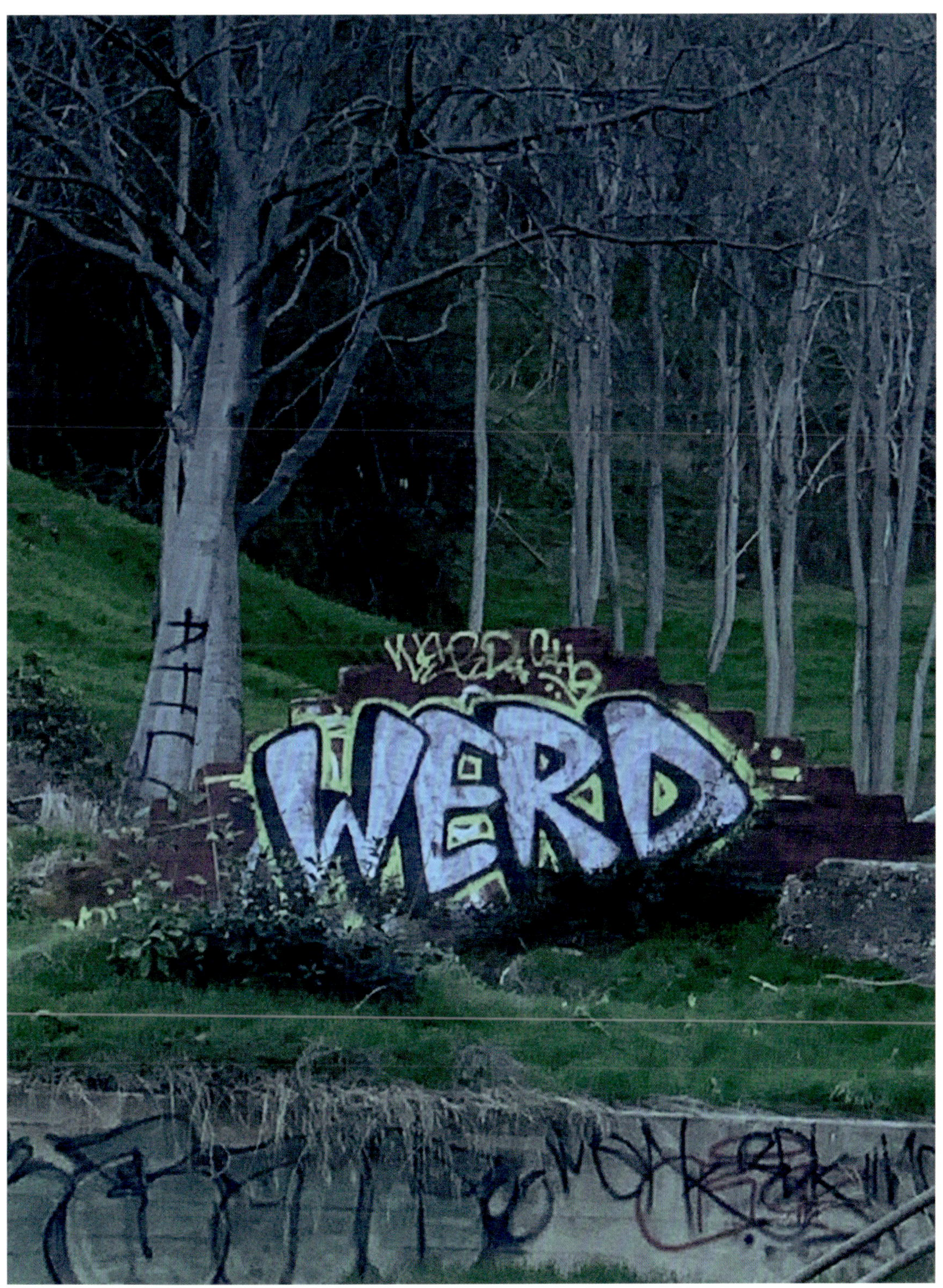
WERD

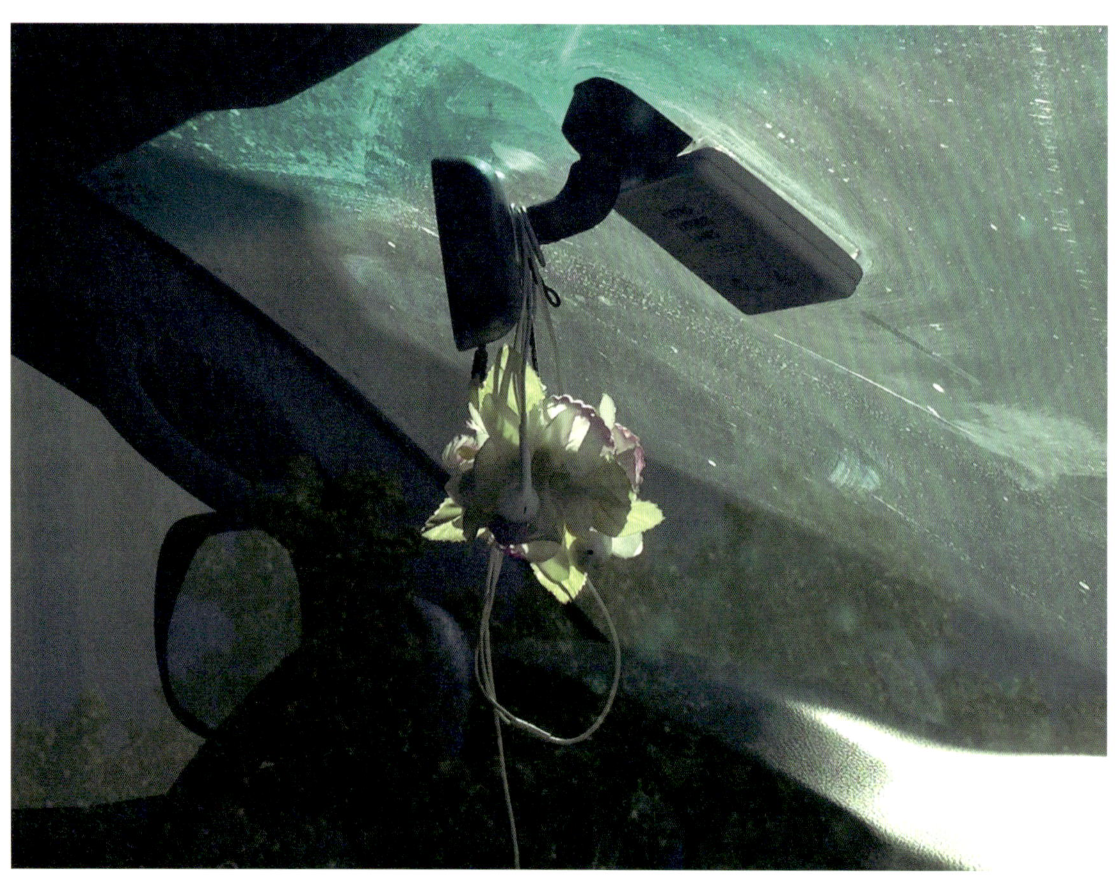

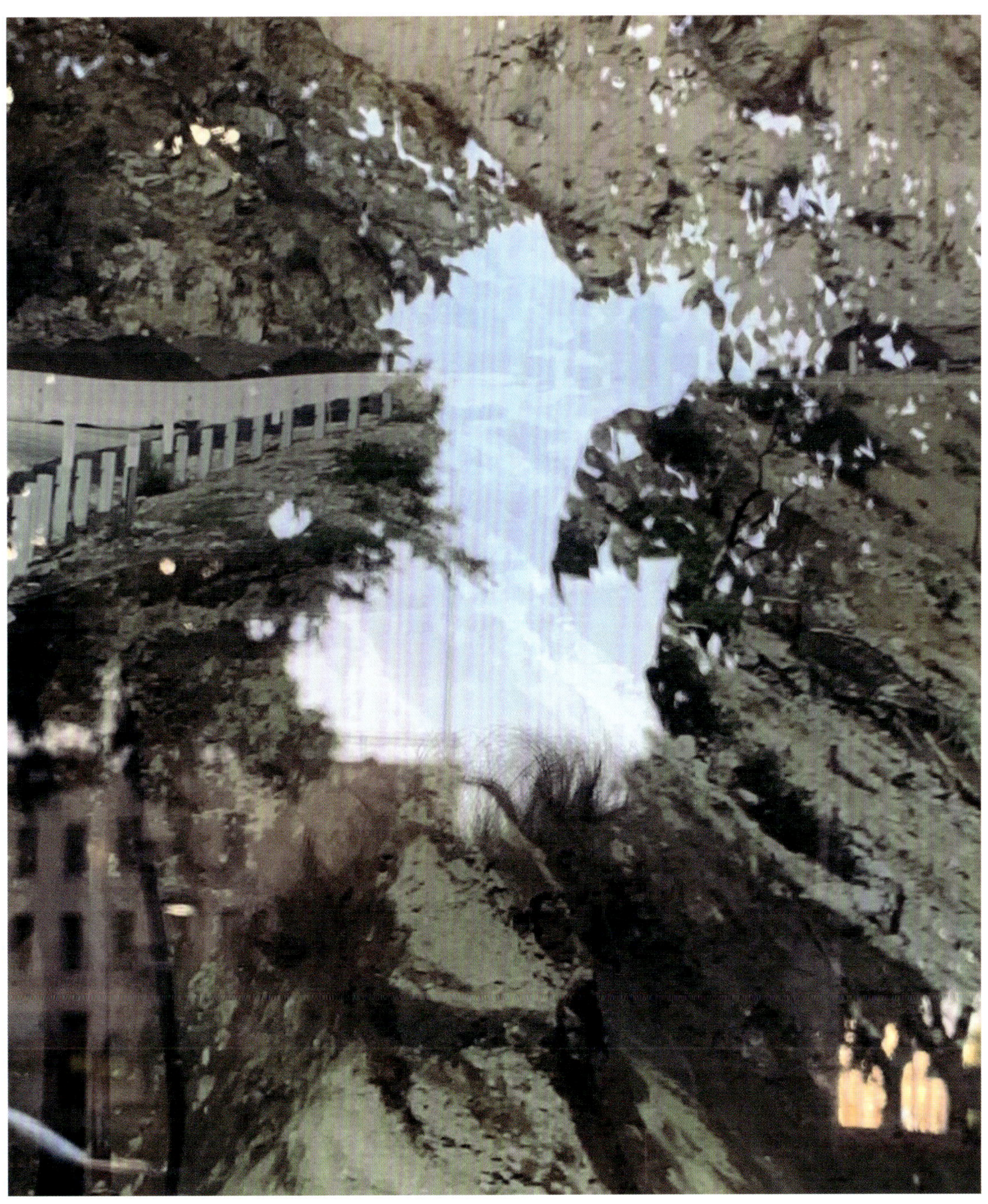

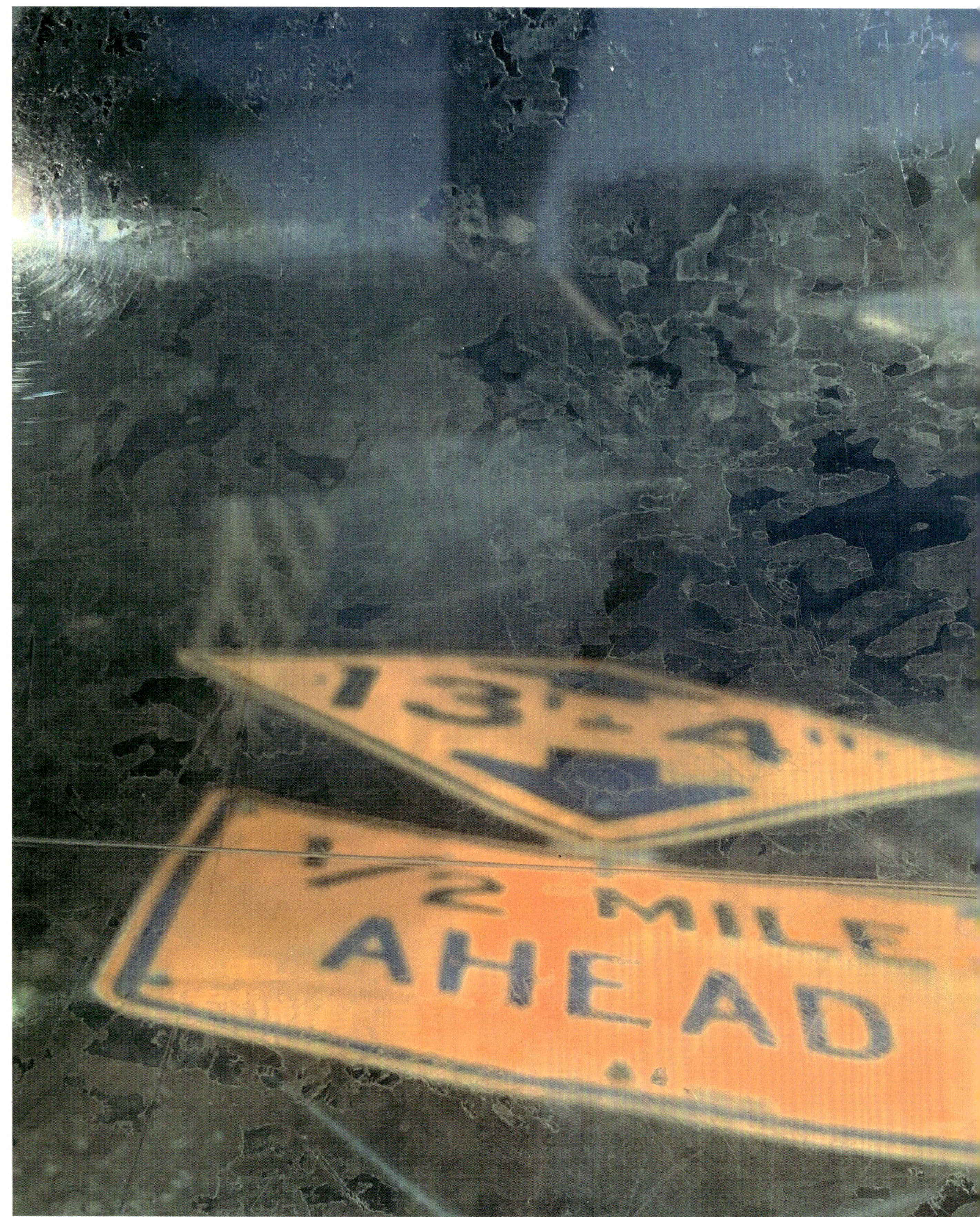

½ MILE
AHEAD

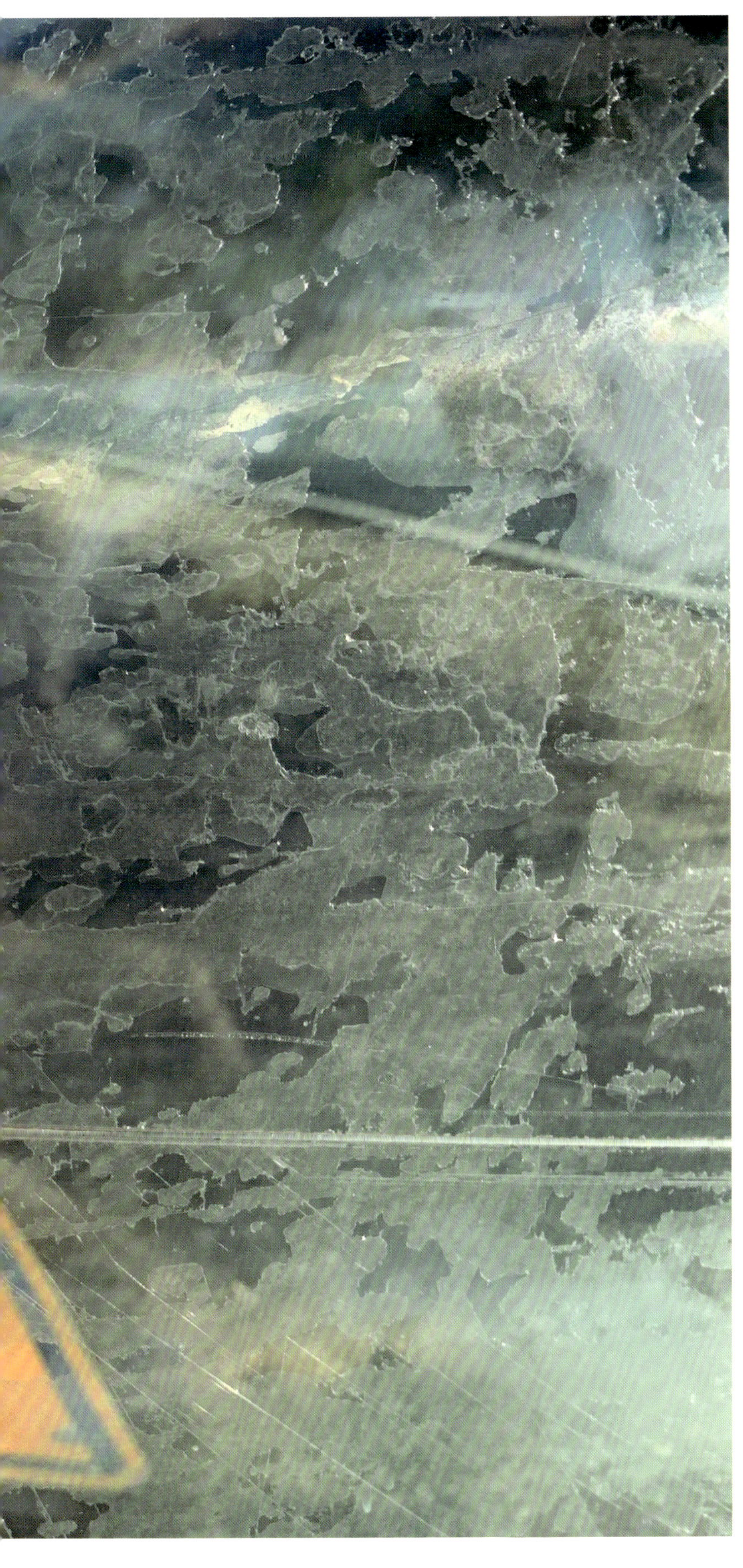

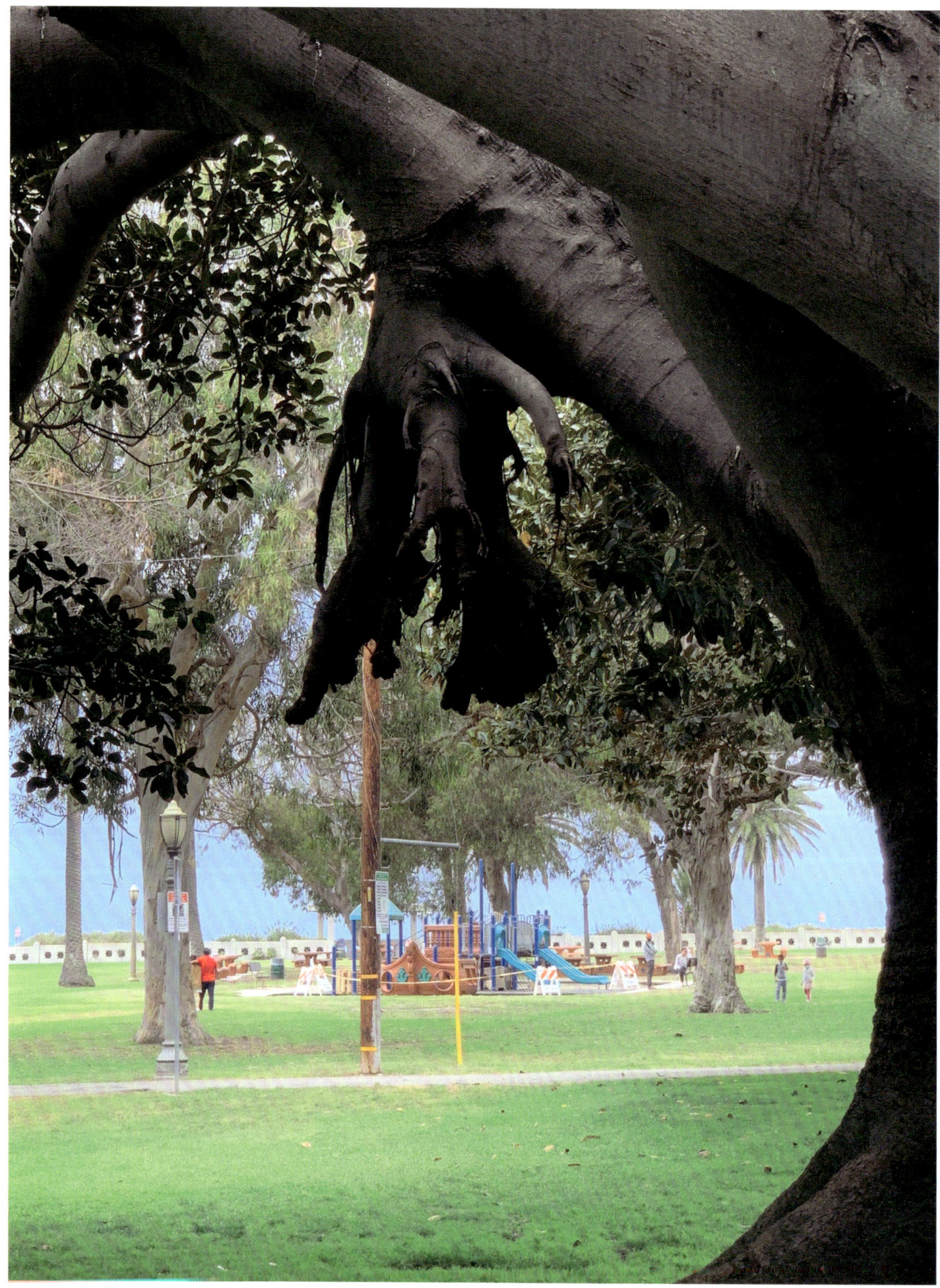

everything changes."

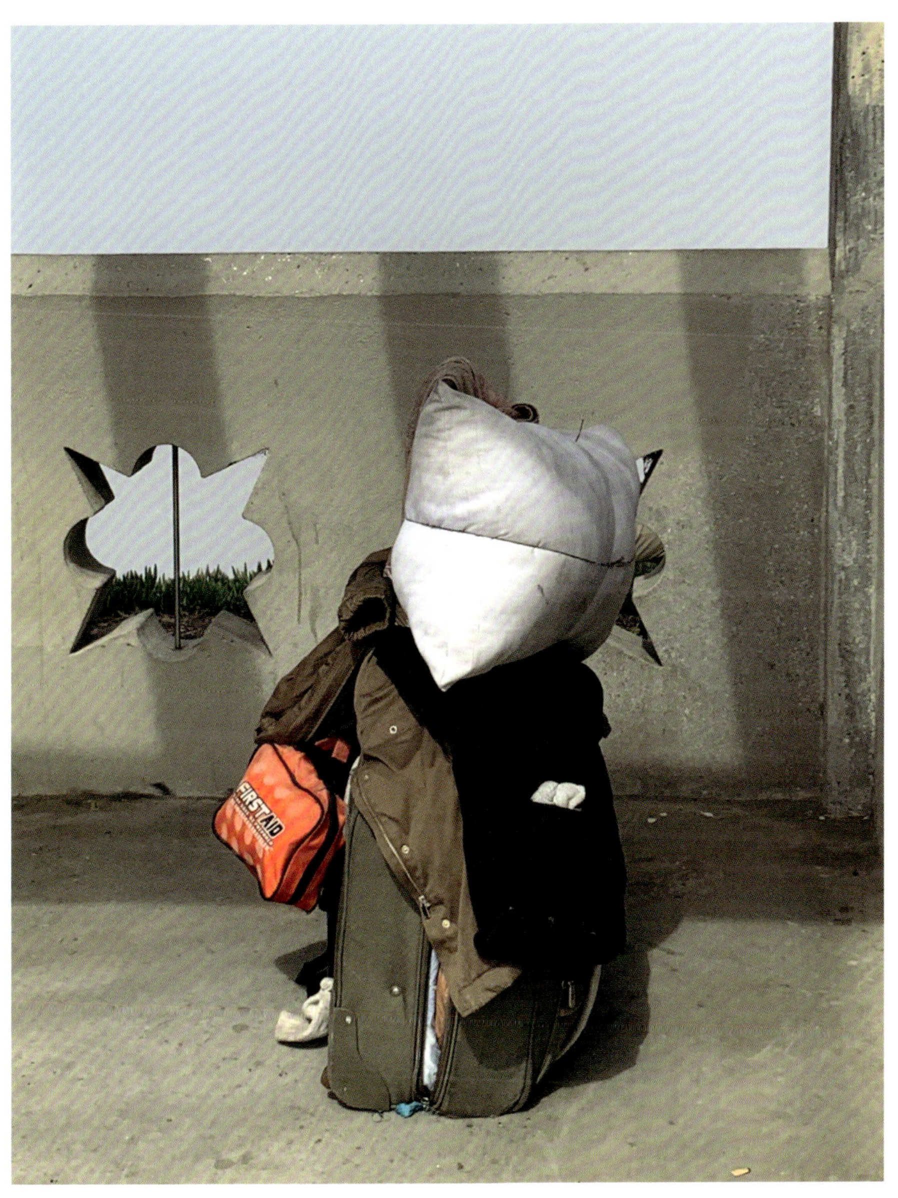
FIRST AID

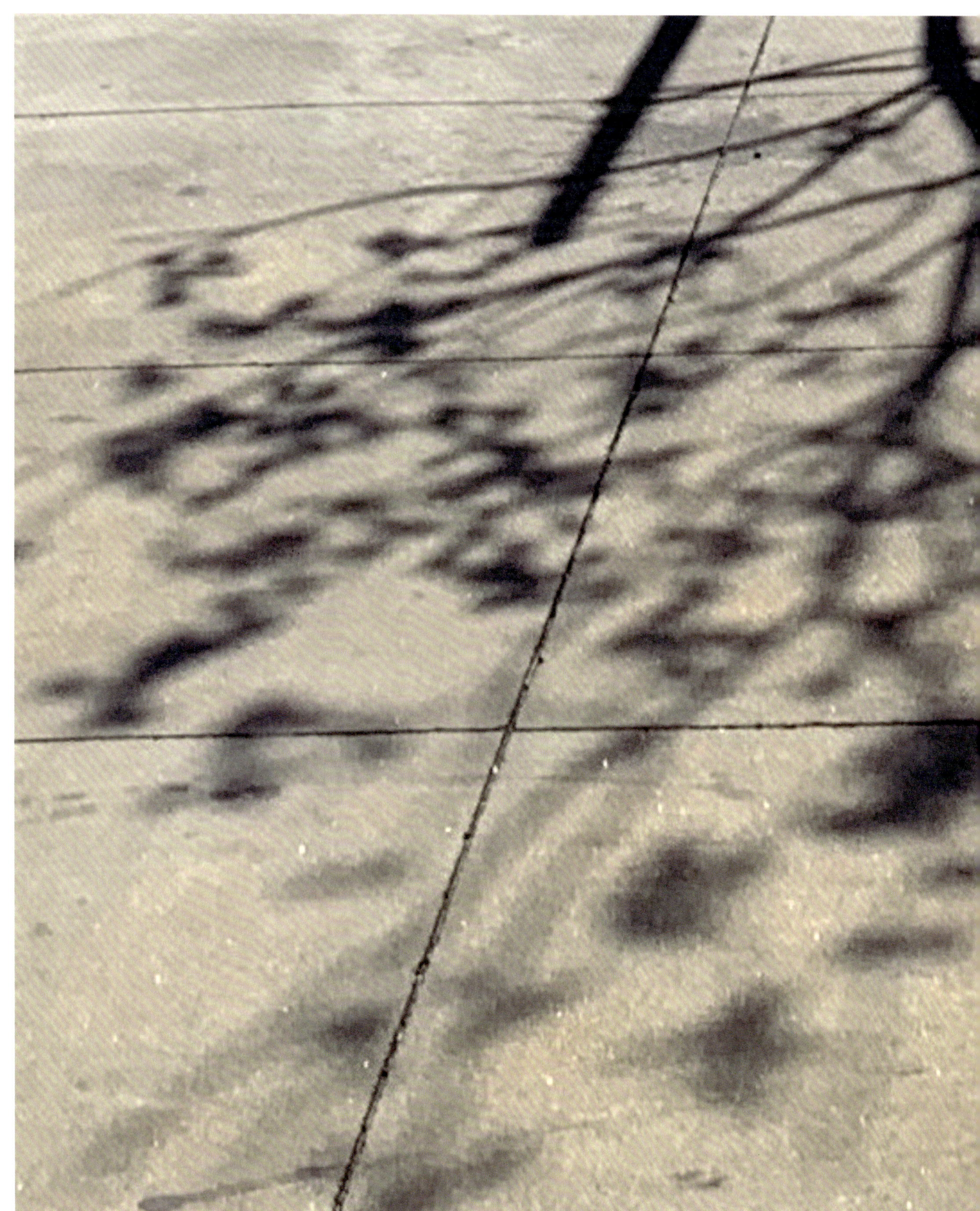

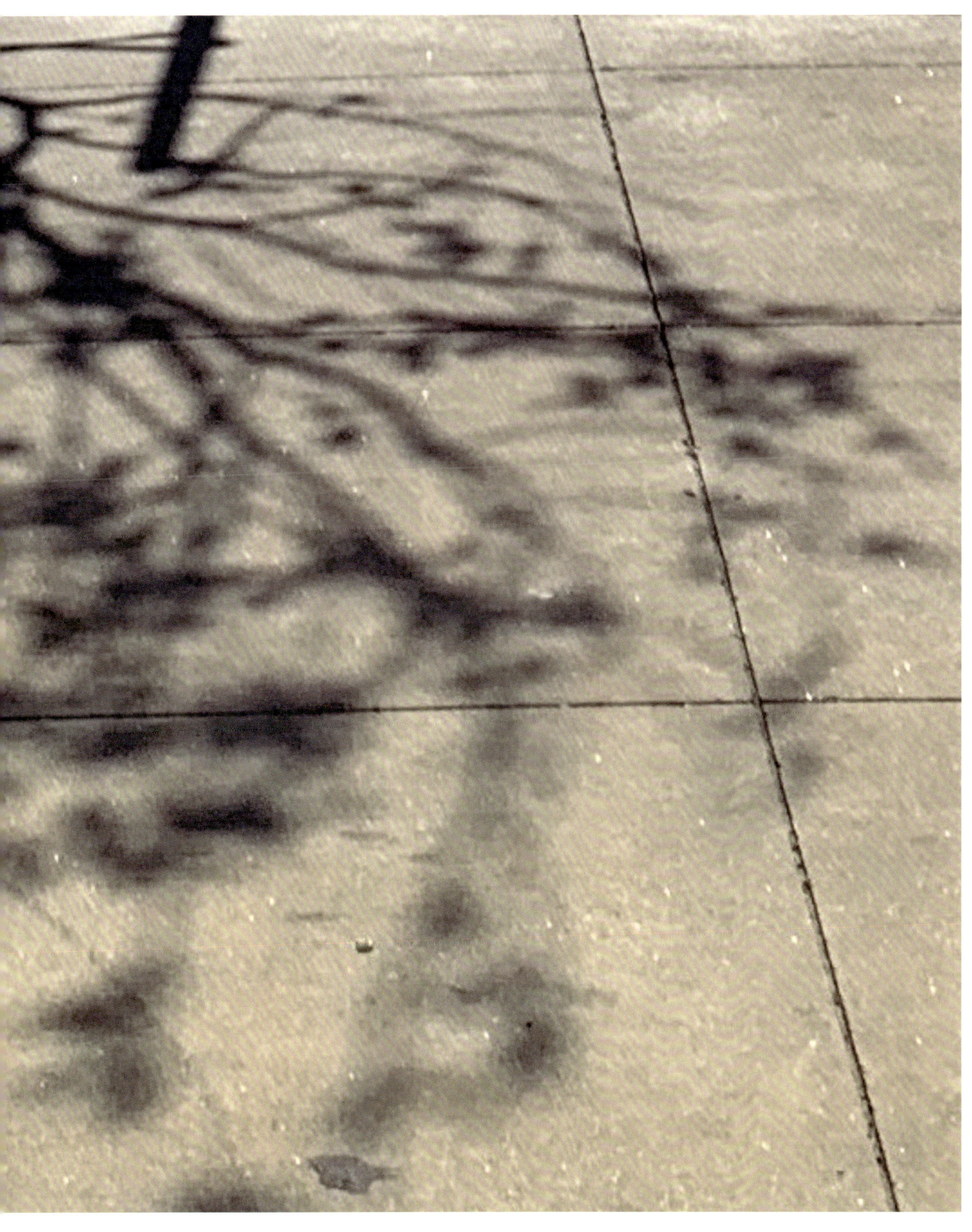

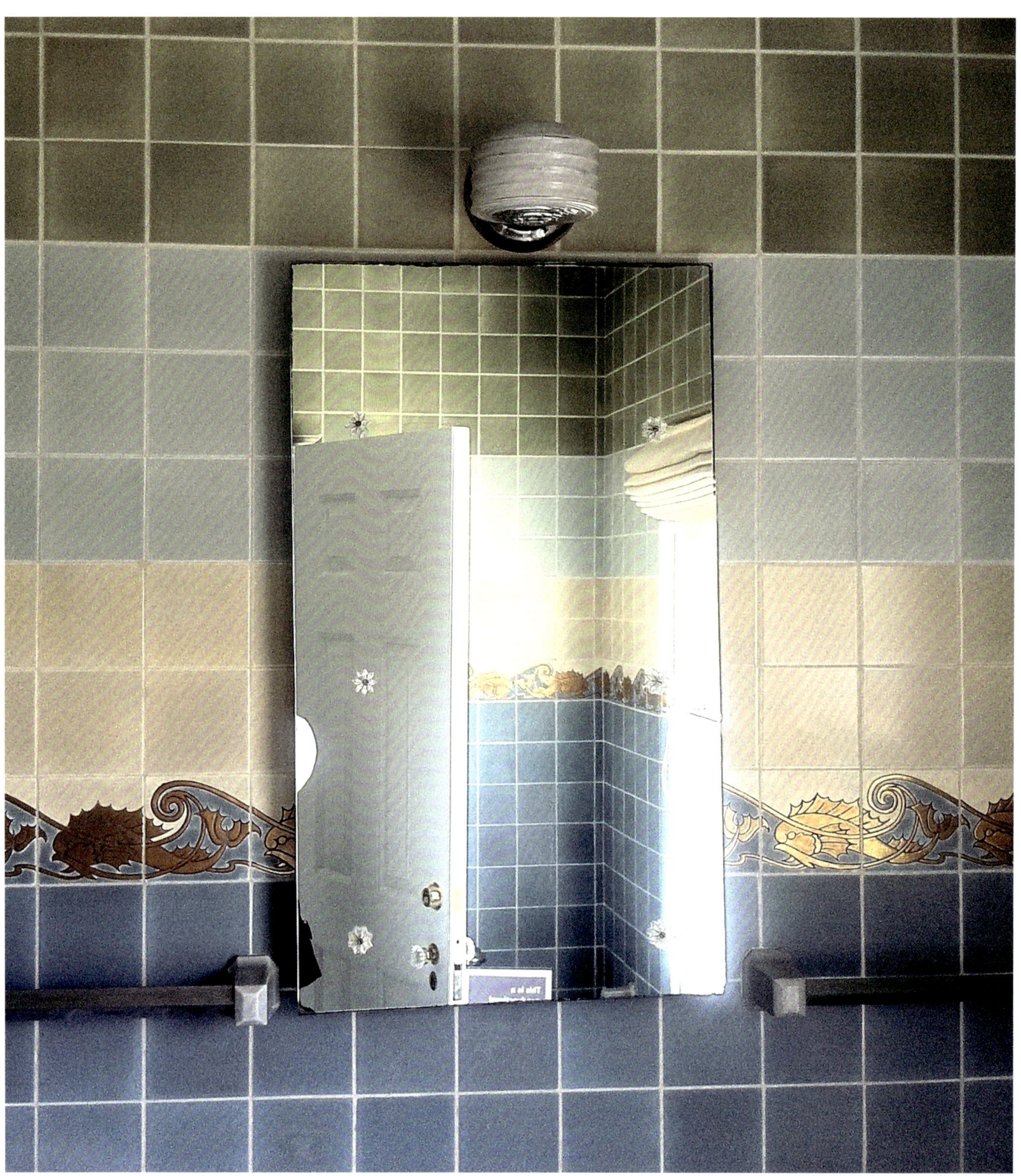

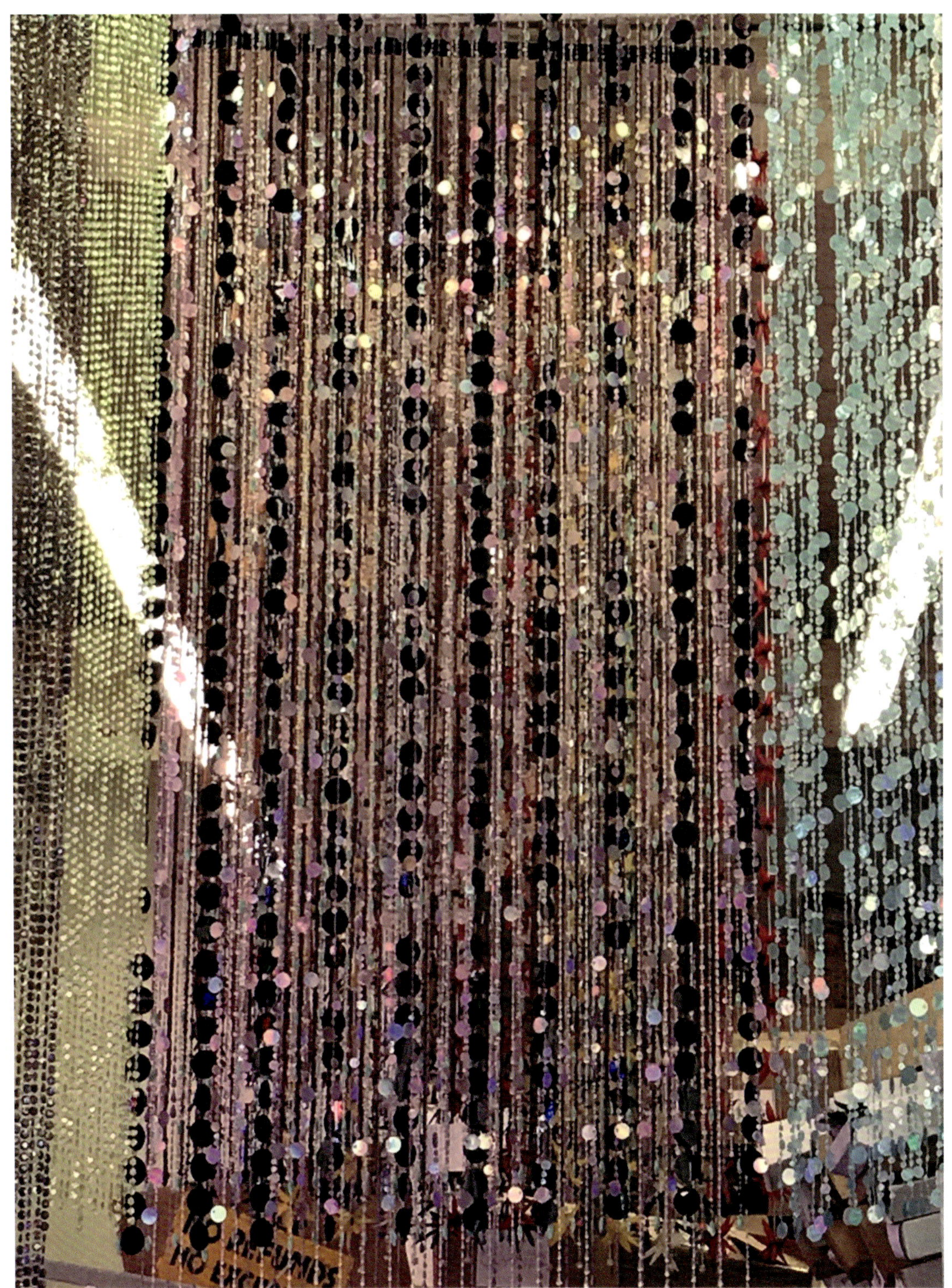

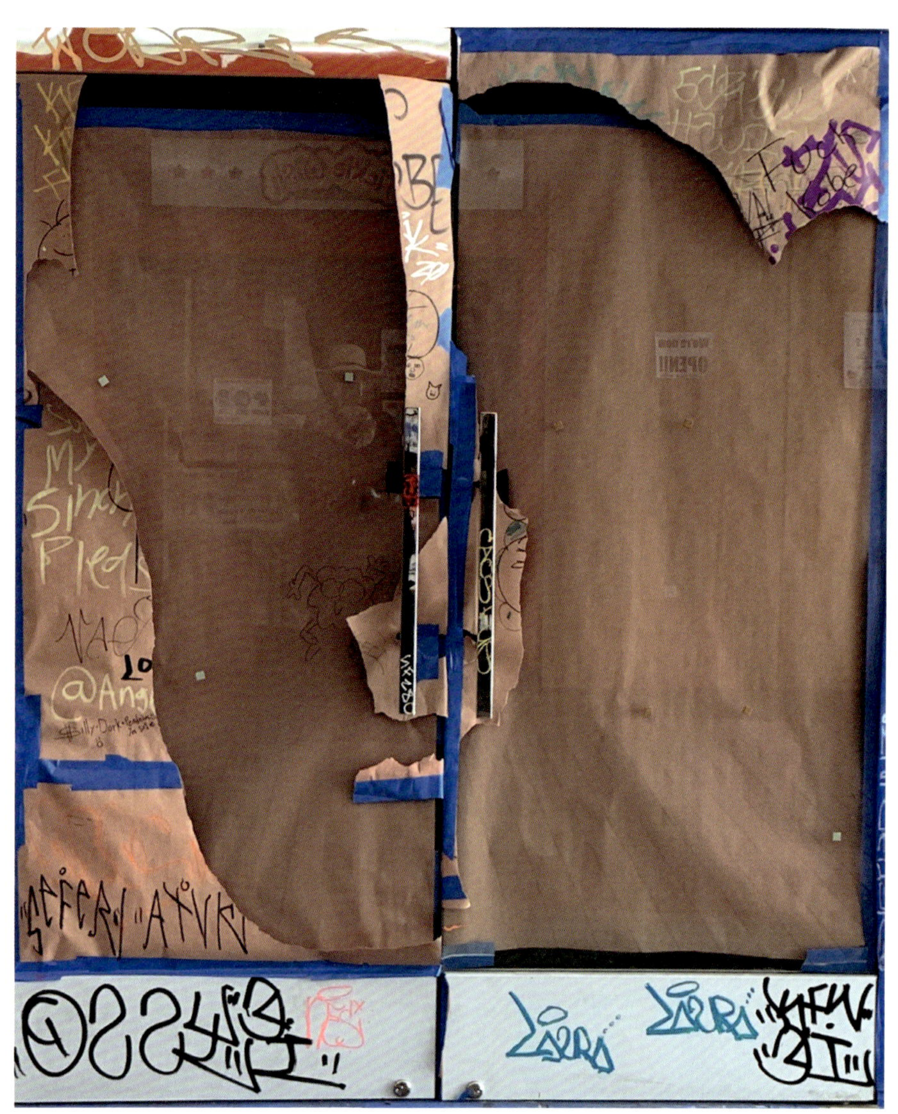

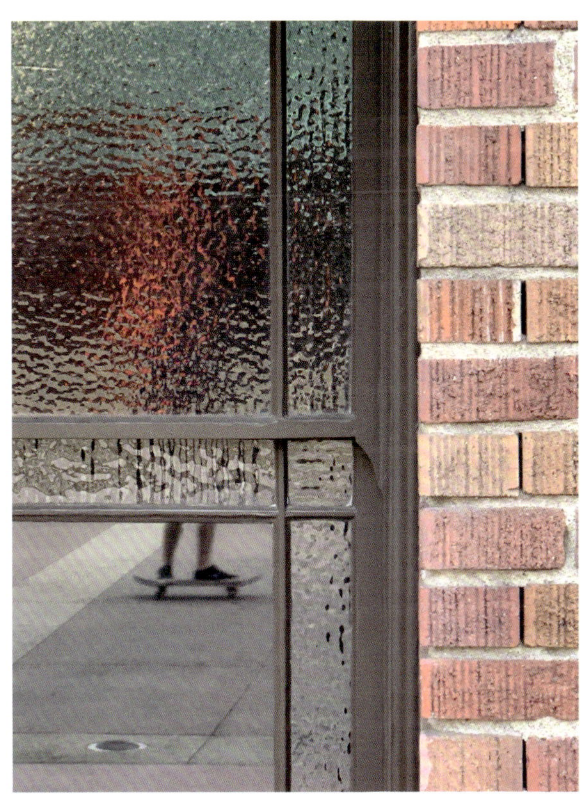

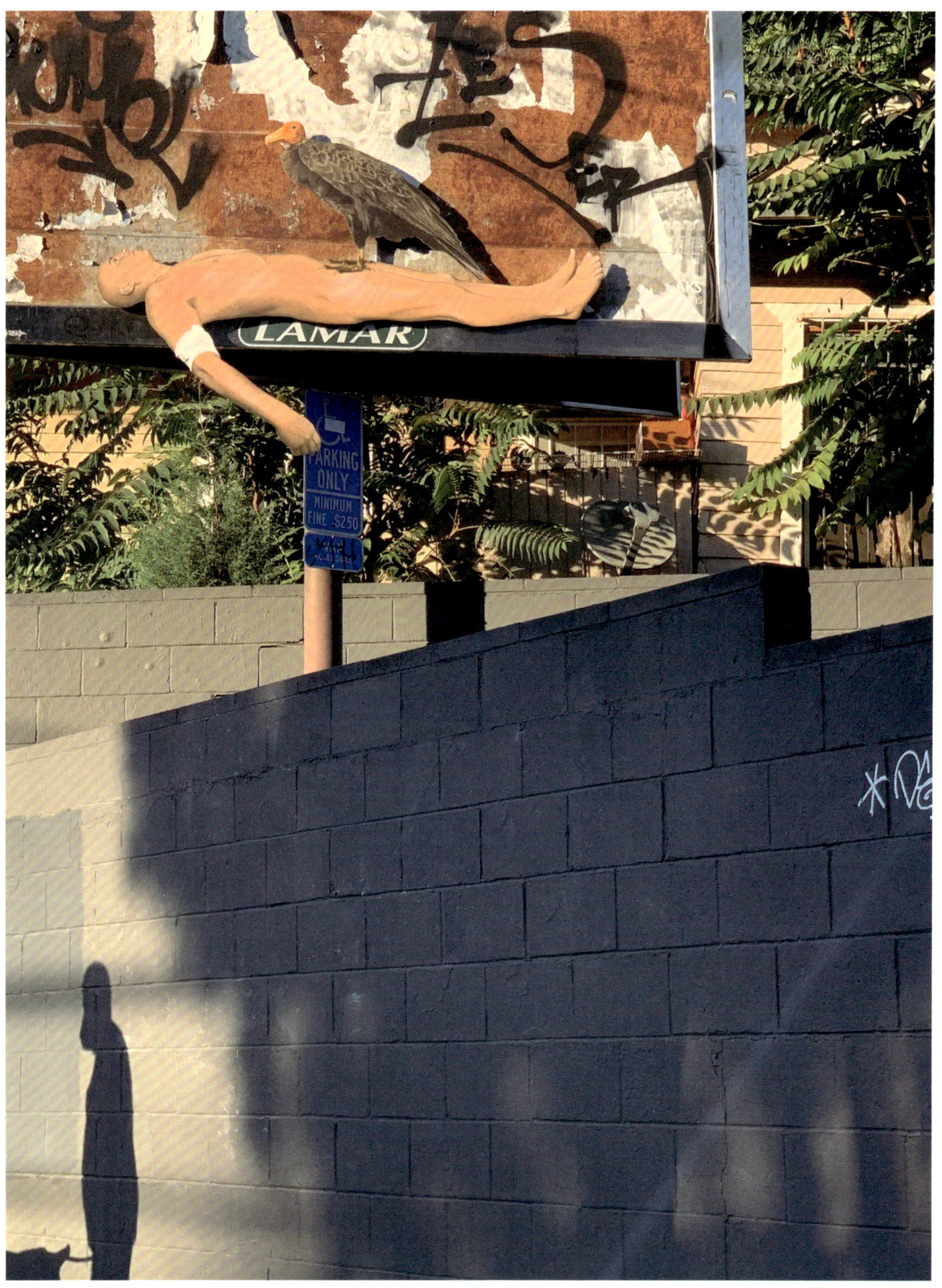
LAMAR
PARKING
ONLY
MINIMUM
FINE $250

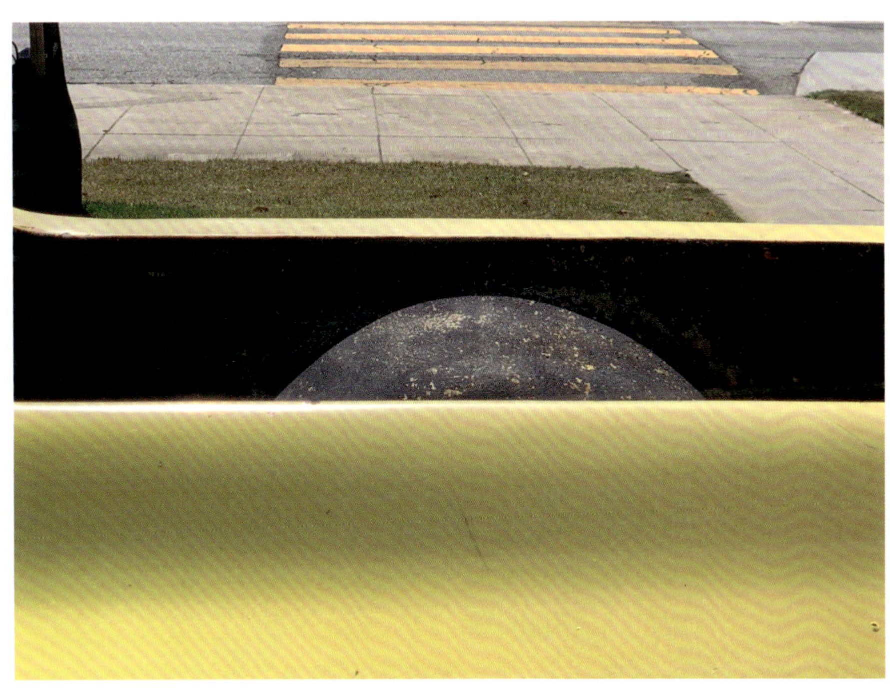

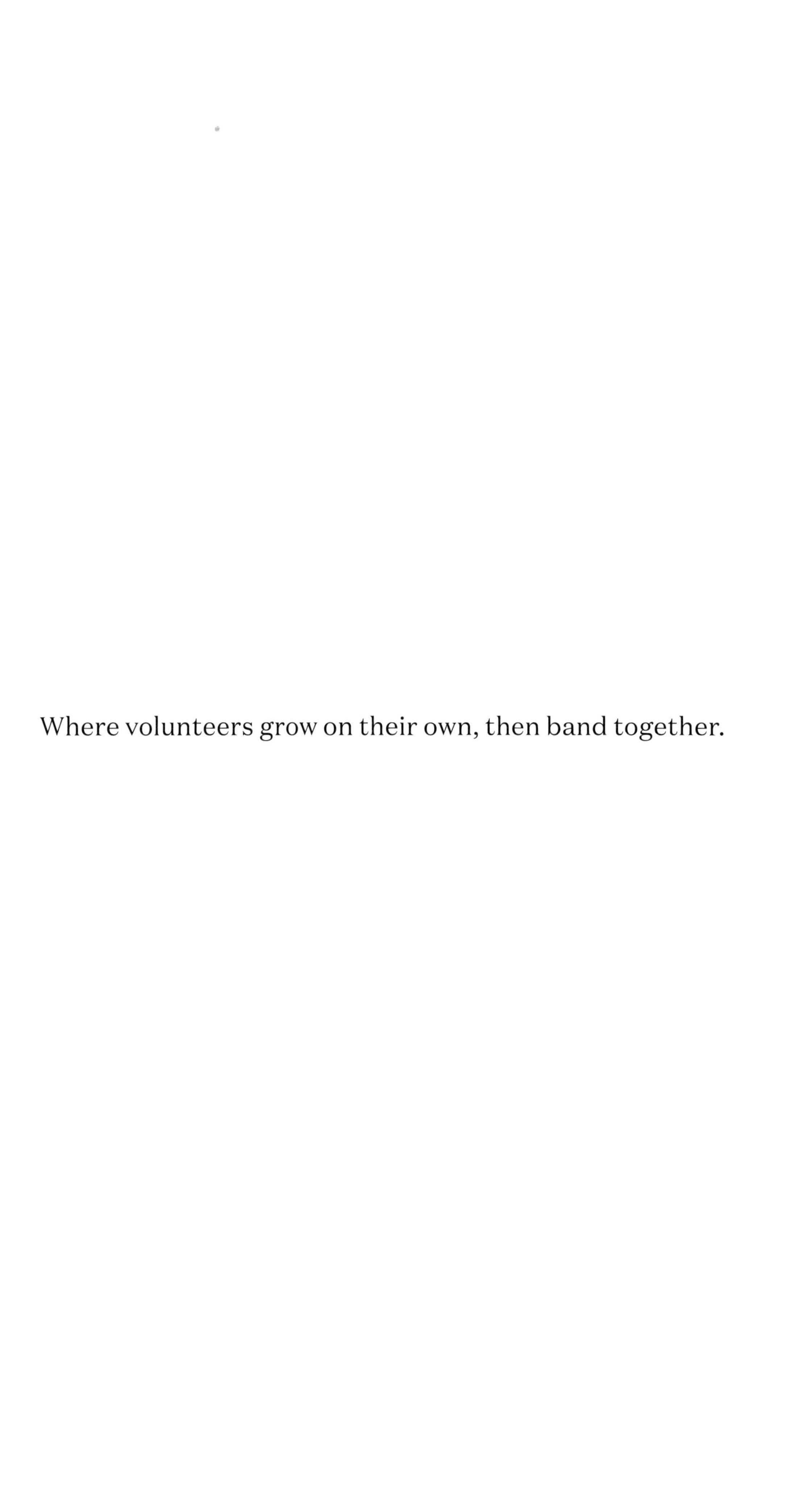

Where volunteers grow on their own, then band together.

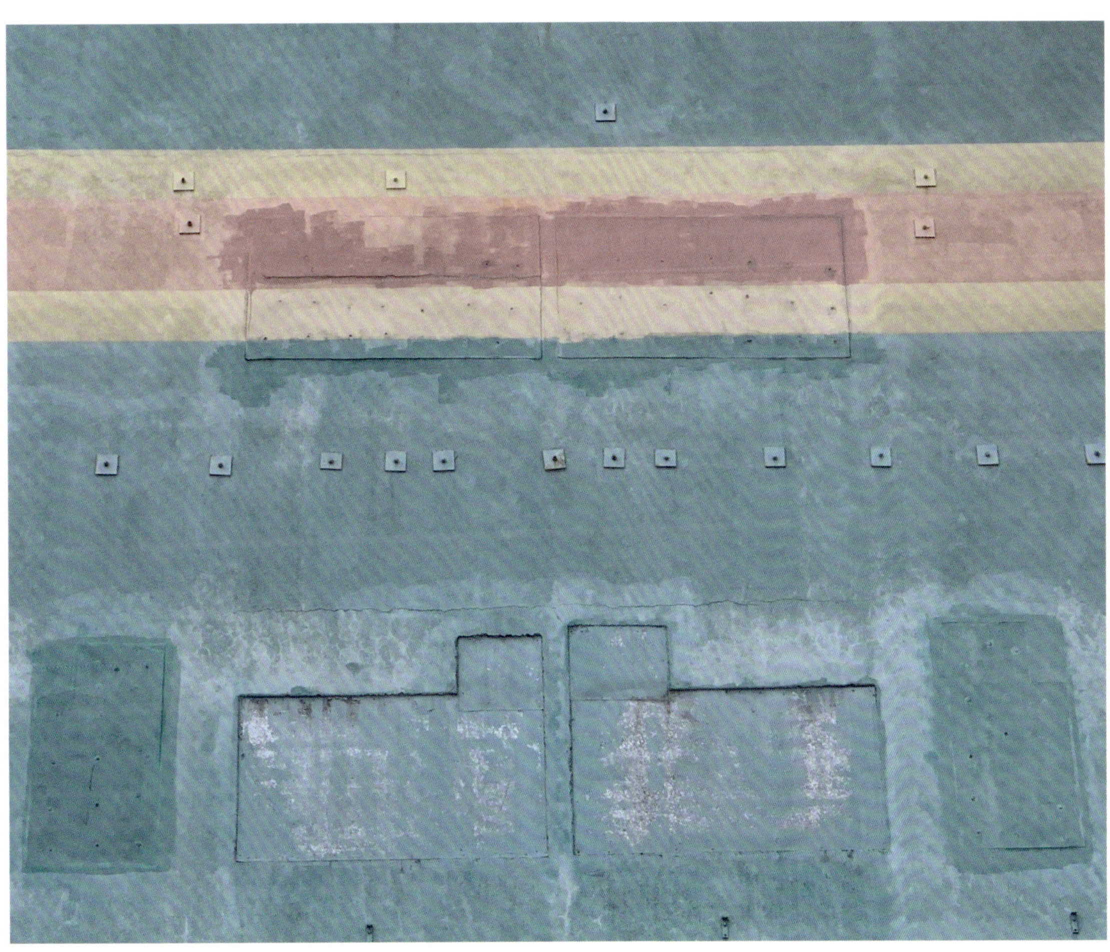

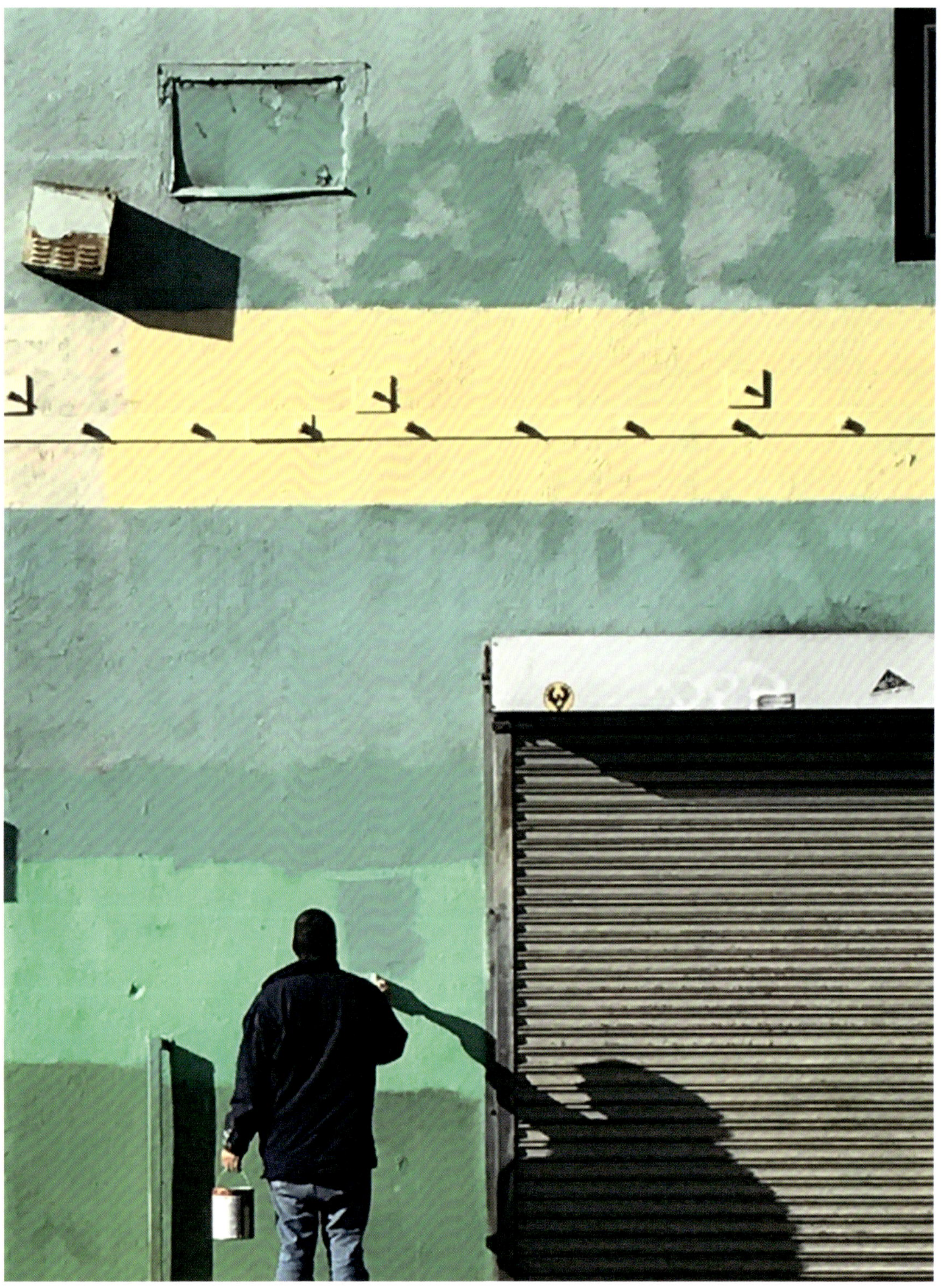

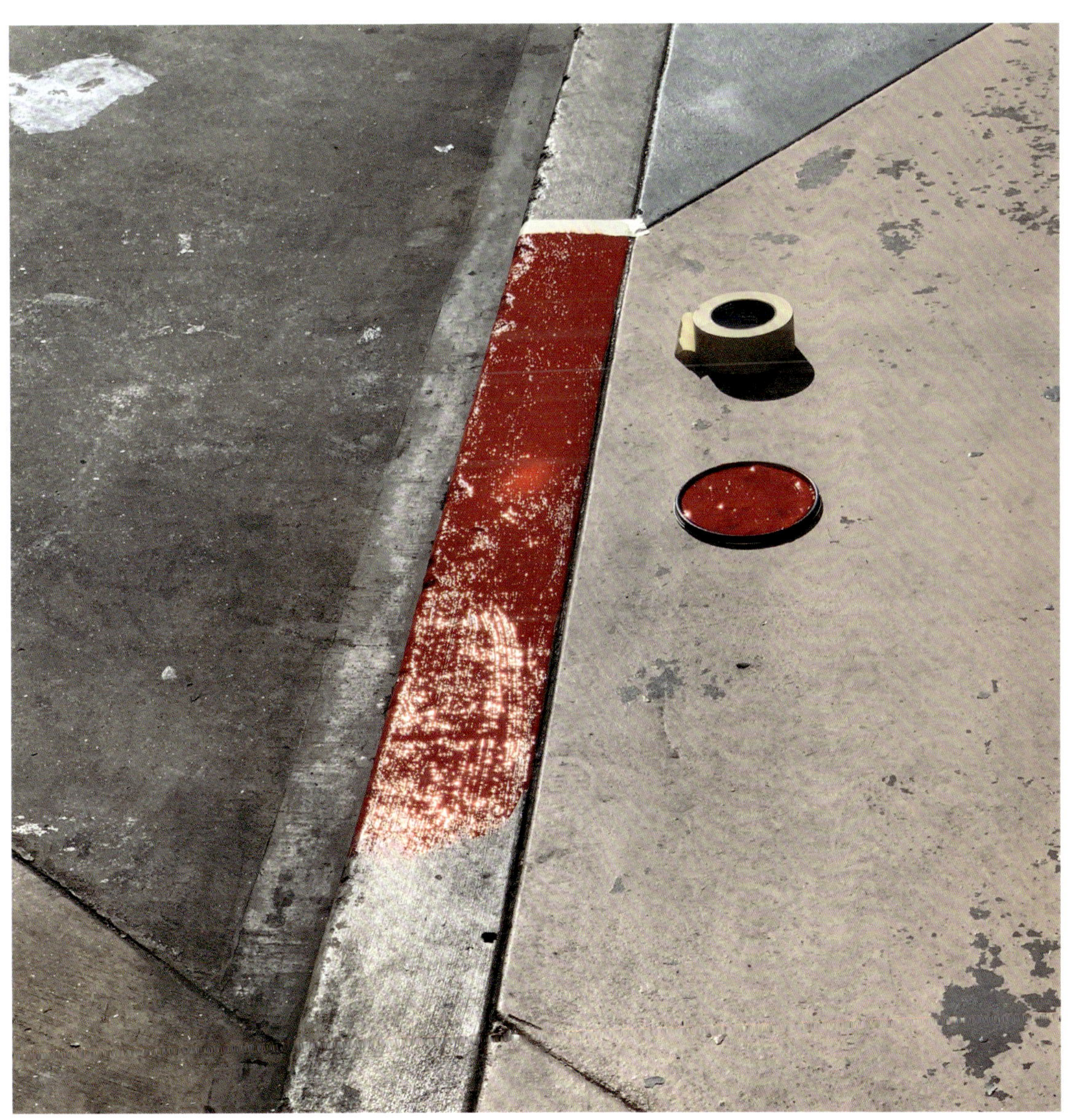

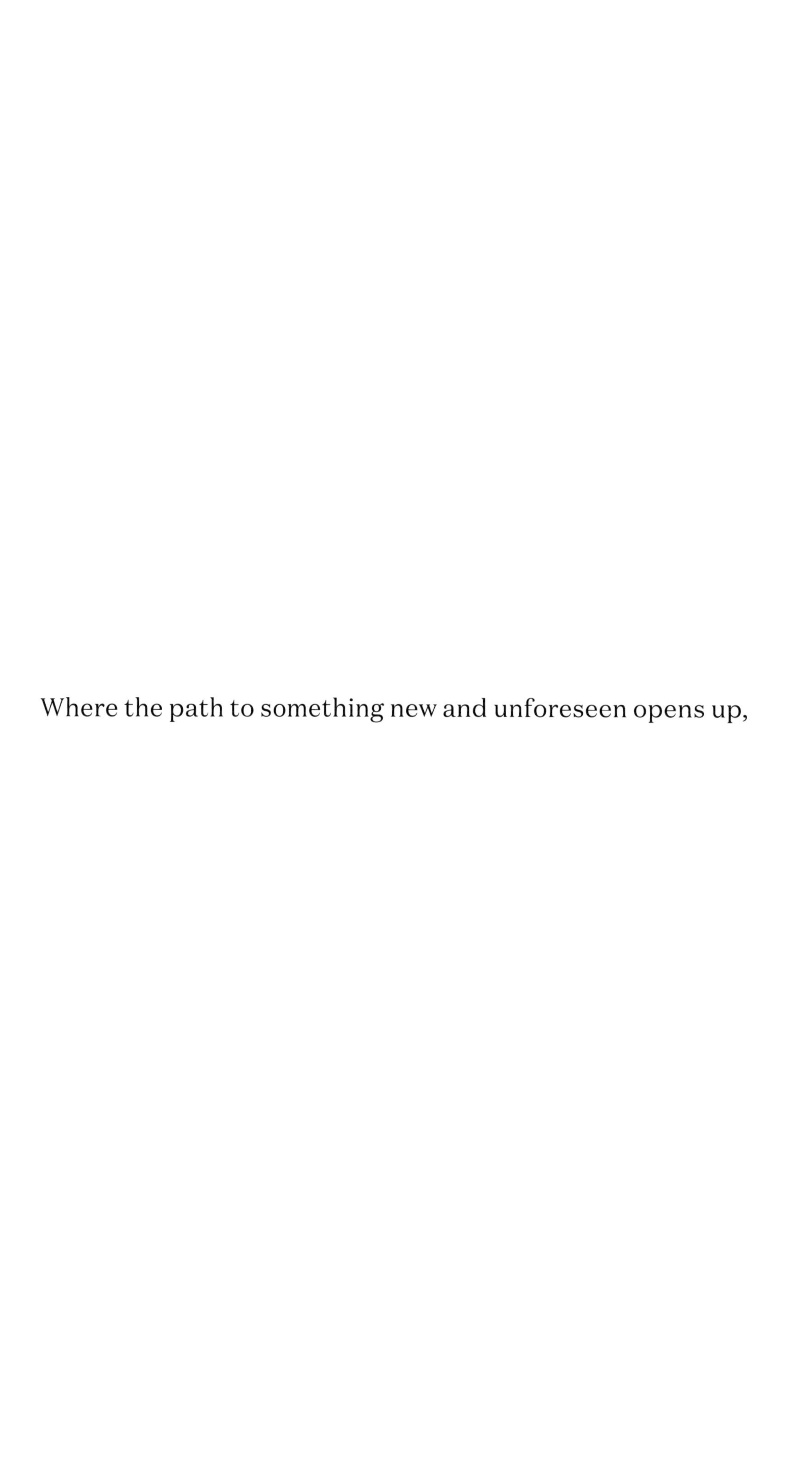

Where the path to something new and unforeseen opens up,

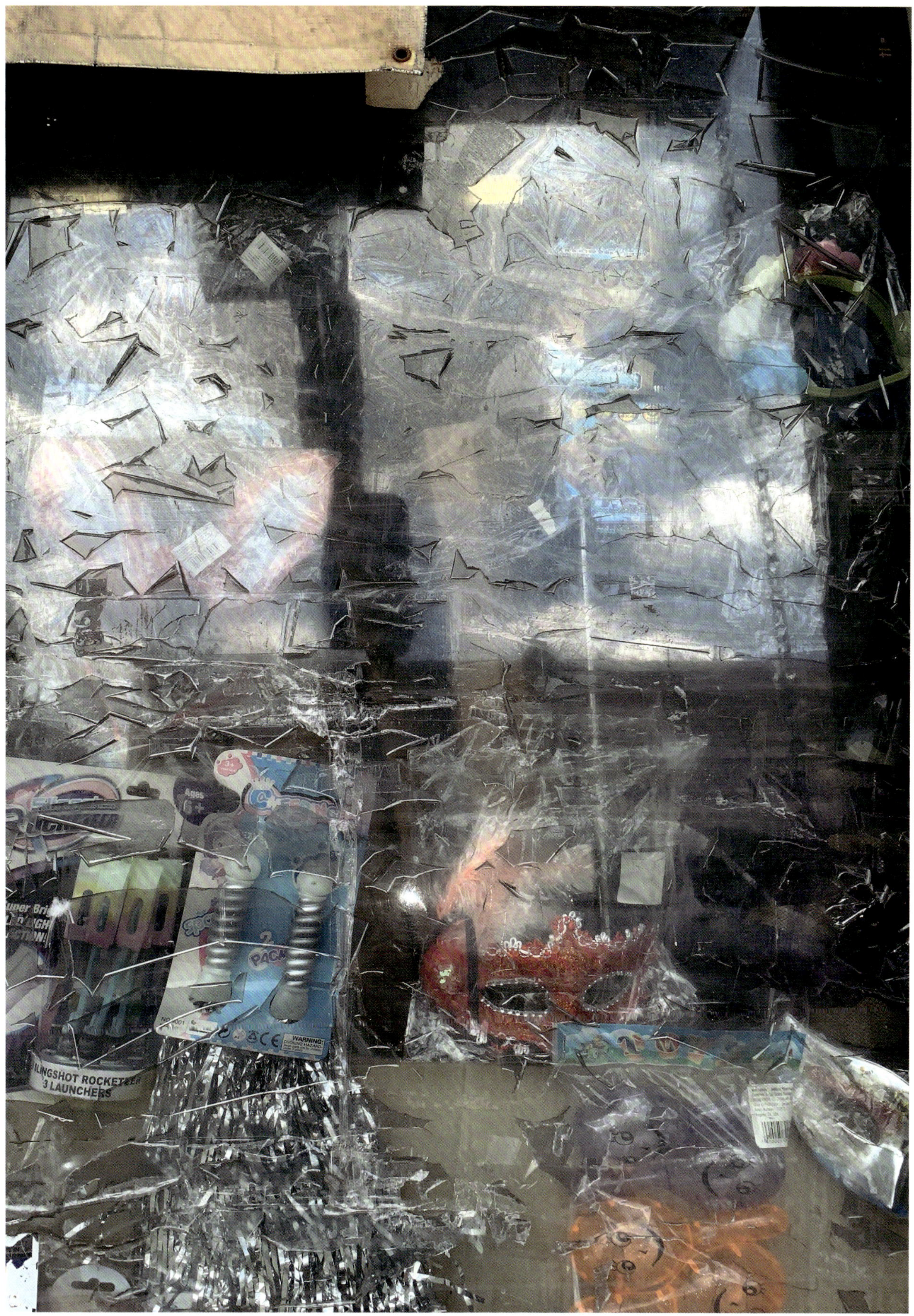

LINGSHOT ROCKETEER
3 LAUNCHERS
WARNING:

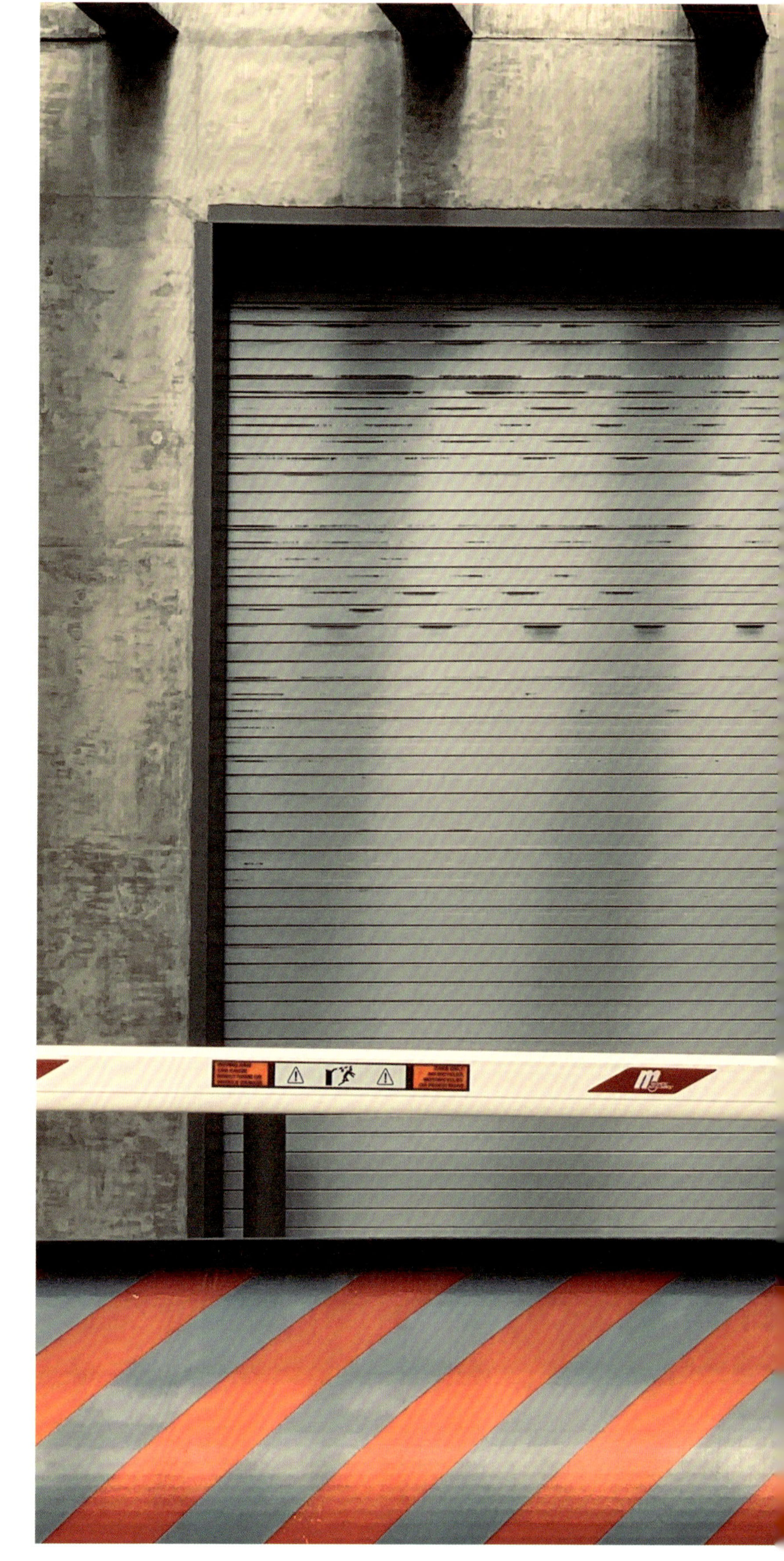

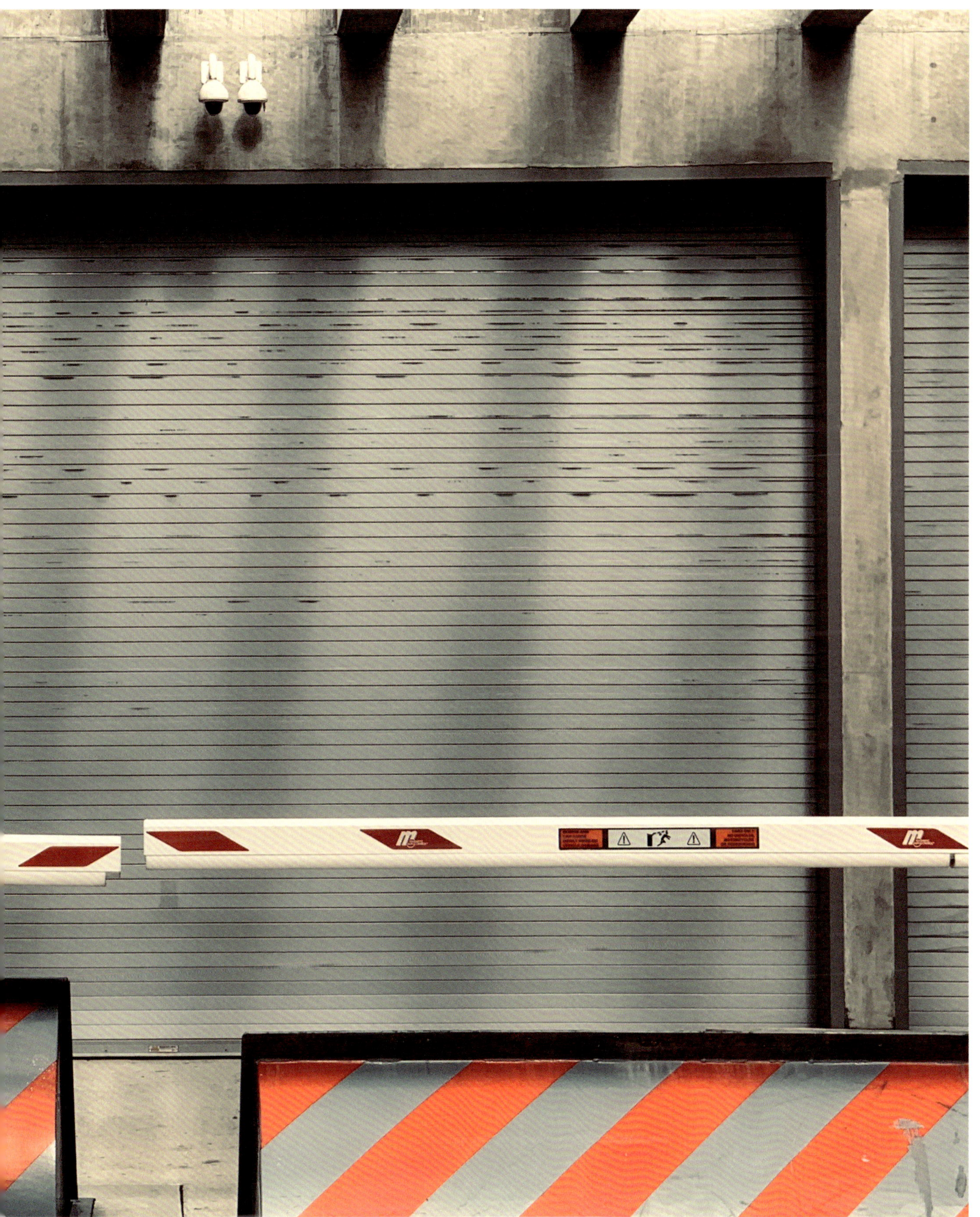

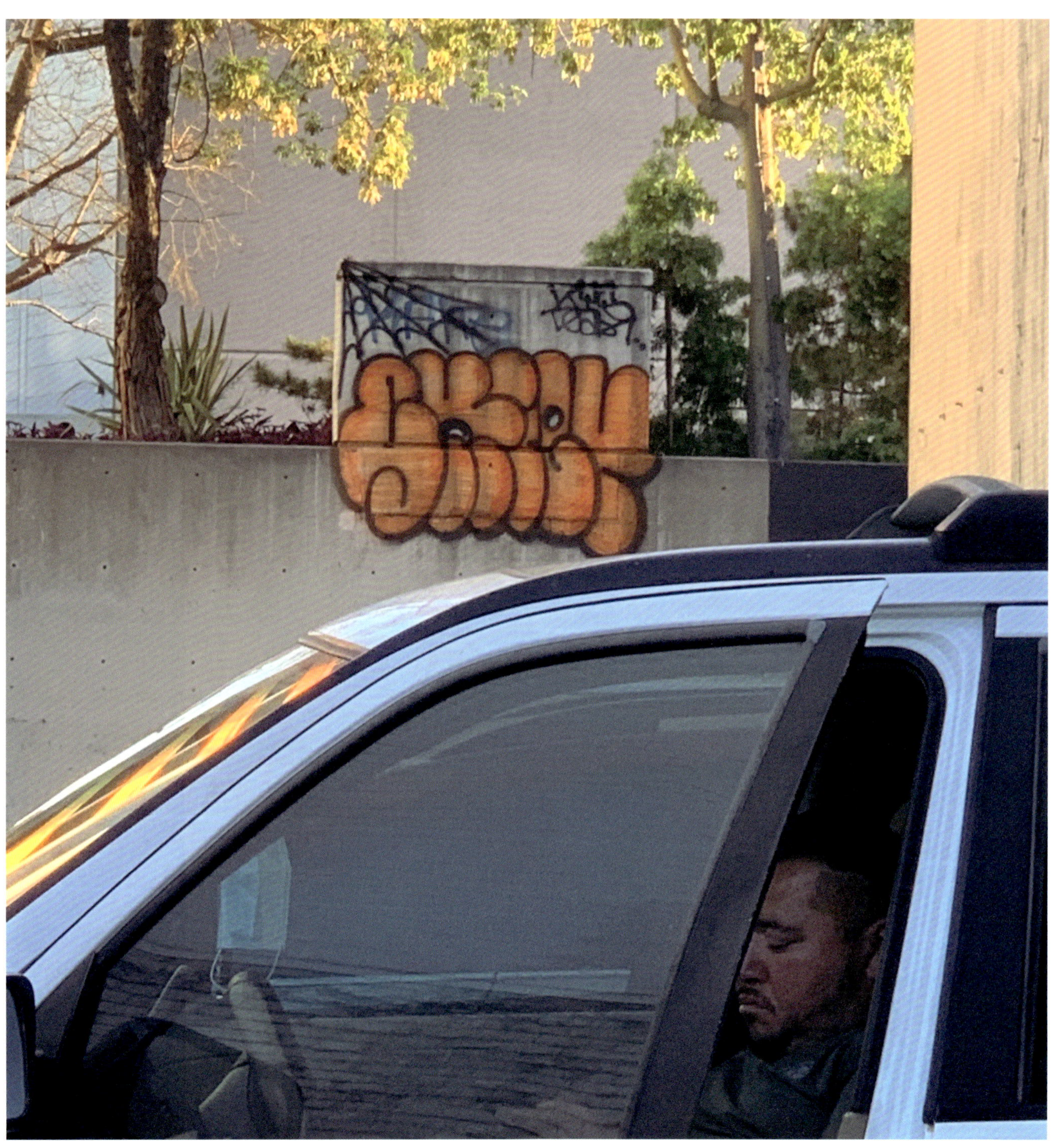

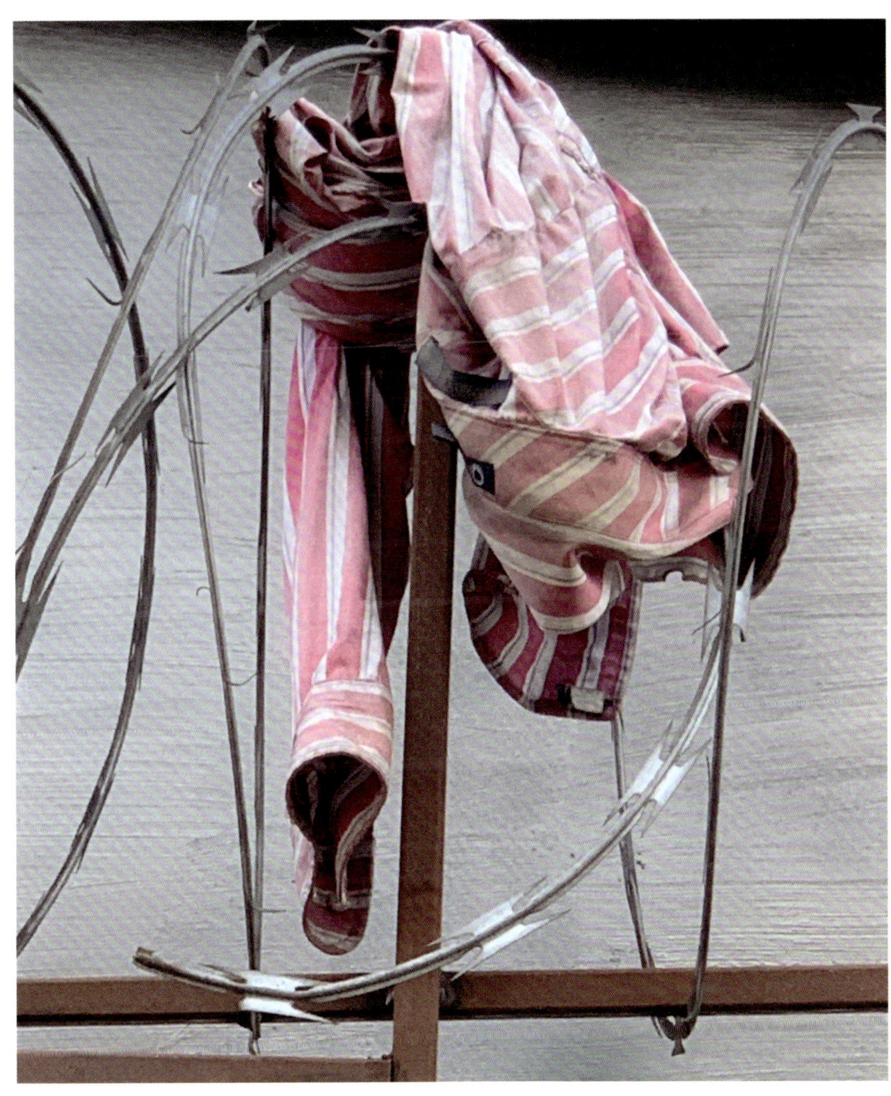

coming into view,

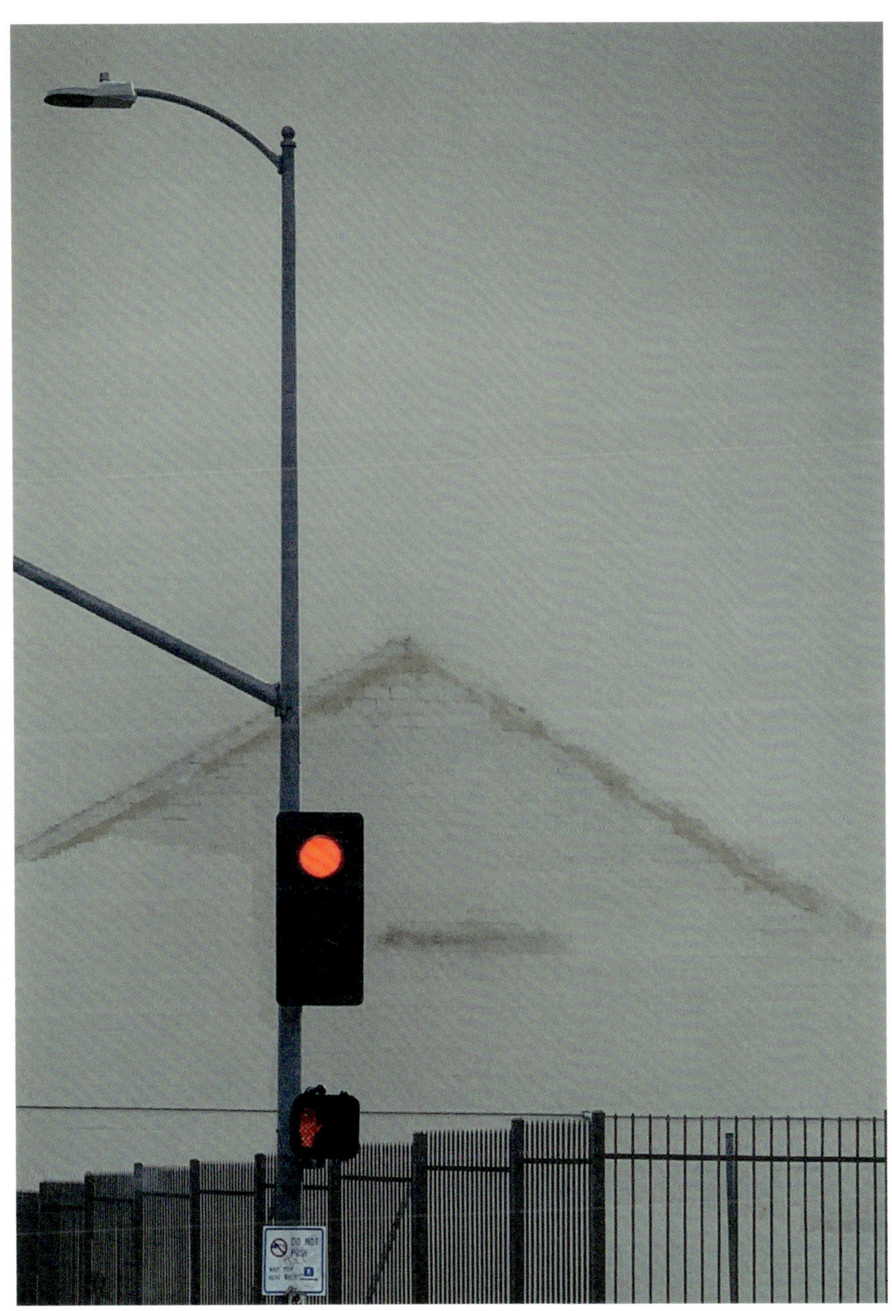
DO NOT
PUSH

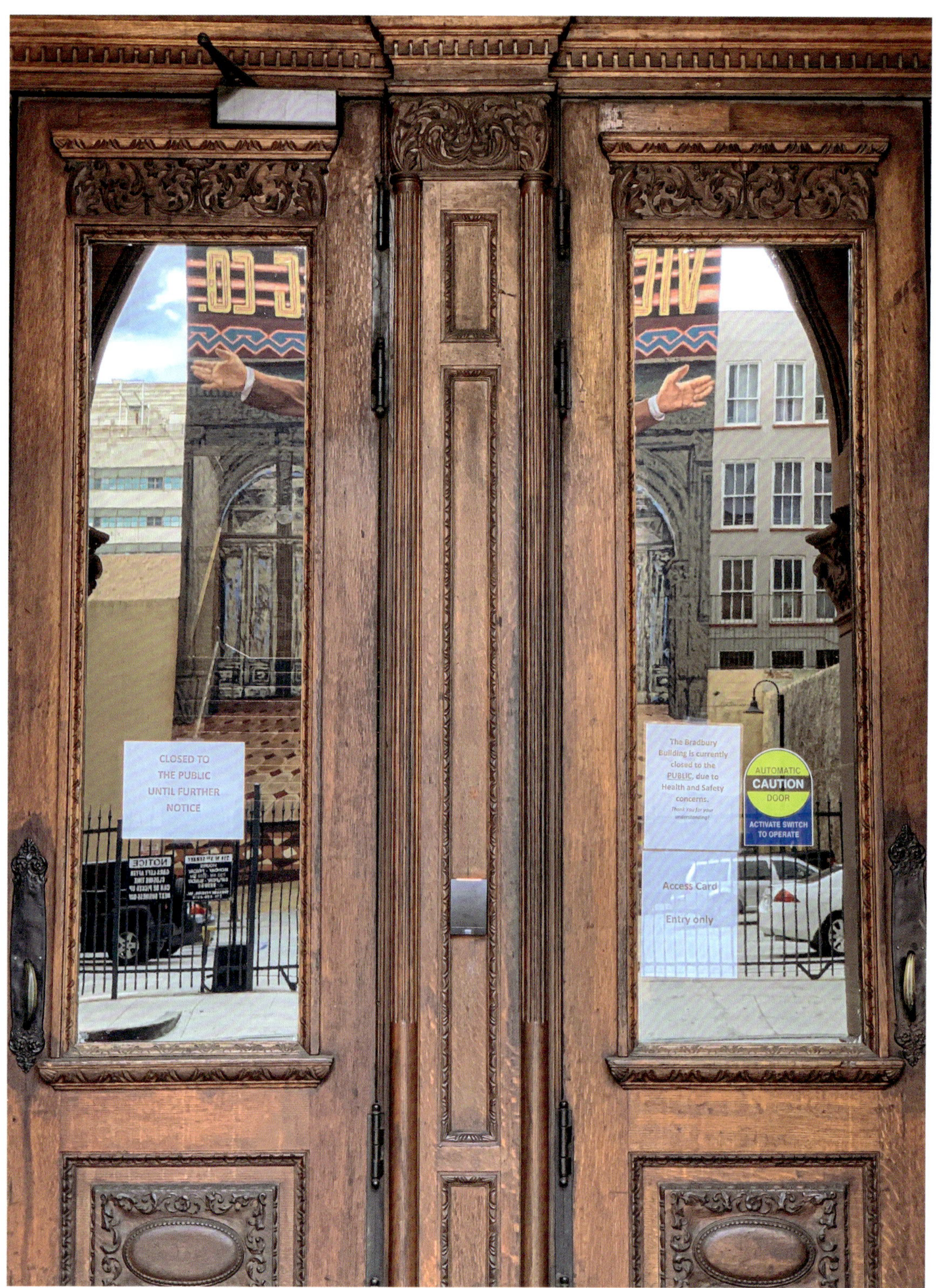
CLOSED TO
THE PUBLIC
UNTIL FURTHER
NOTICE
The Bradbury
Building is currently
closed to the
PUBLIC, due to
Health and Safety
concerns.
Thank you for your
understanding!
AUTOMATIC
CAUTION
DOOR
ACTIVATE SWITCH
TO OPERATE
Access Card
Entry only

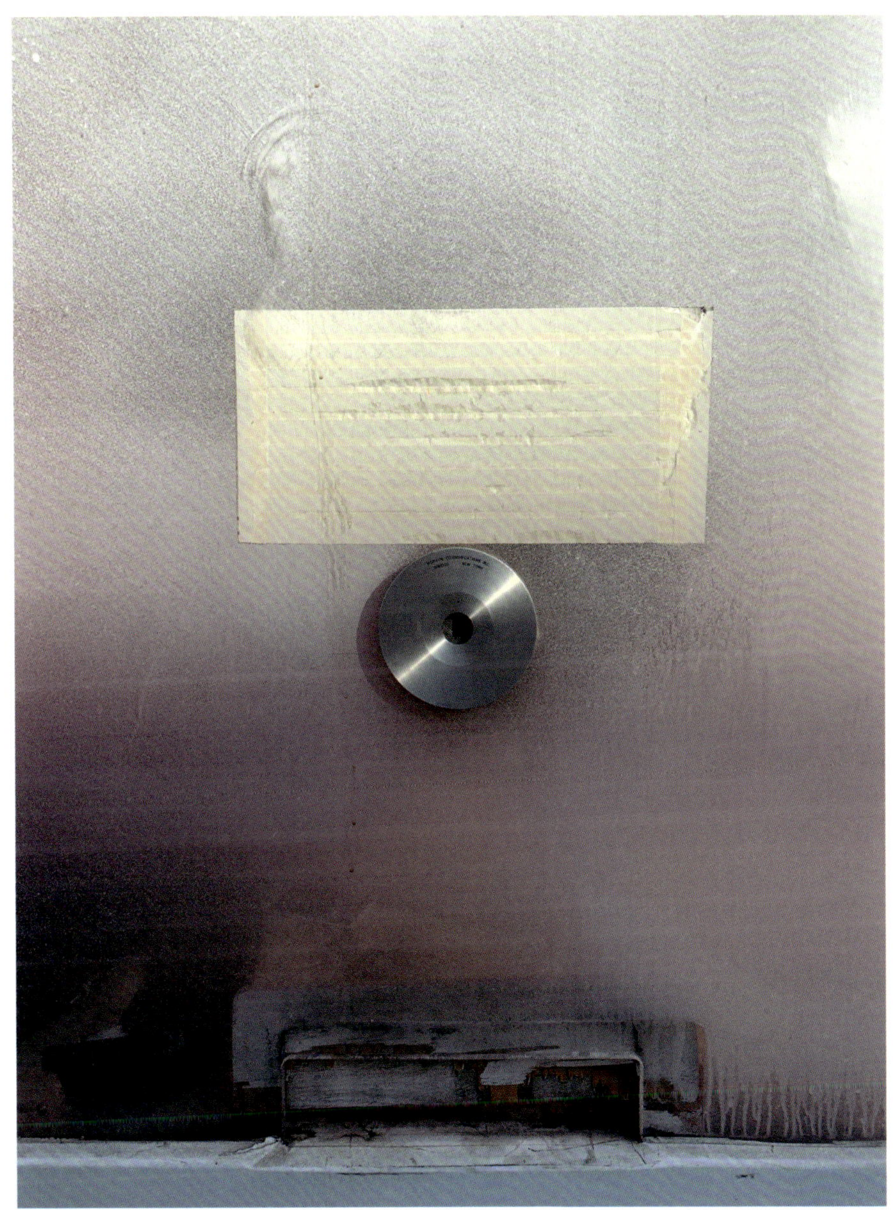

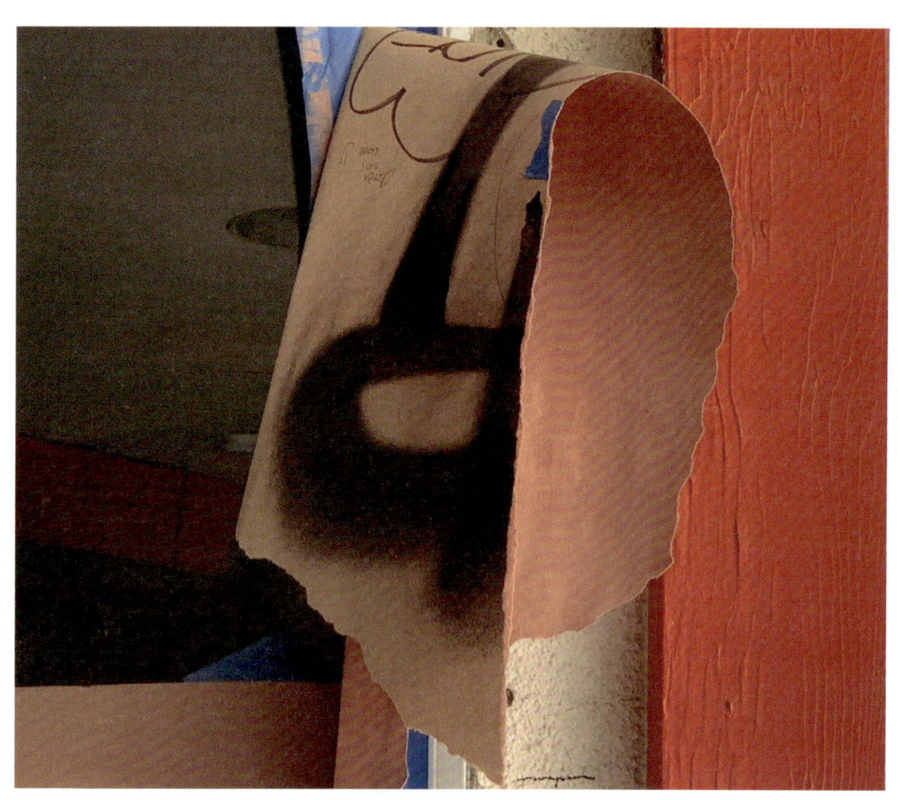

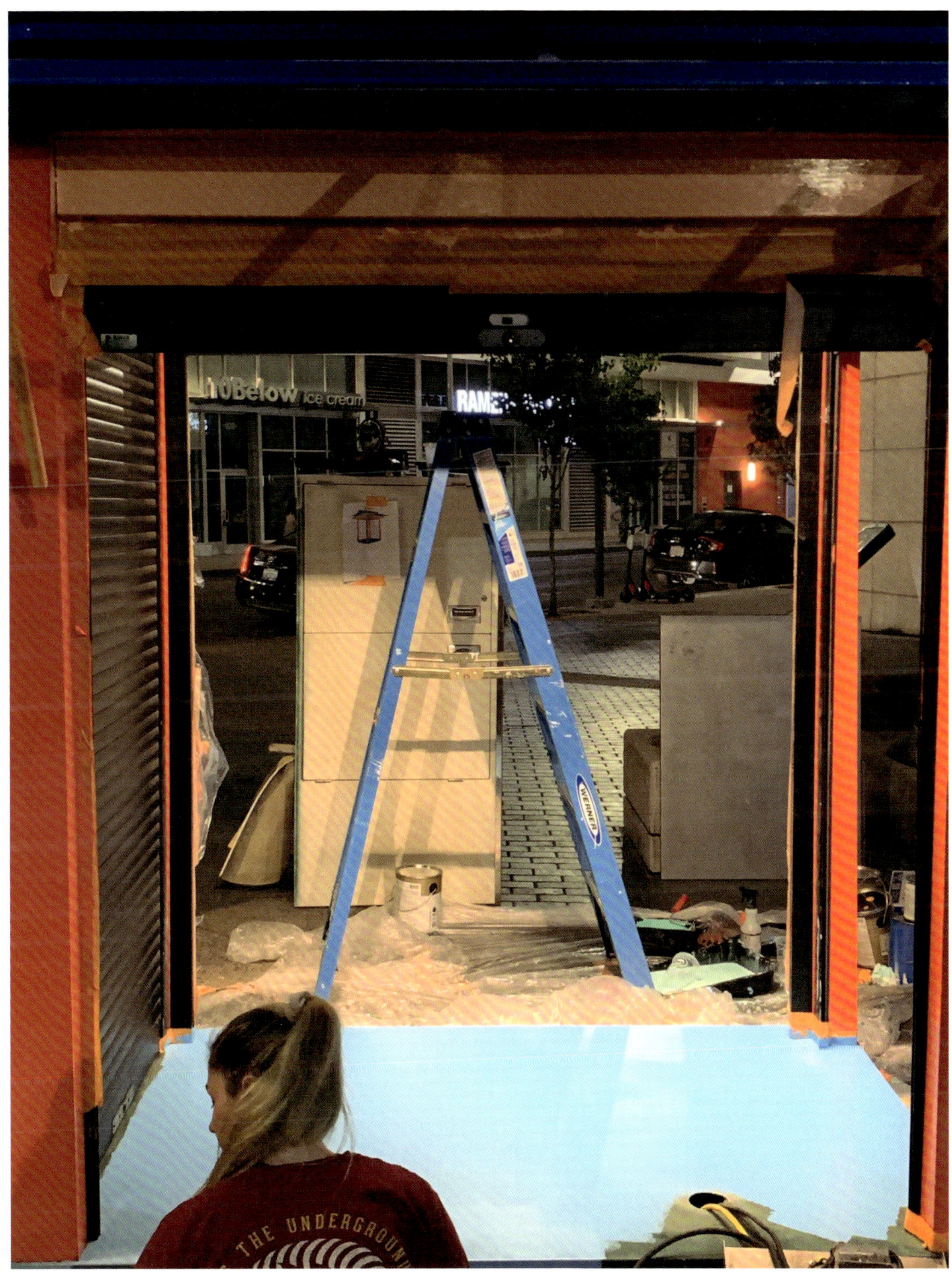
10Below ice cream
WERNER

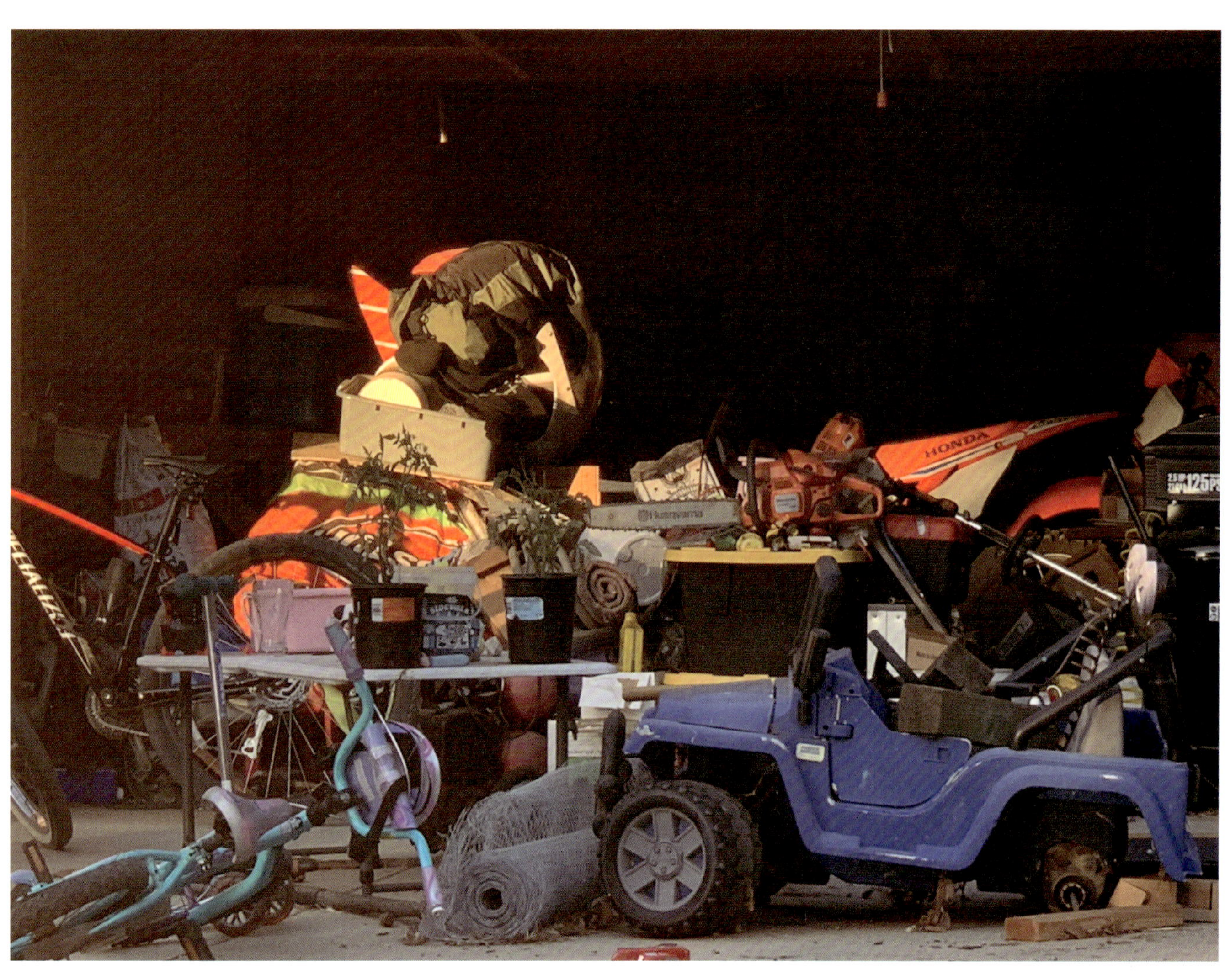
Husqvarna
HONDA

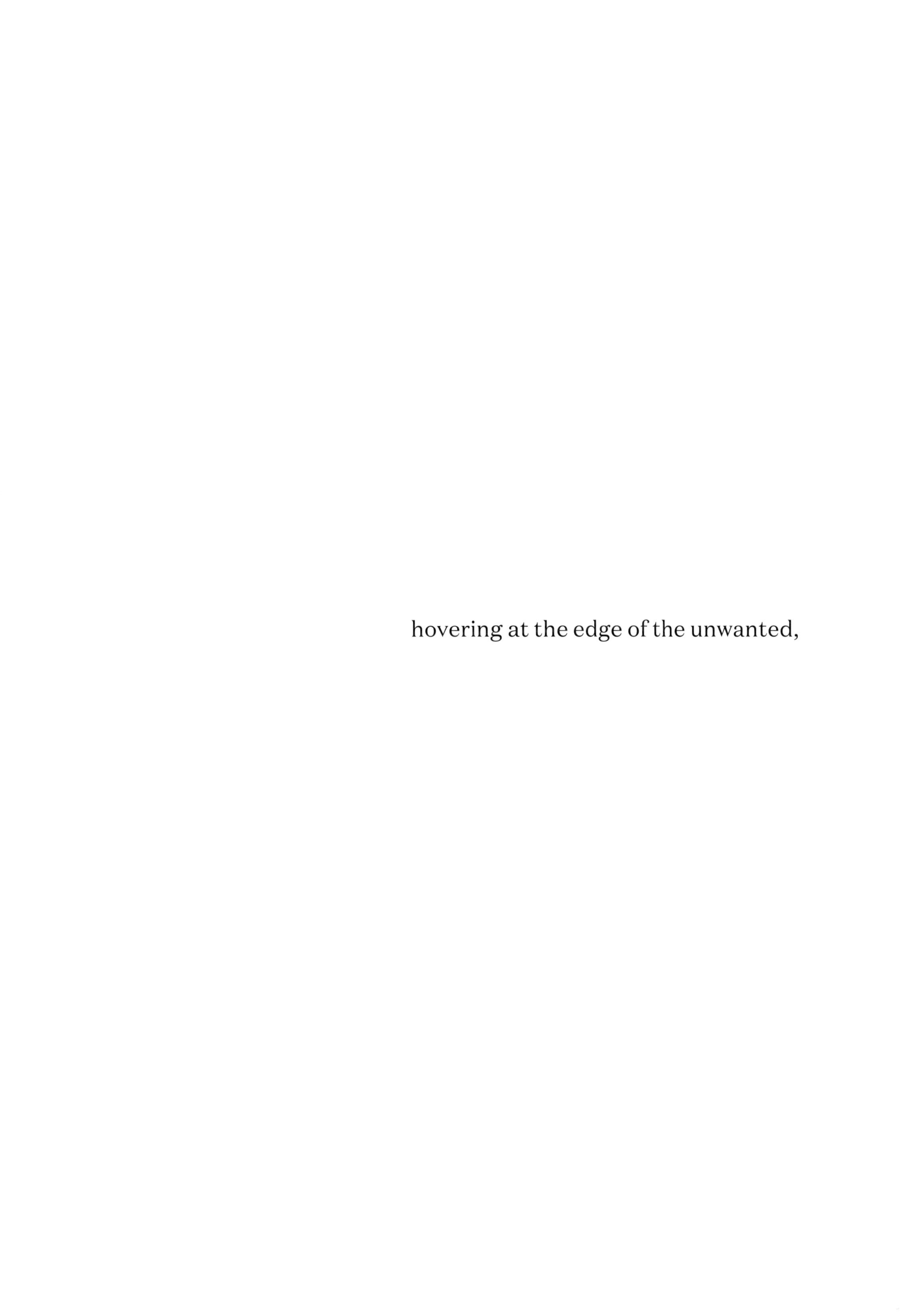

hovering at the edge of the unwanted,

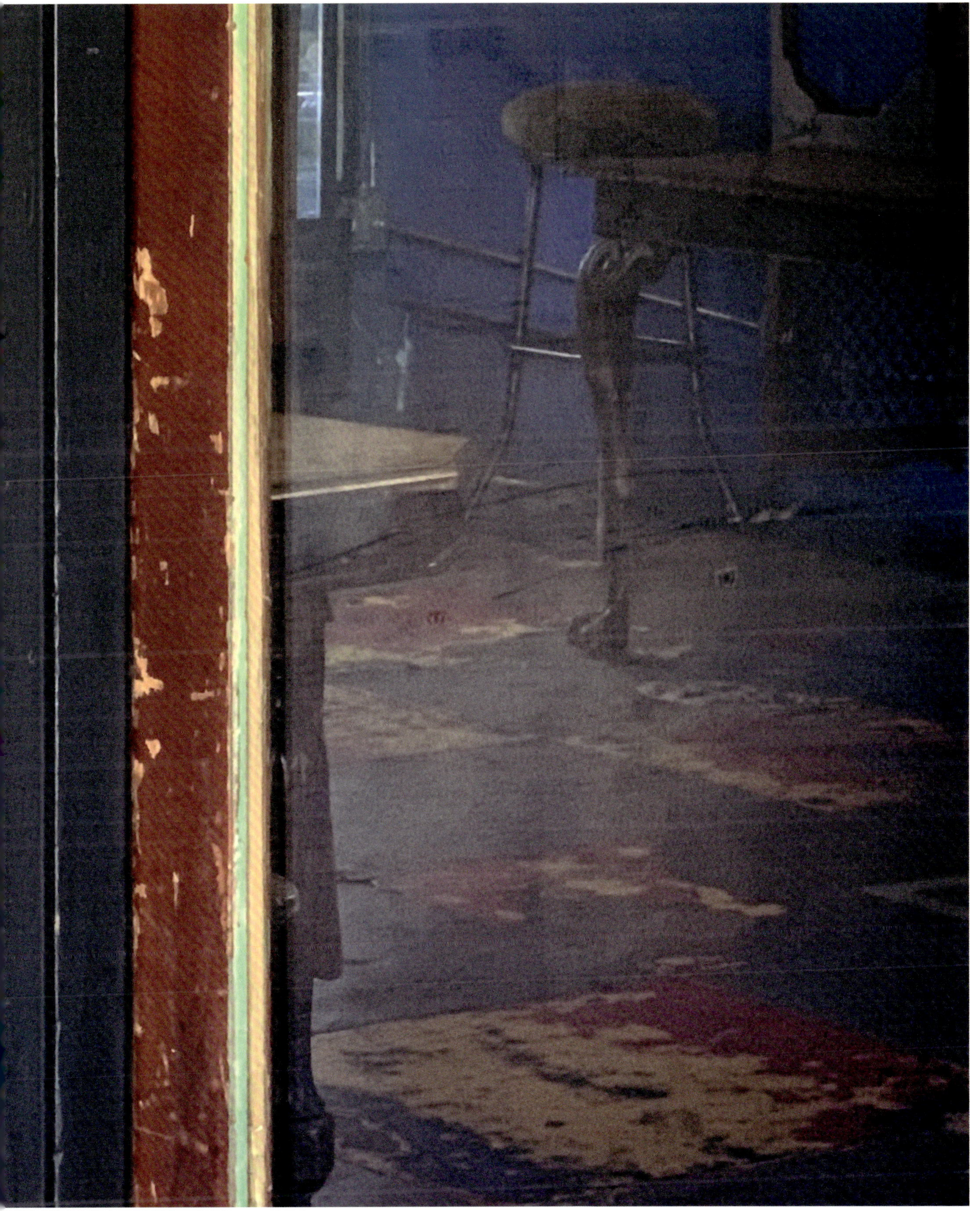

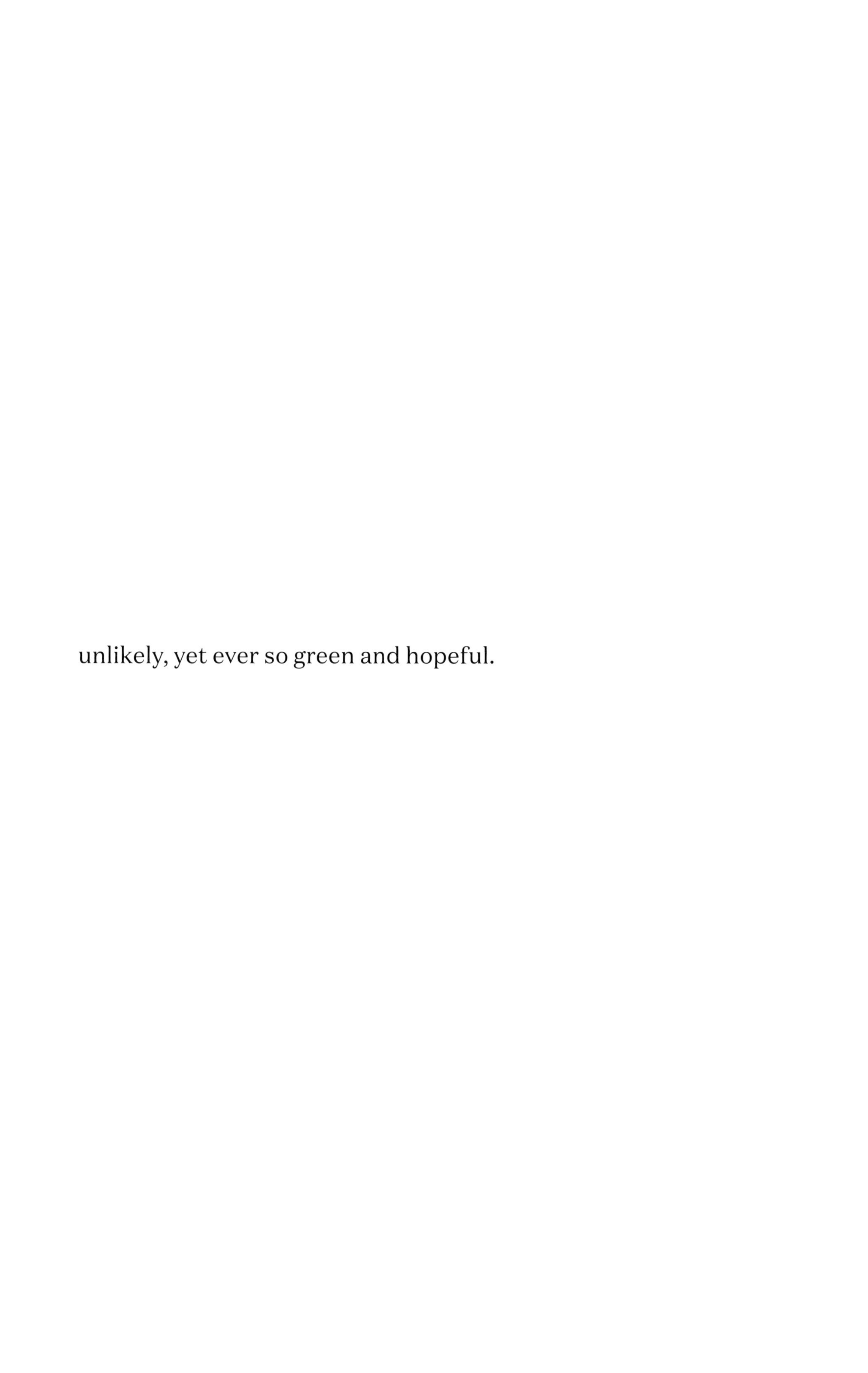

unlikely, yet ever so green and hopeful.

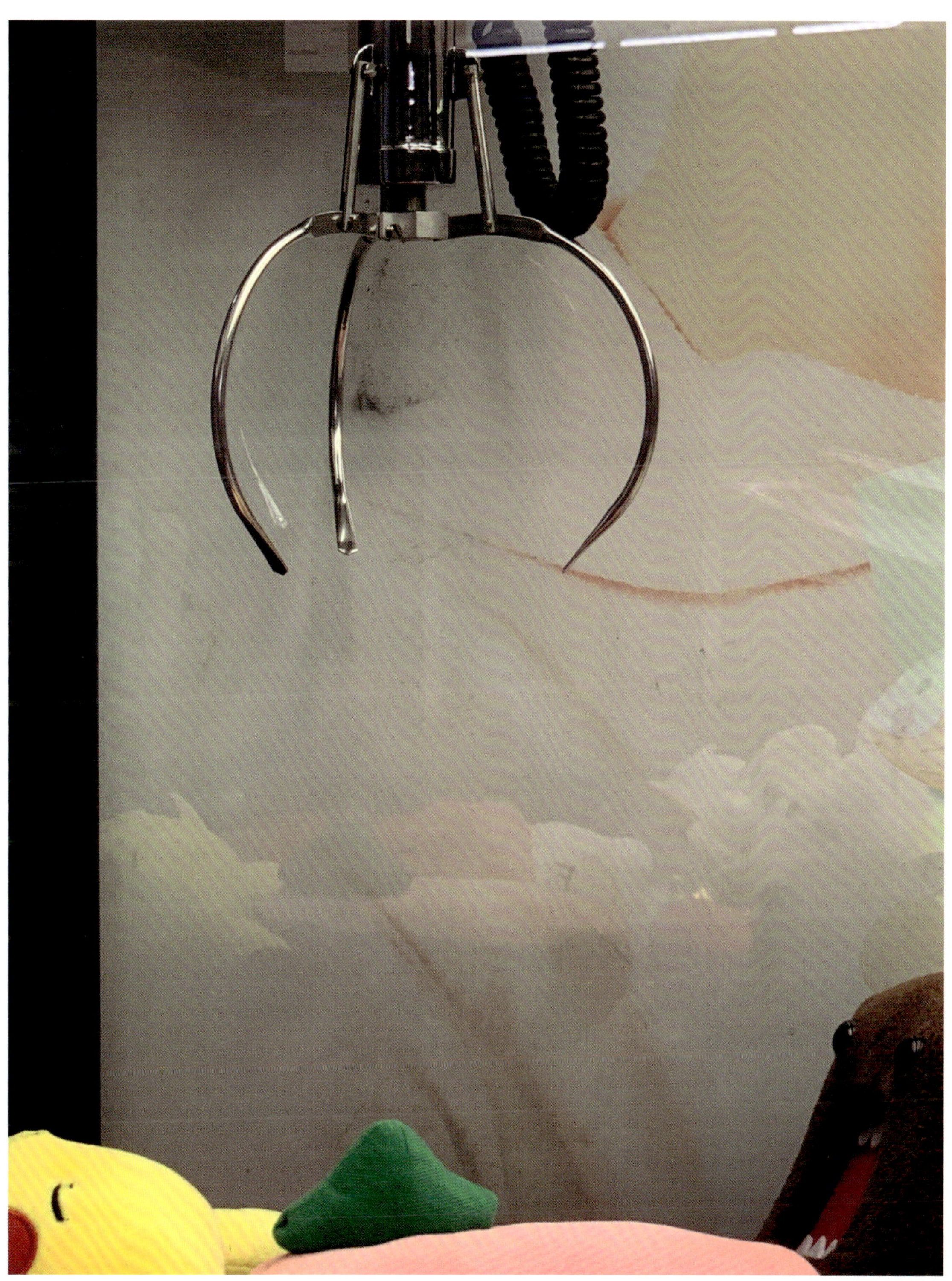

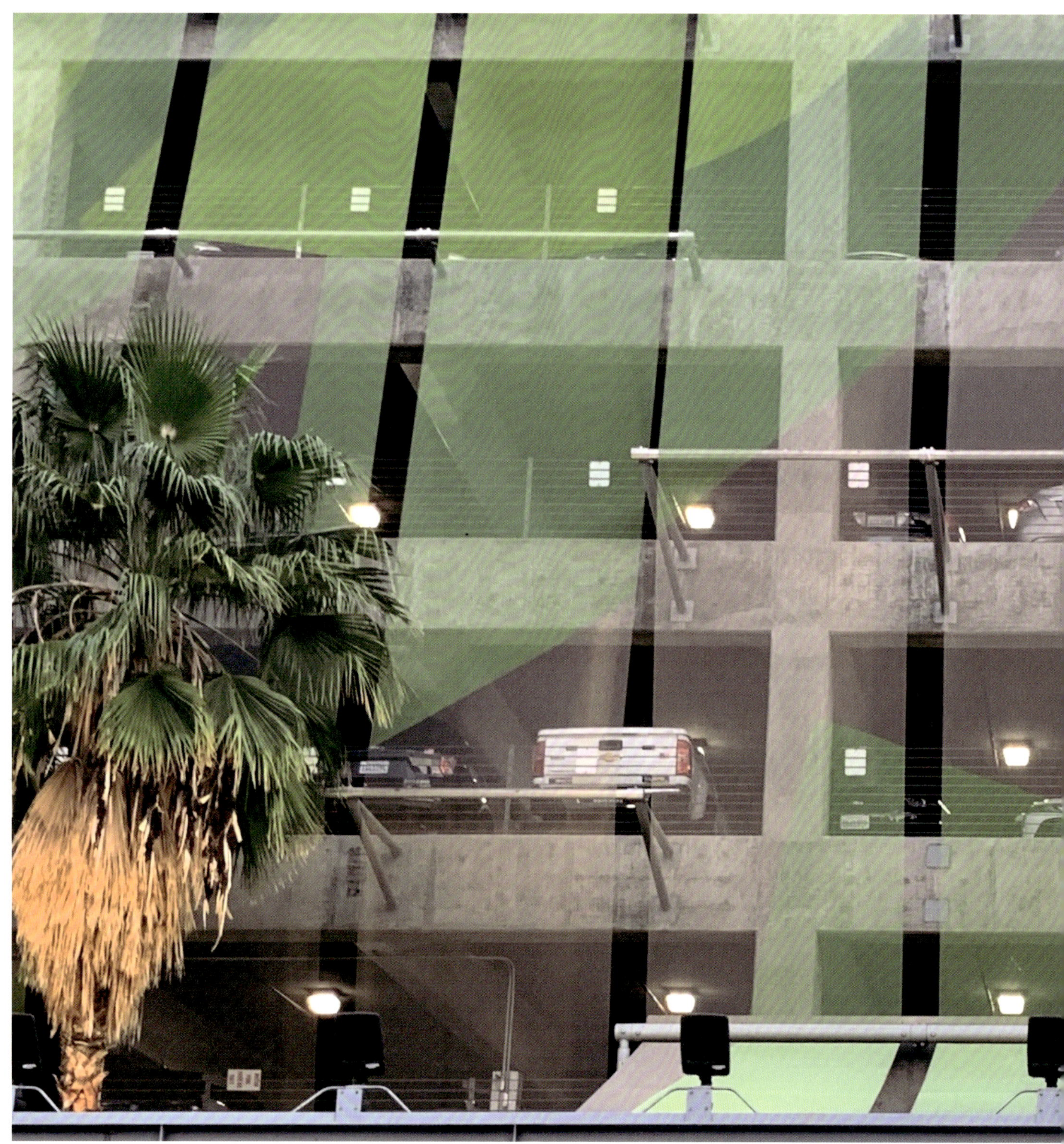

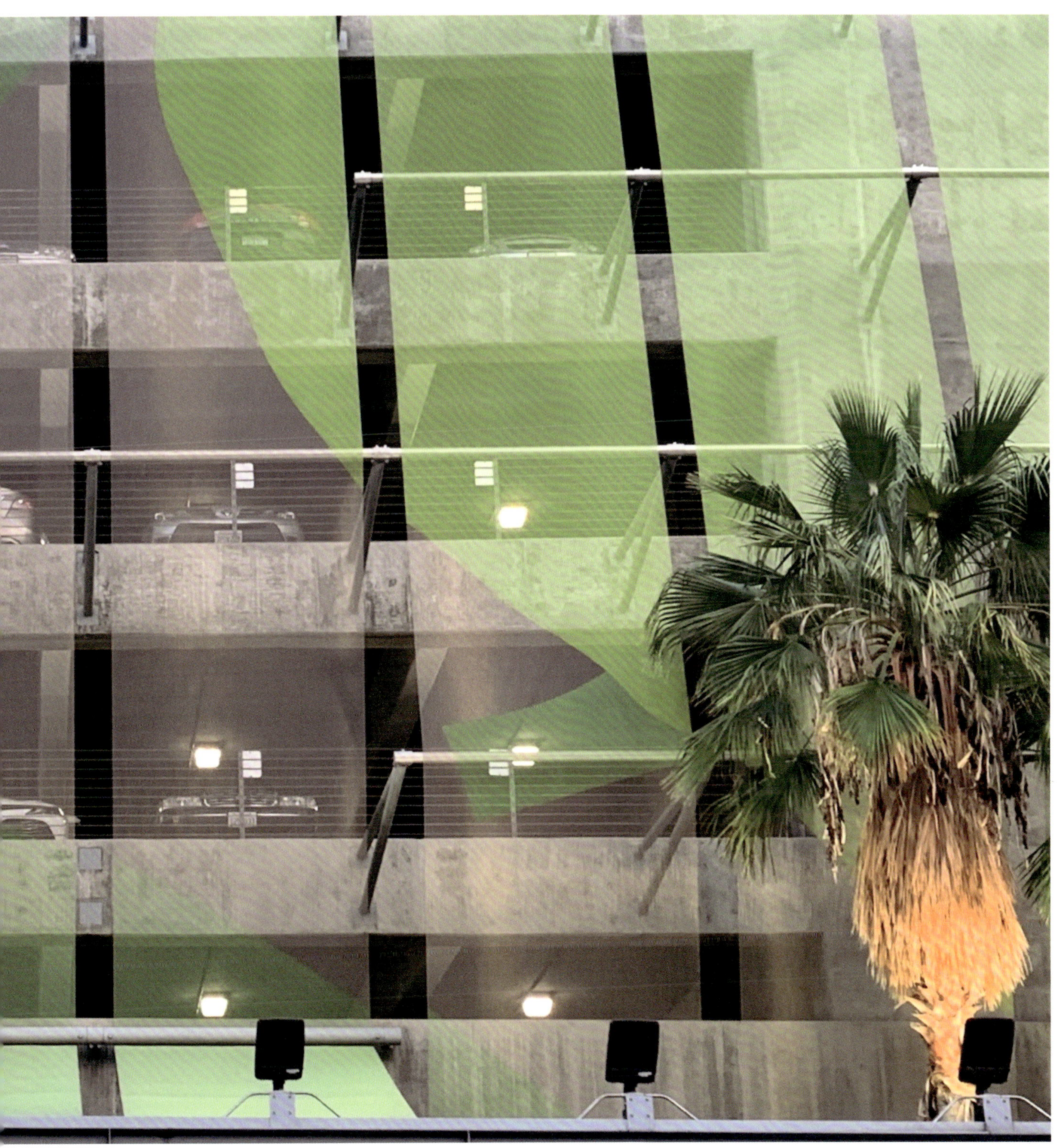

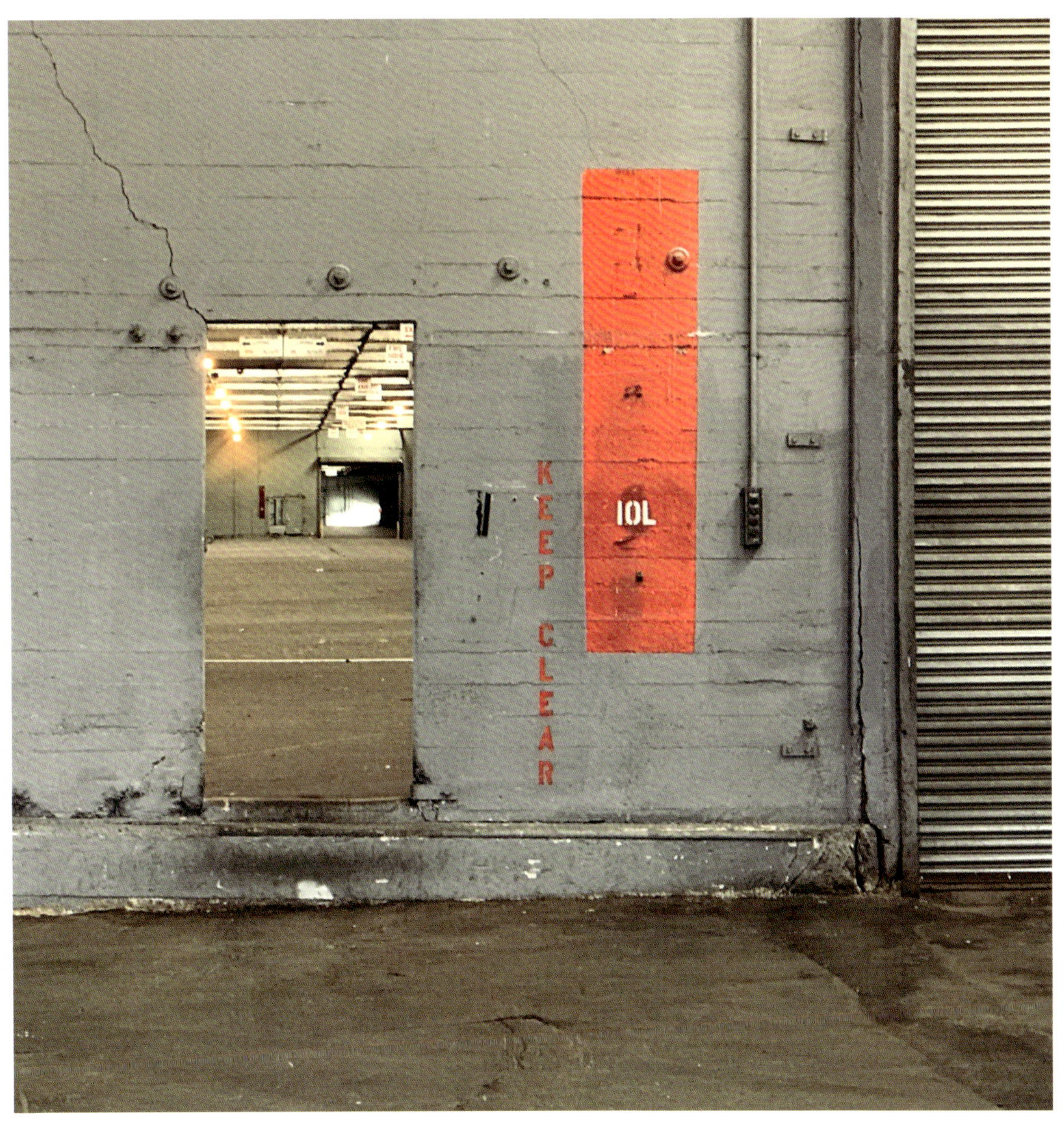
KEEP CLEAR
IOL

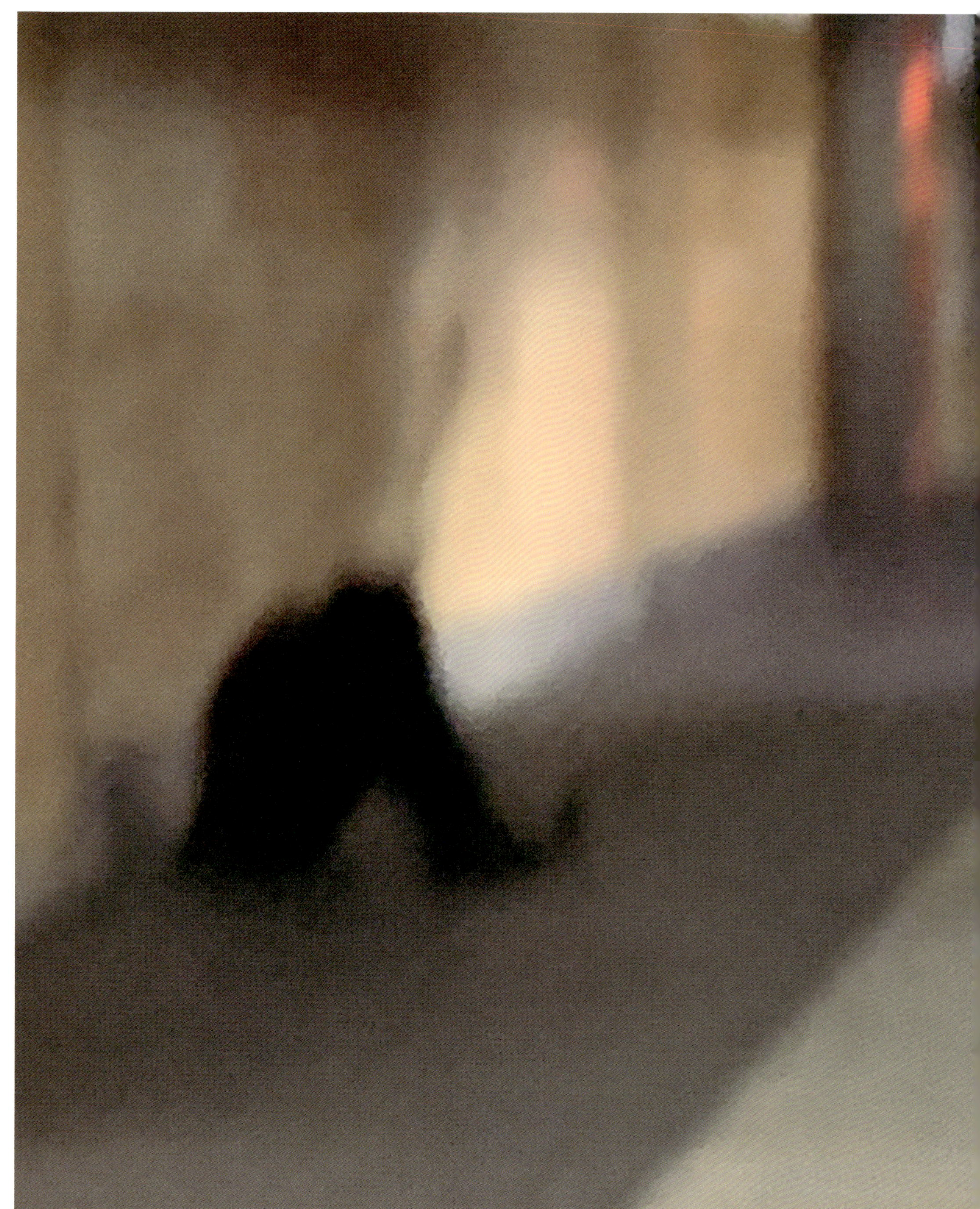

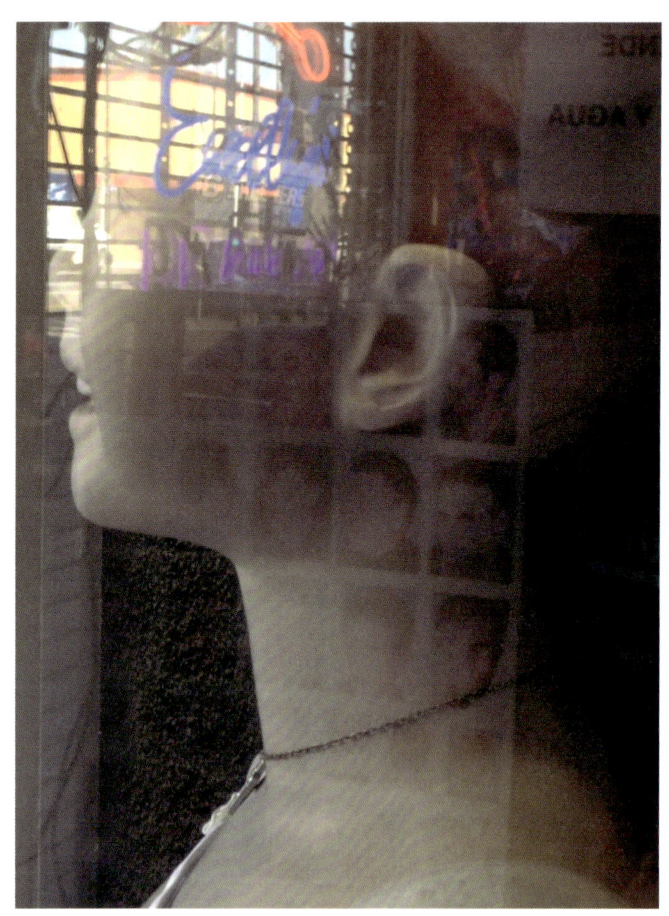

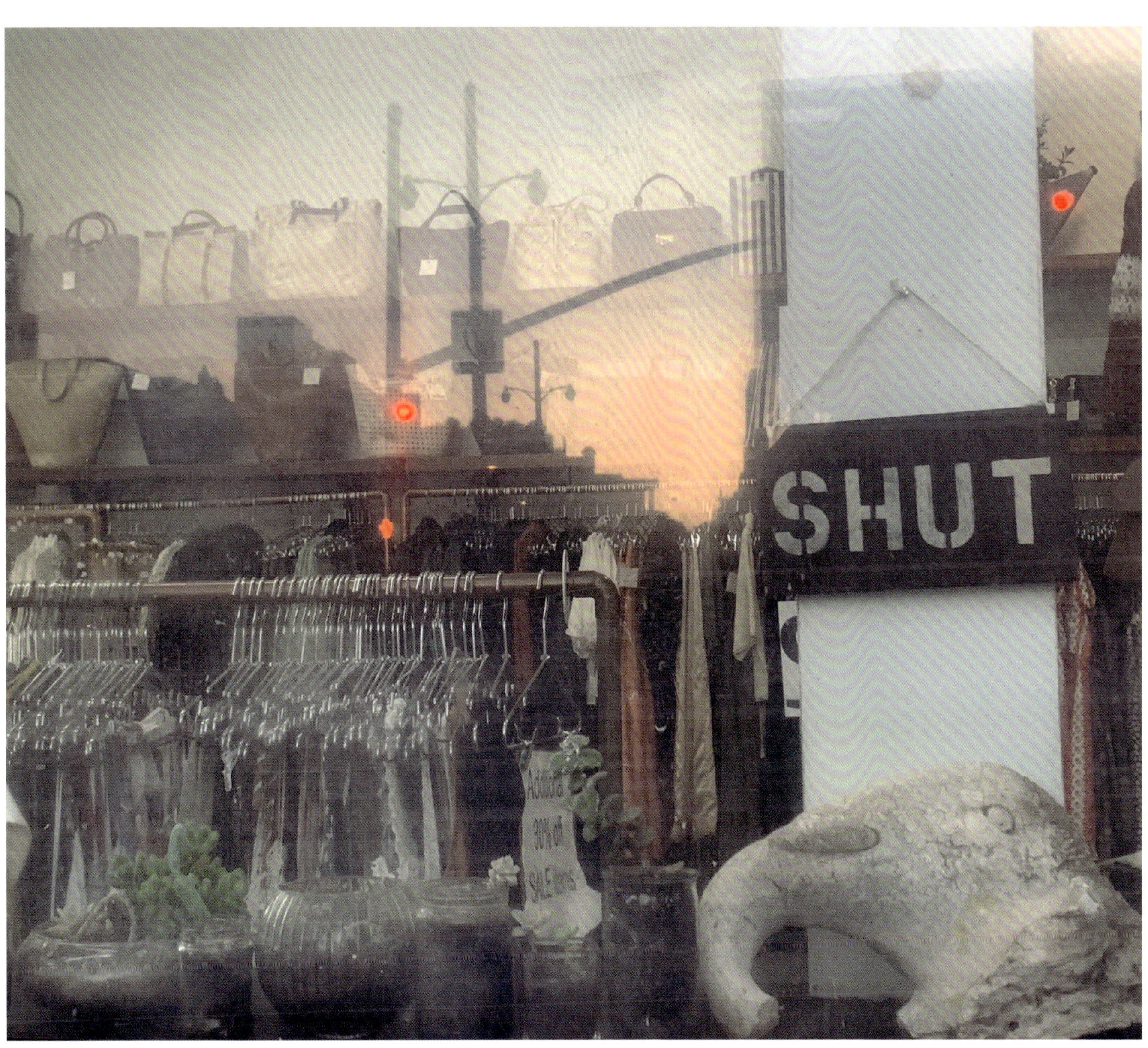
SHUT
30% off

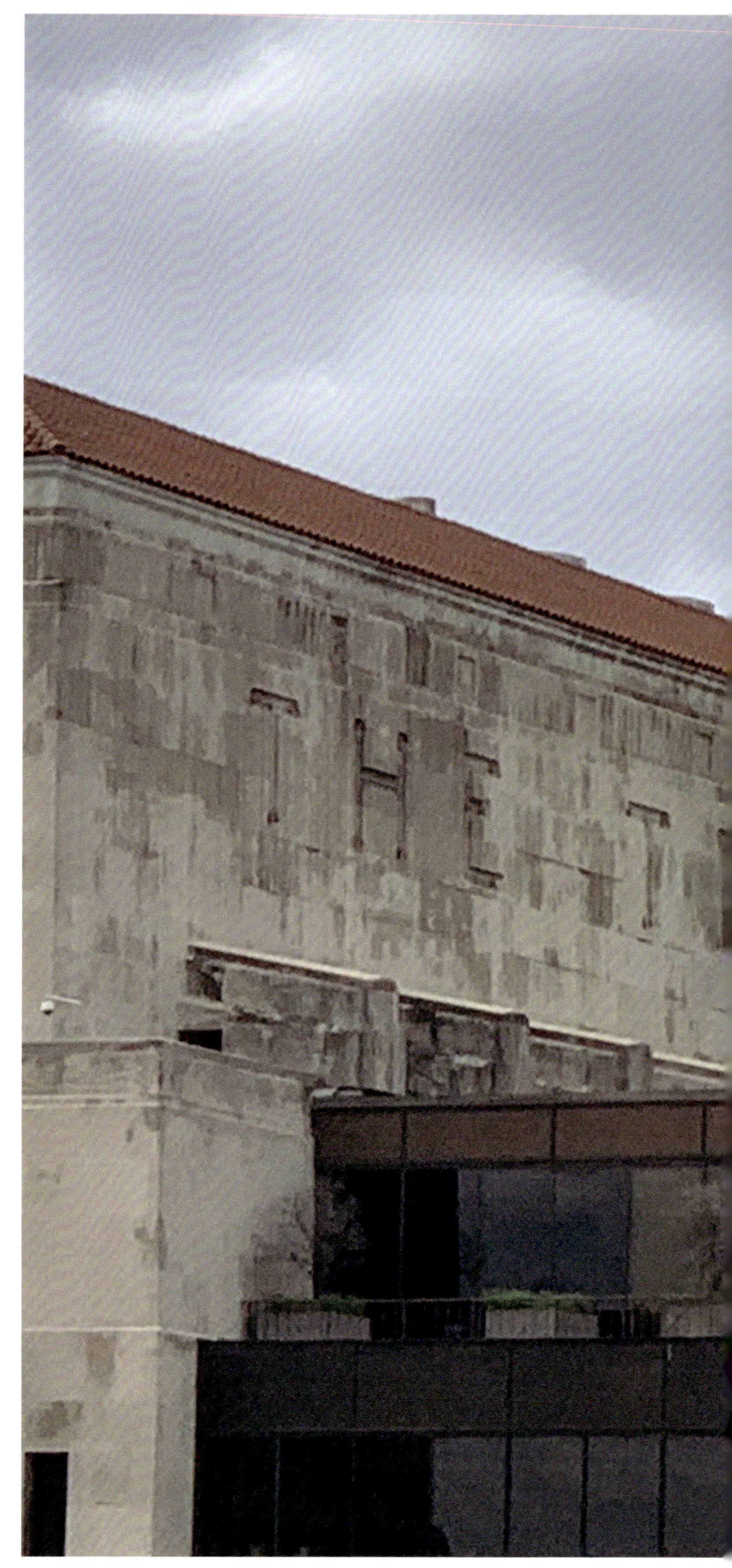
THE

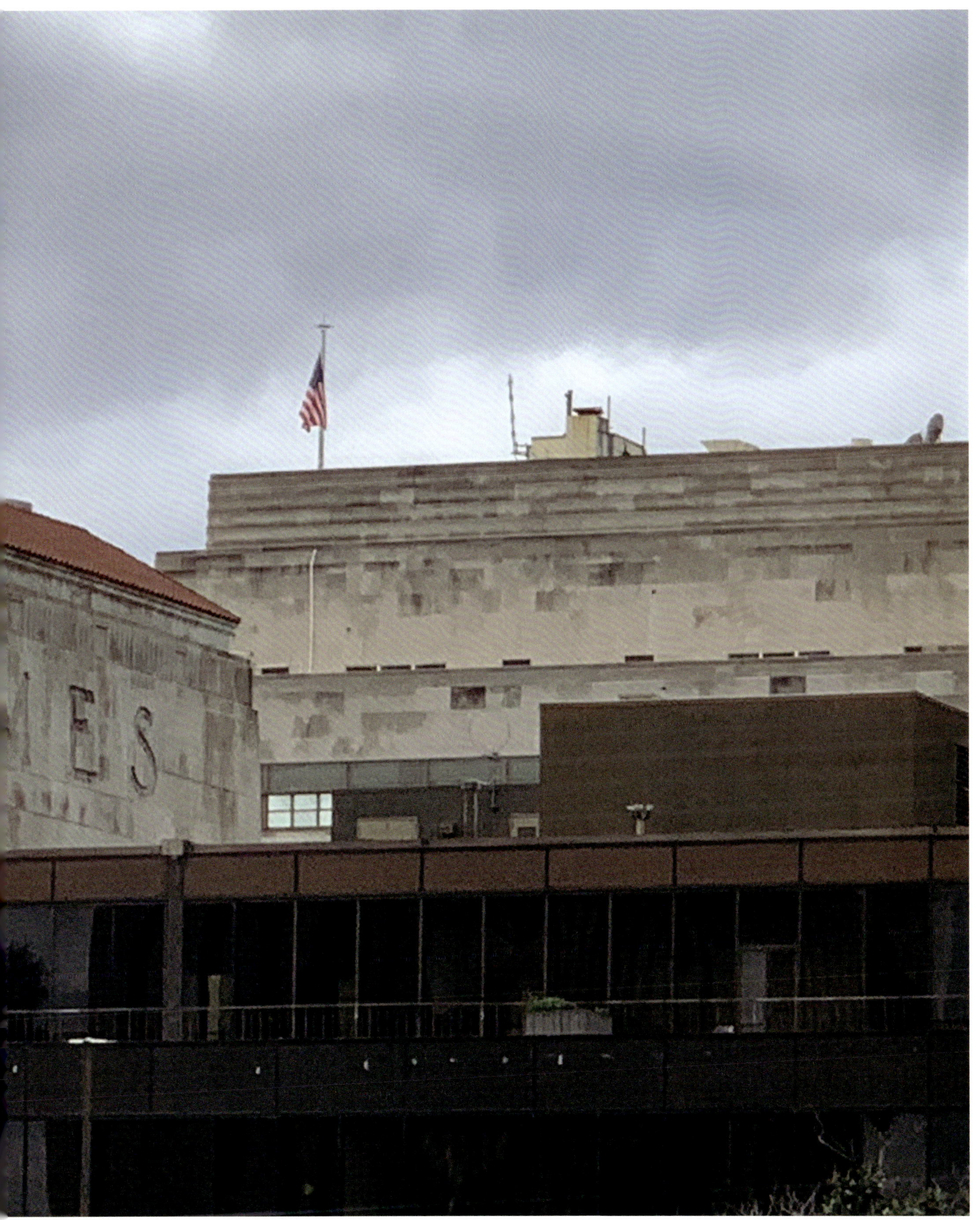

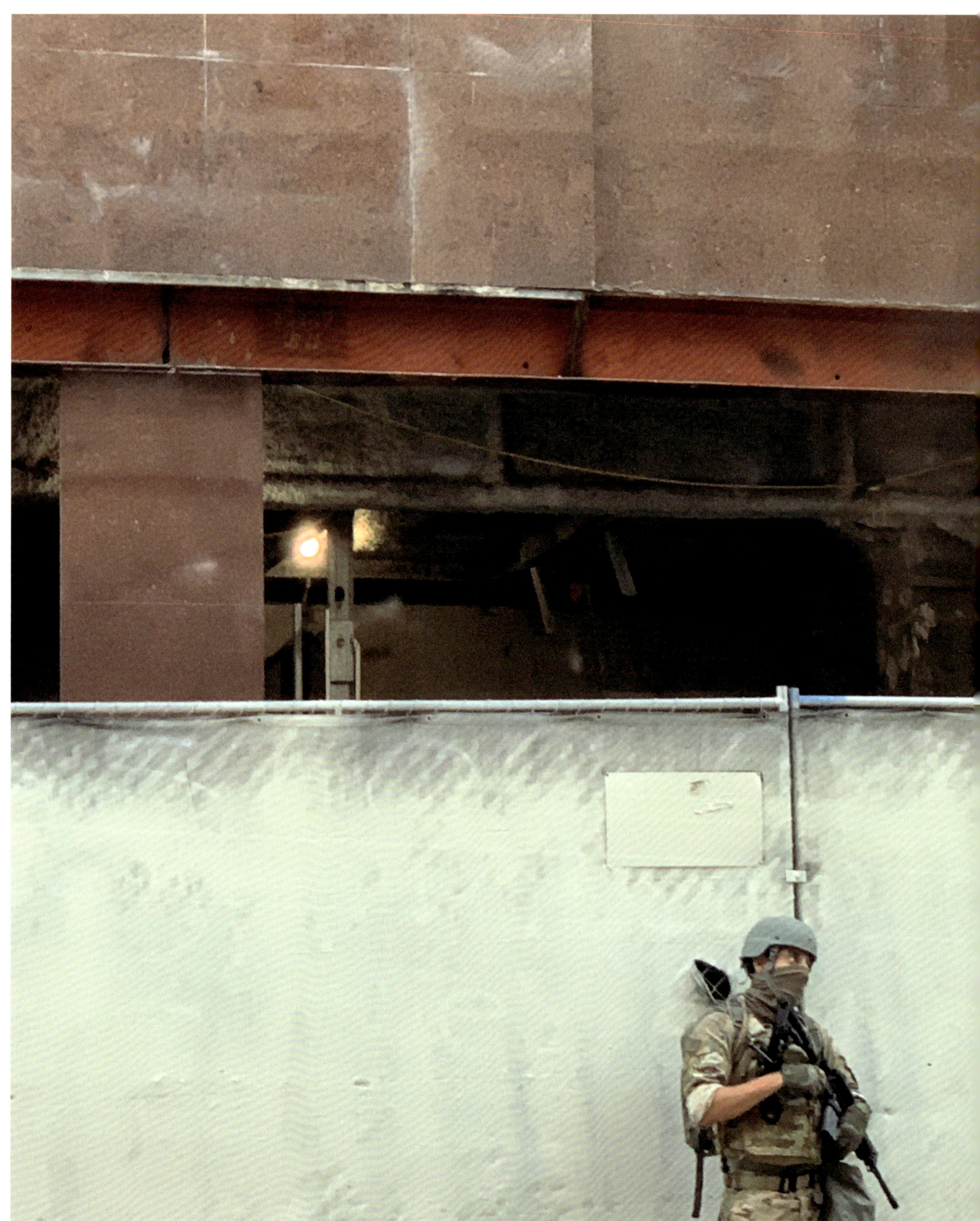

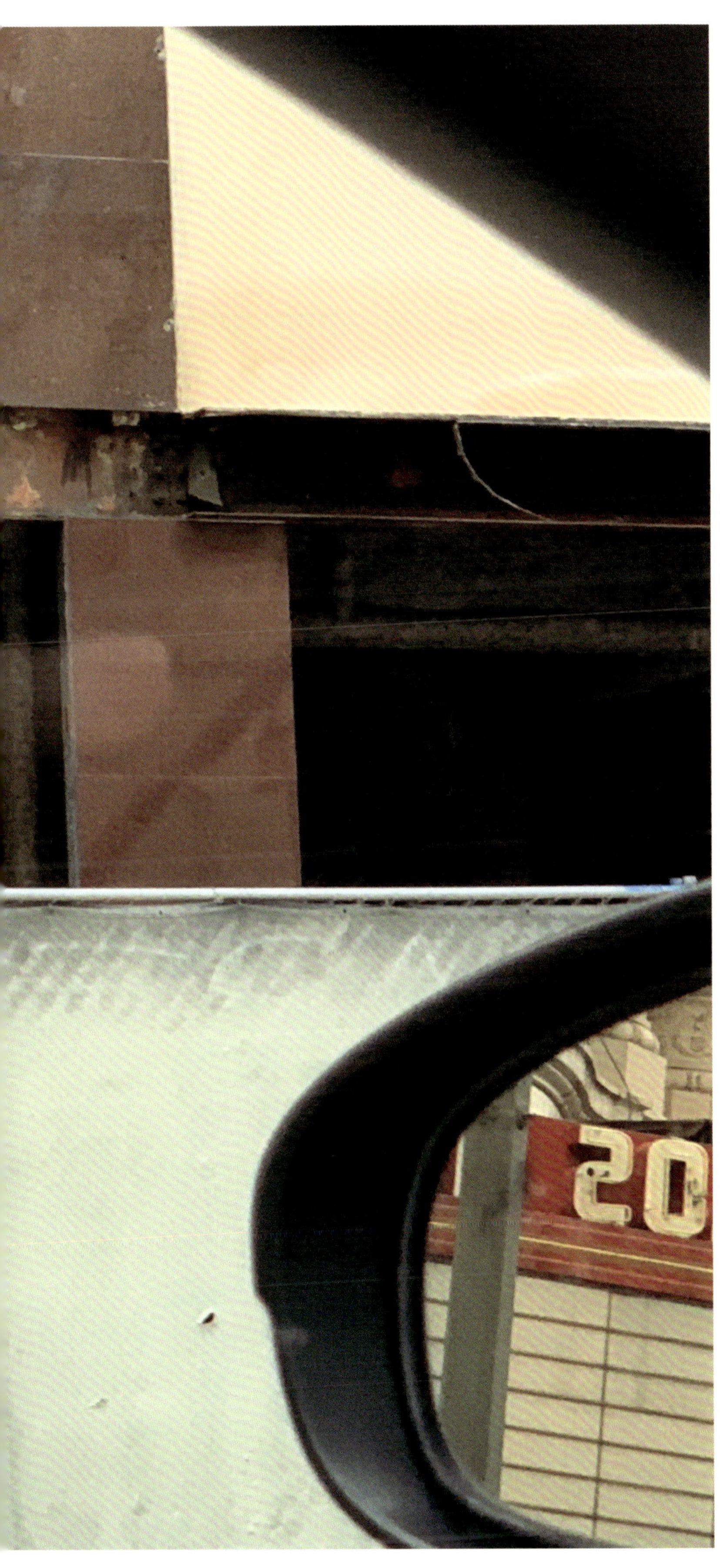
20

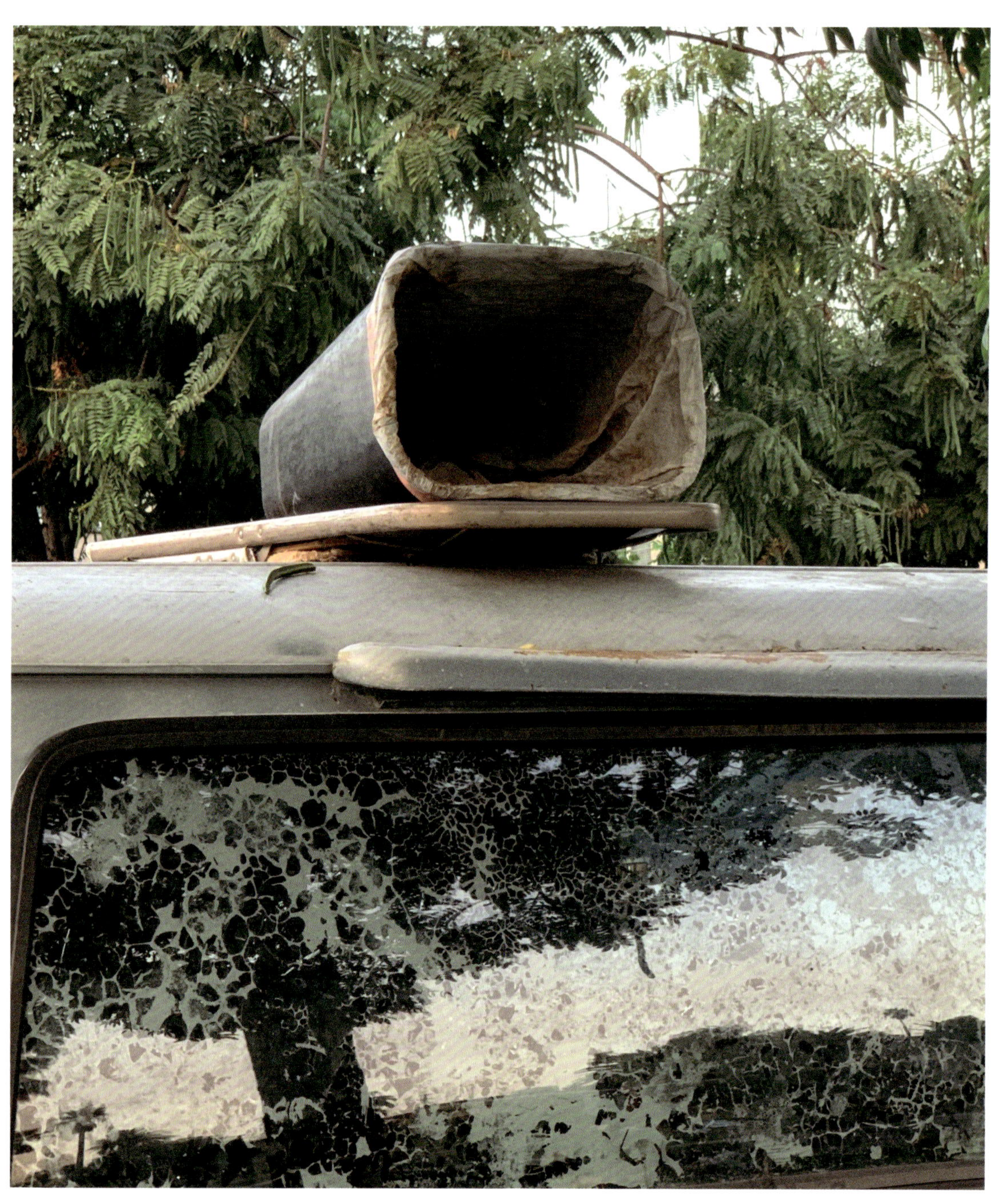

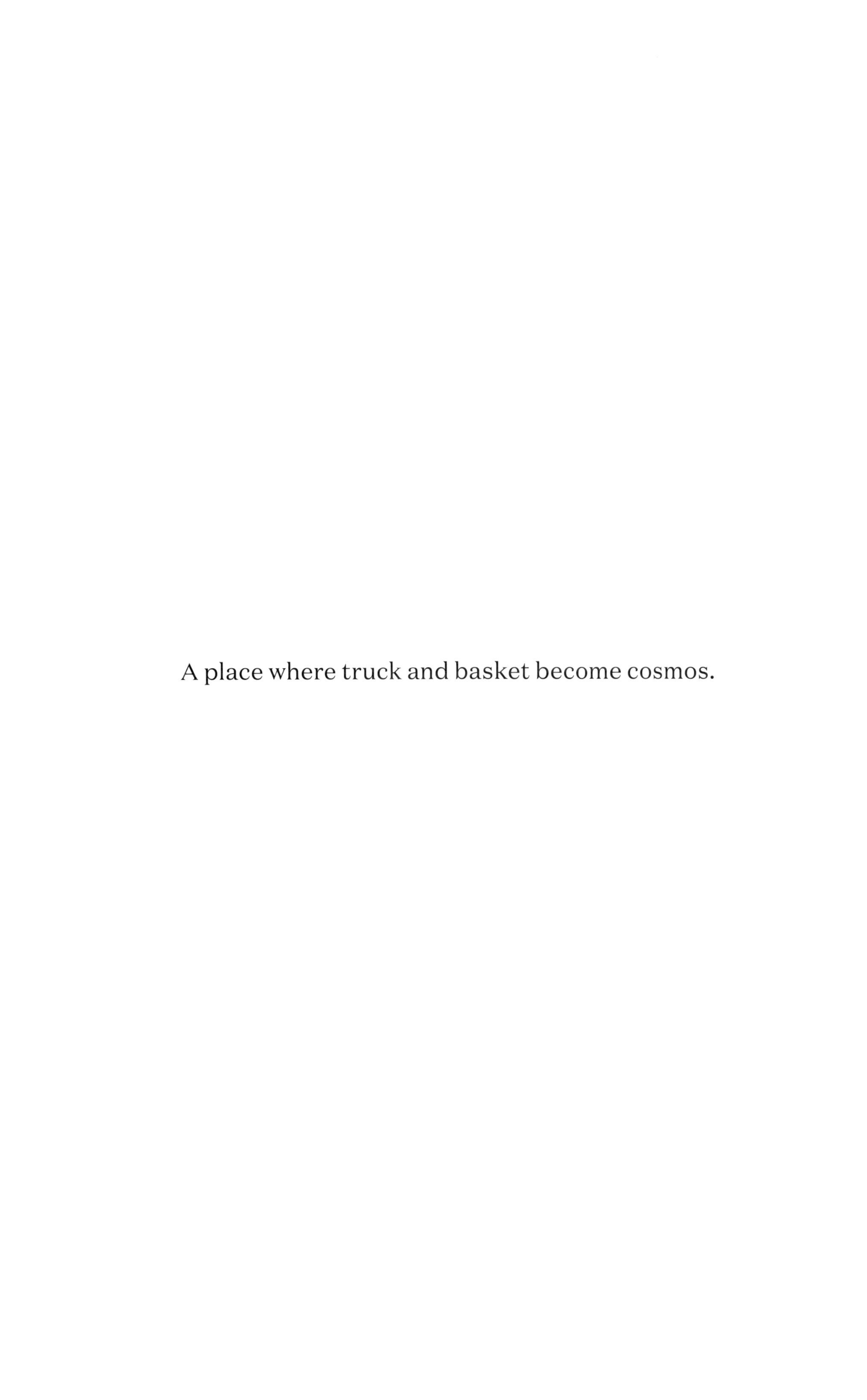

A place where truck and basket become cosmos.

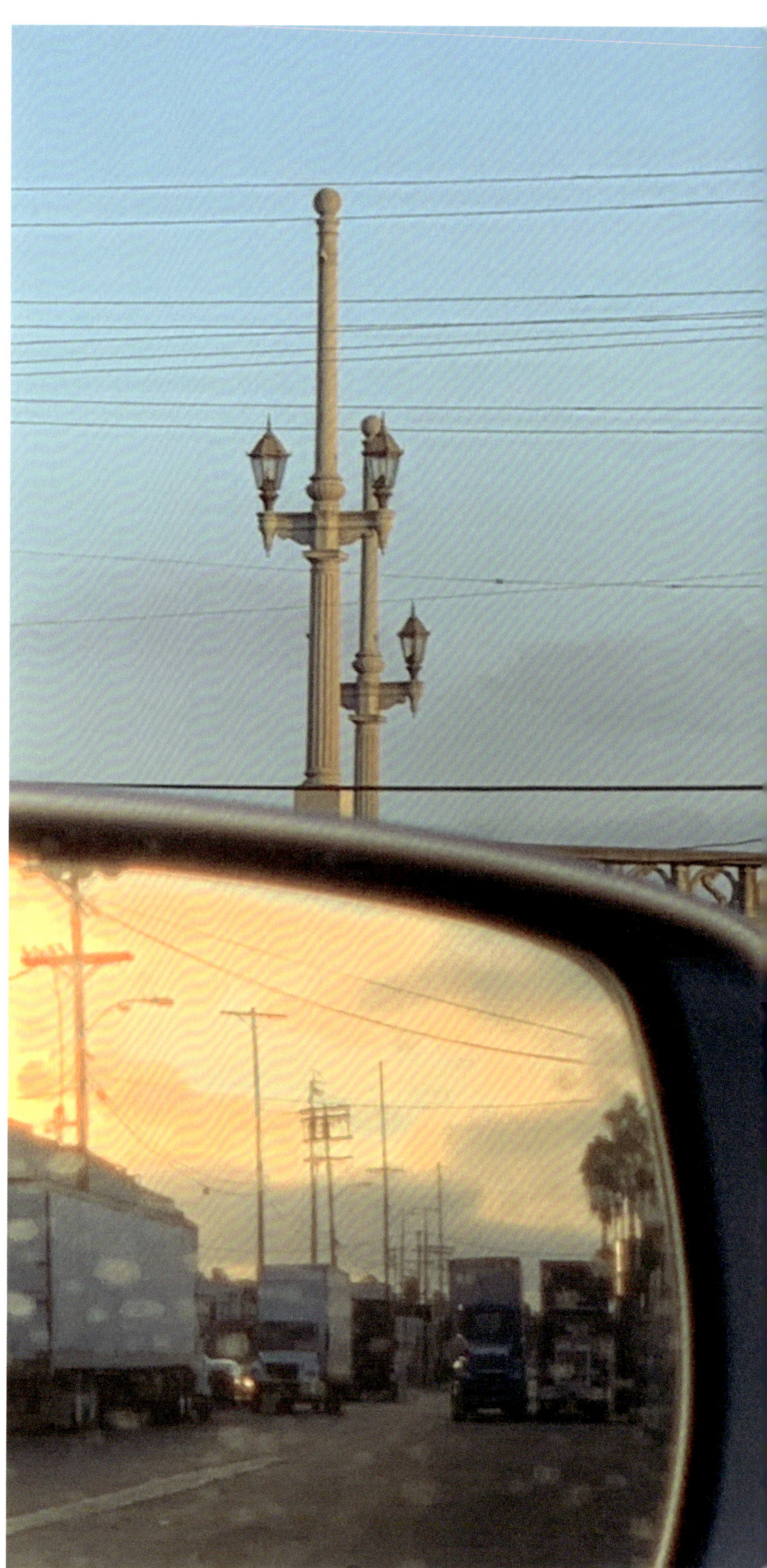

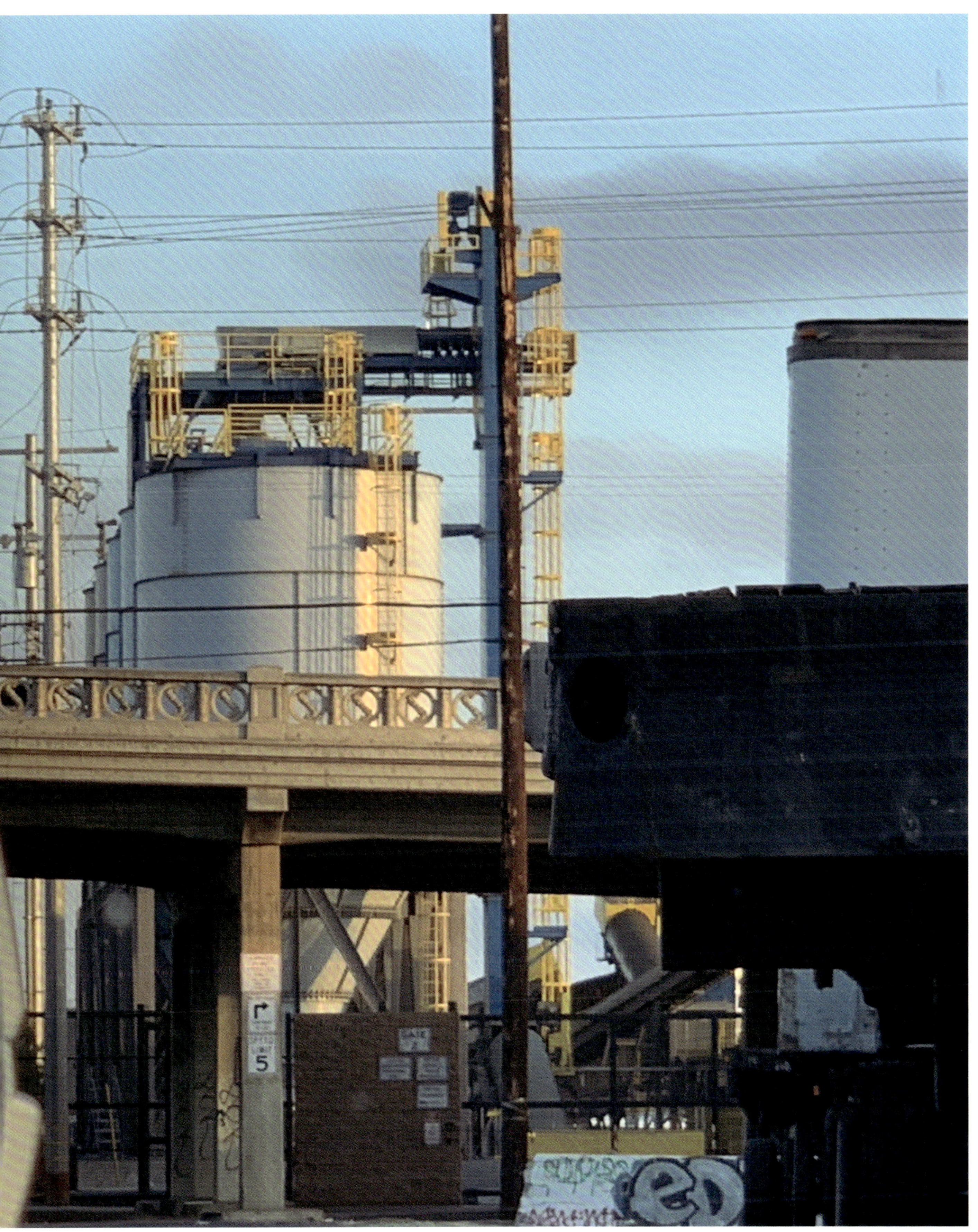
GATE
5

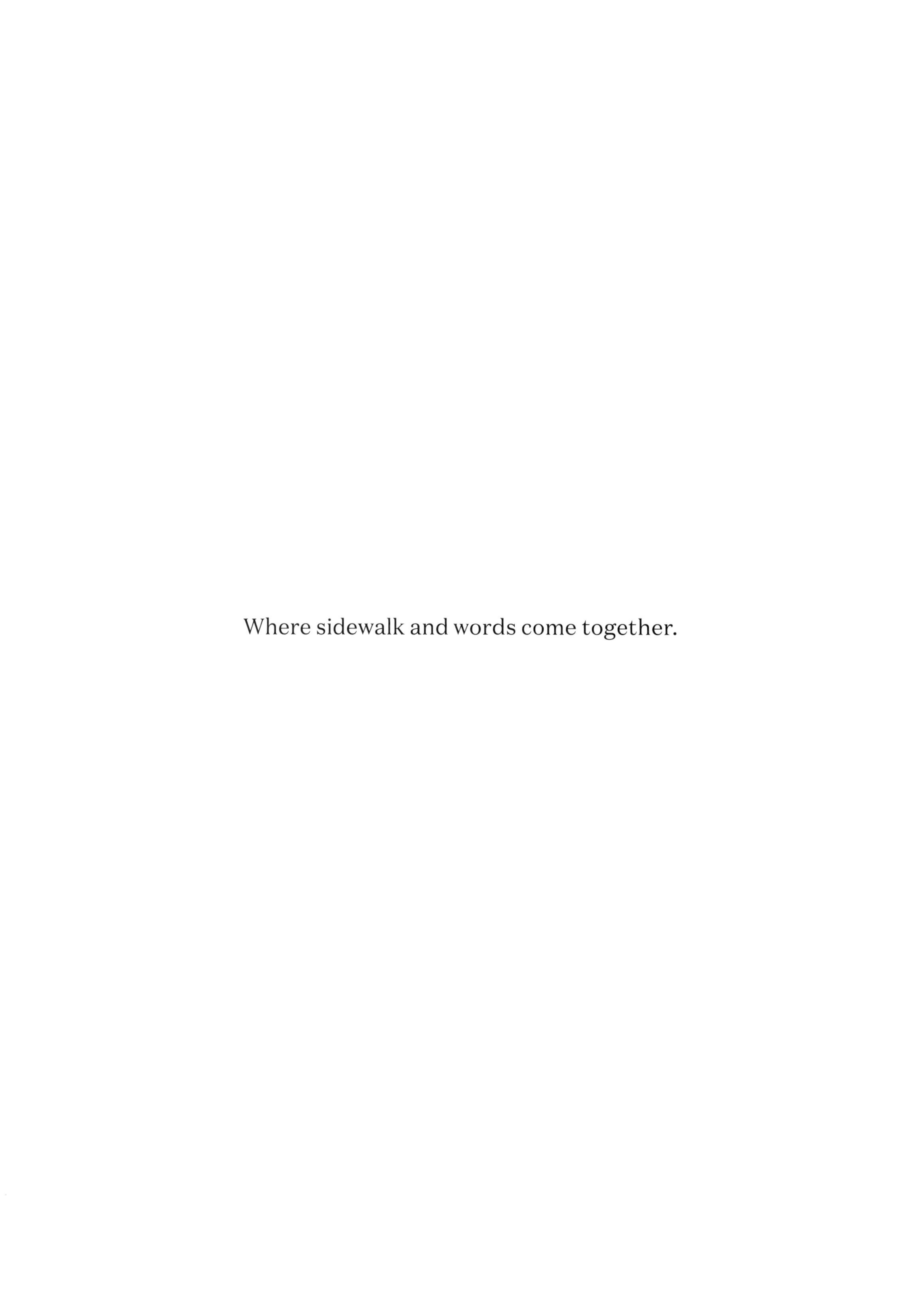

Where sidewalk and words come together.

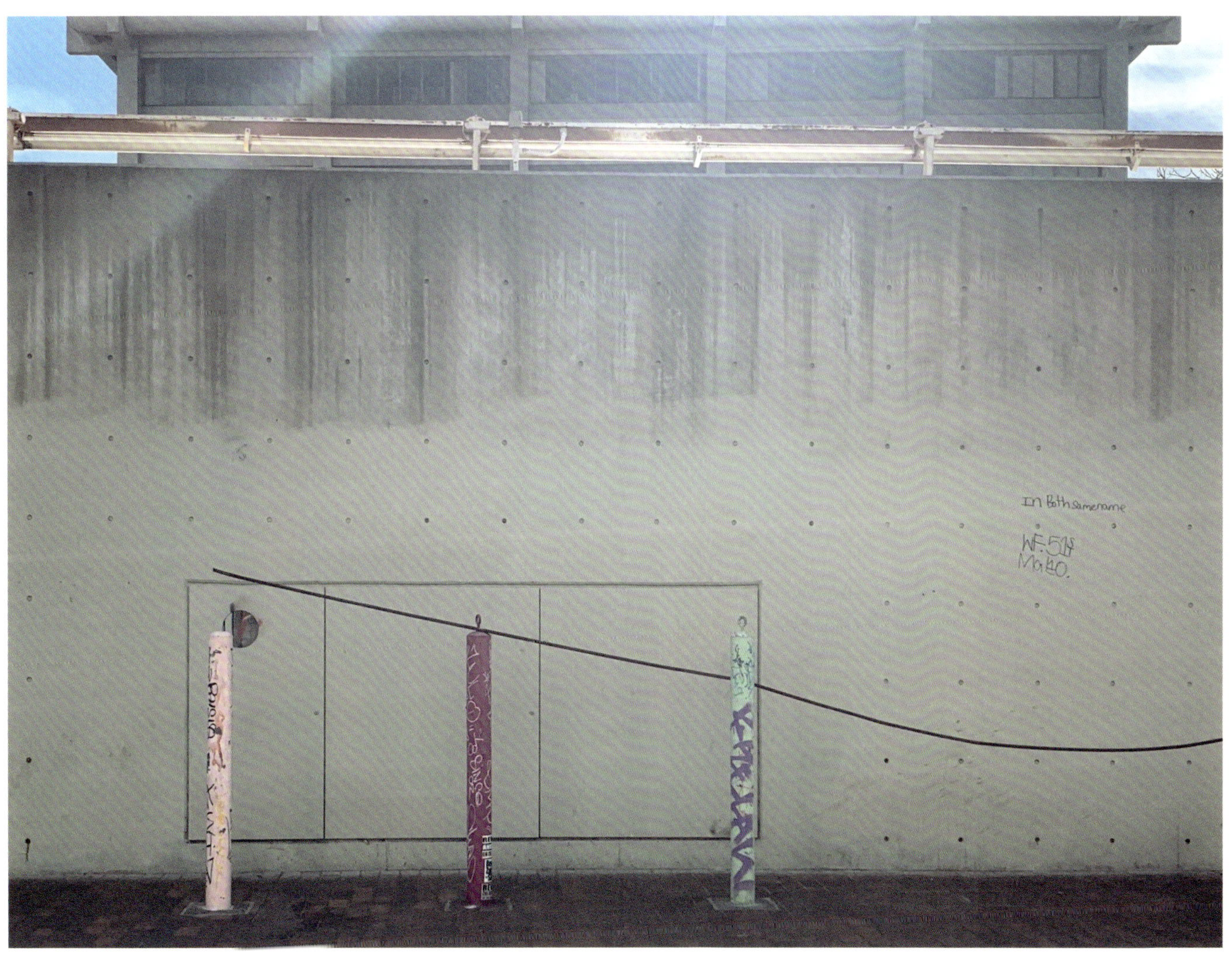
In Both samename

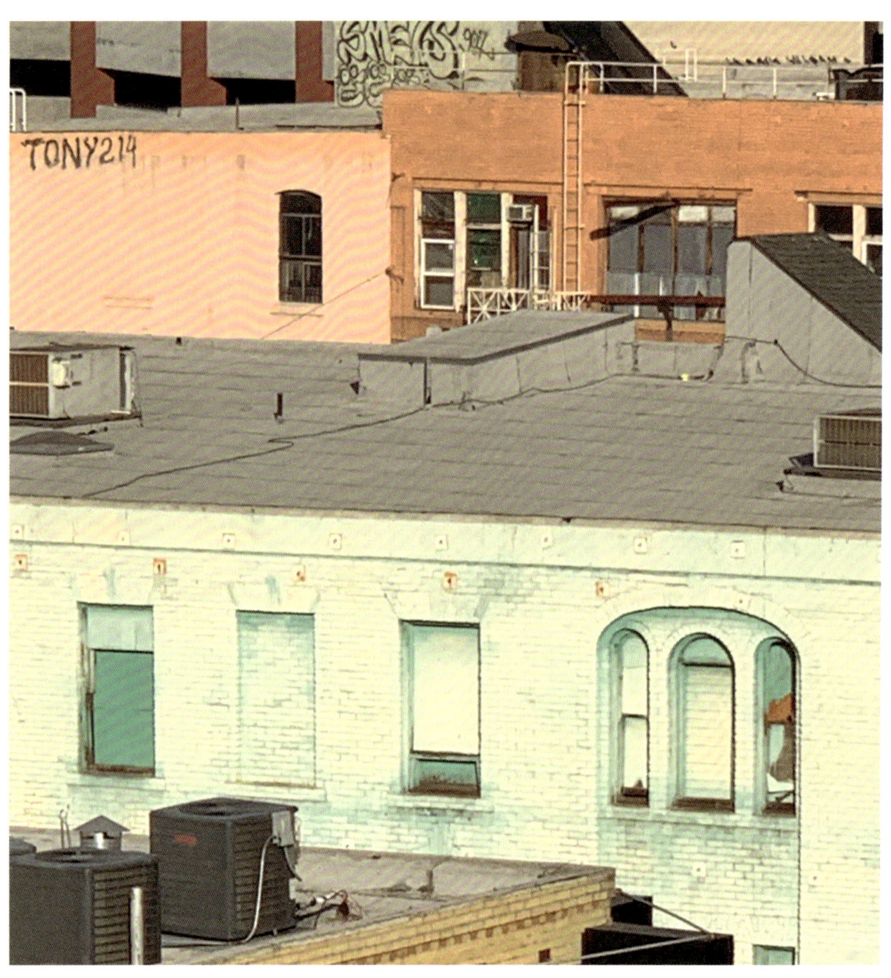
TONY214

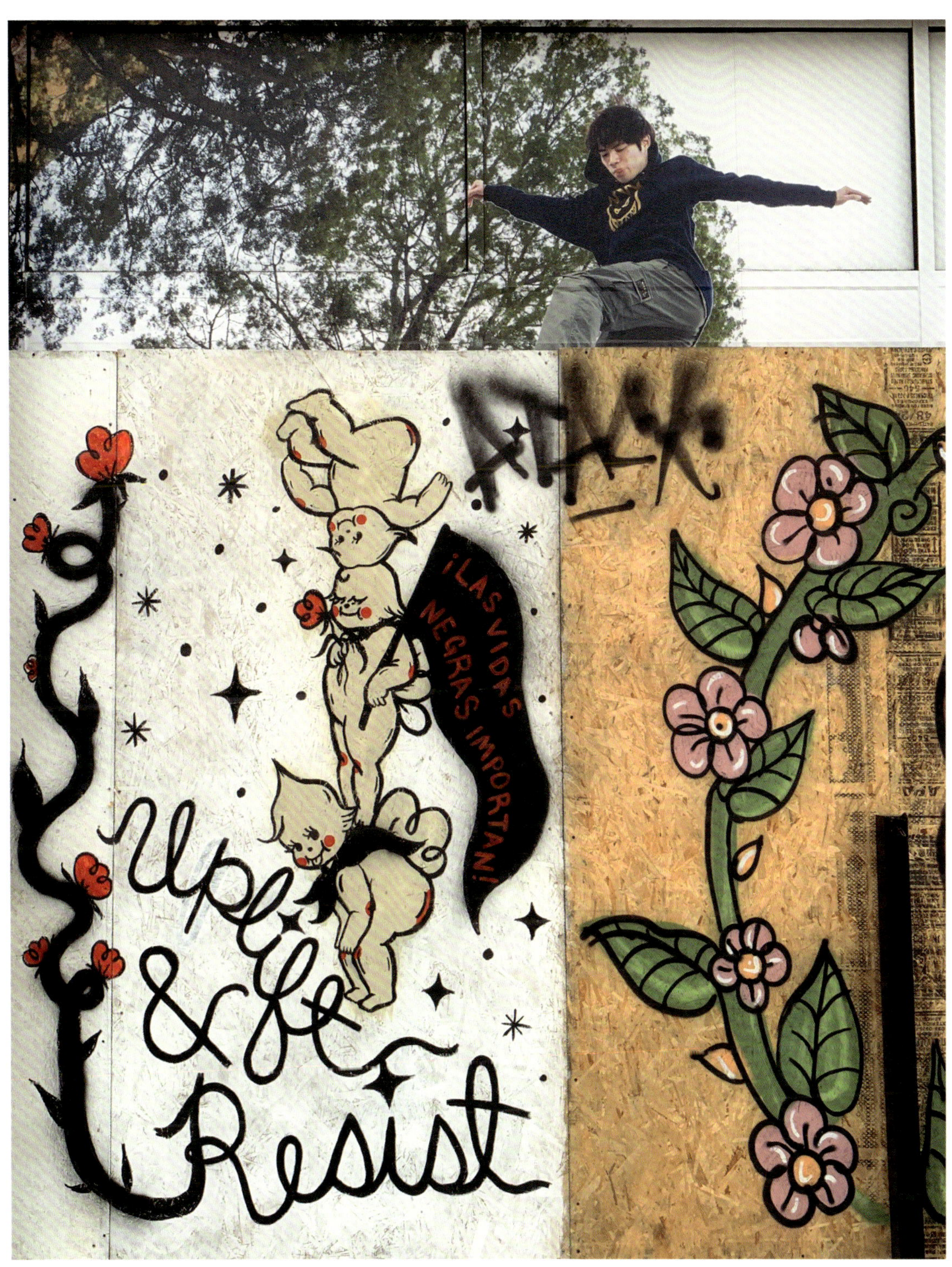
¡LAS VIDAS NEGRAS IMPORTAN!
Uplift & Resist

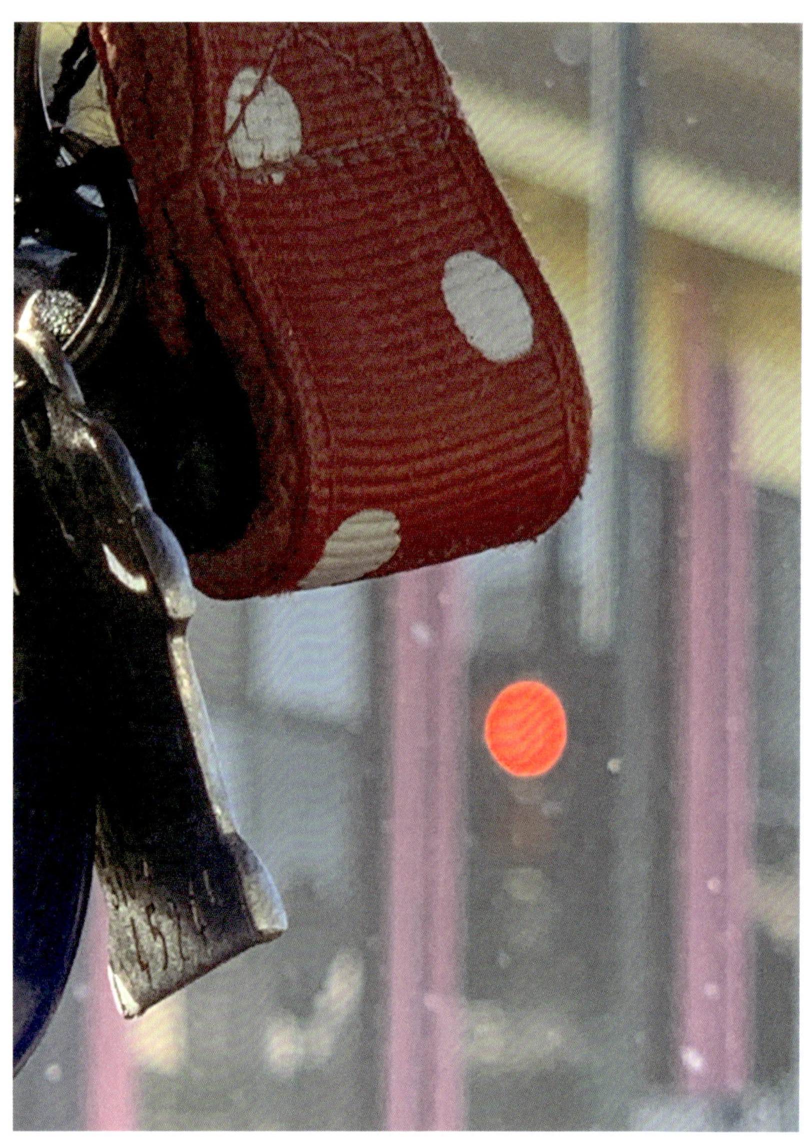

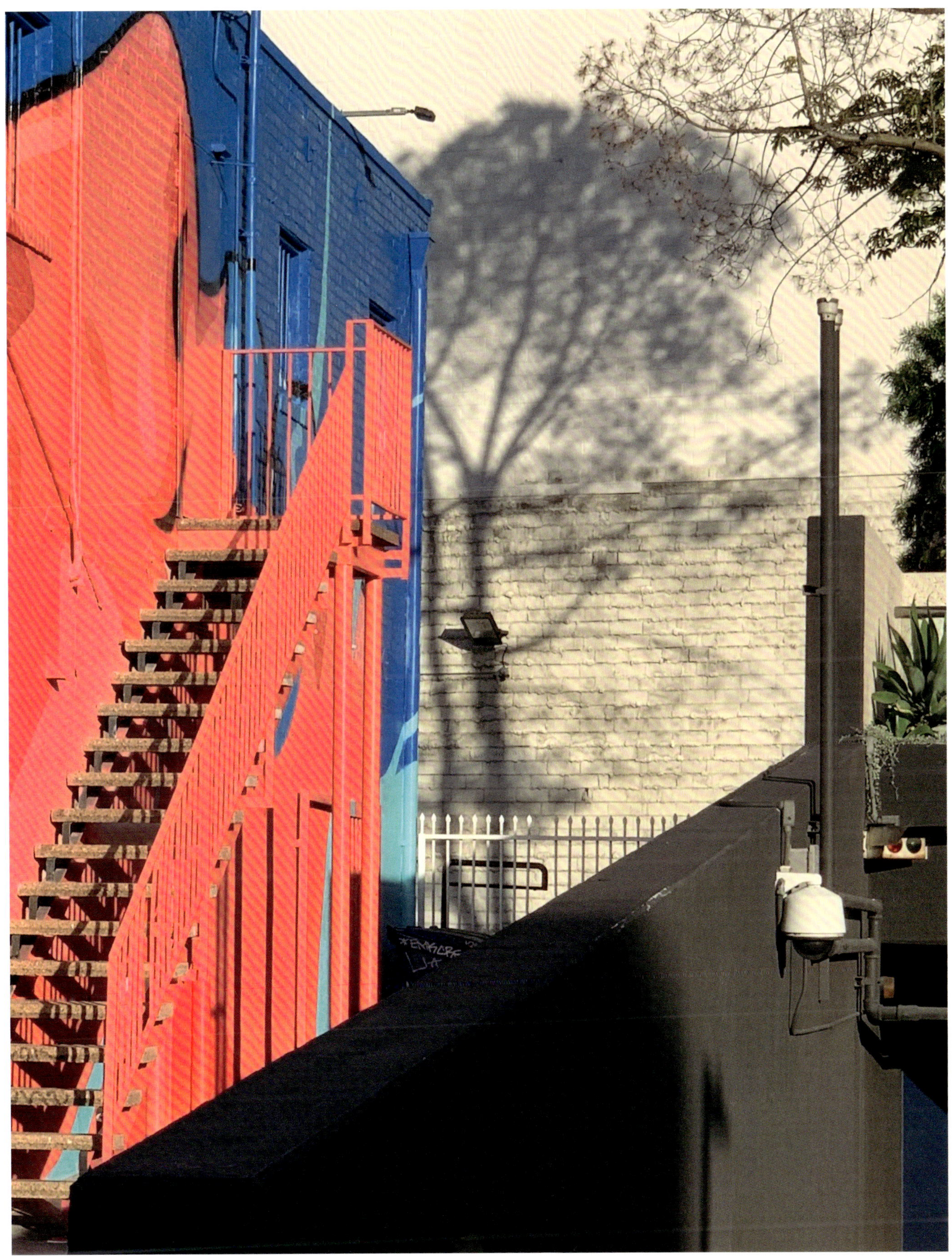

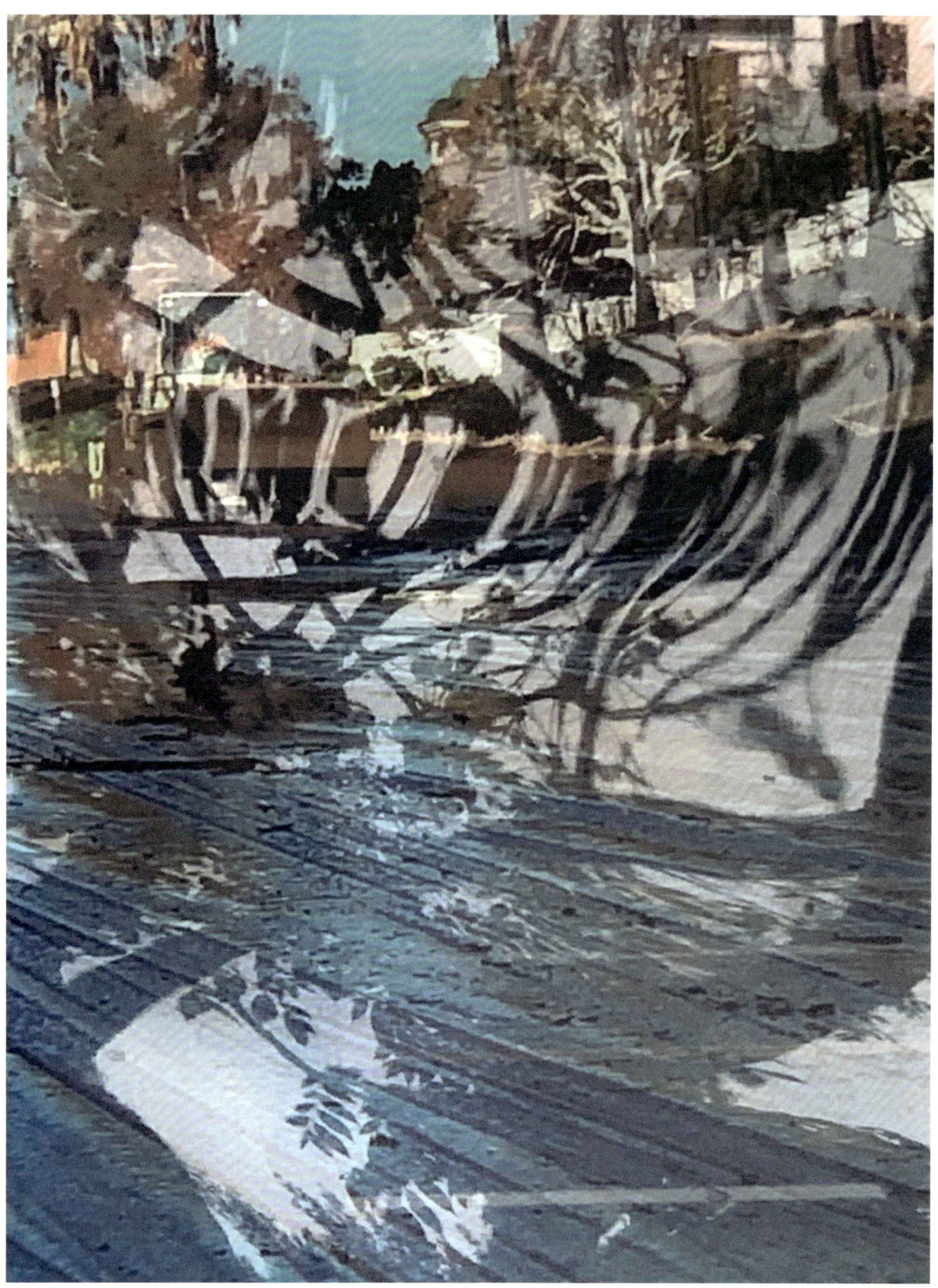

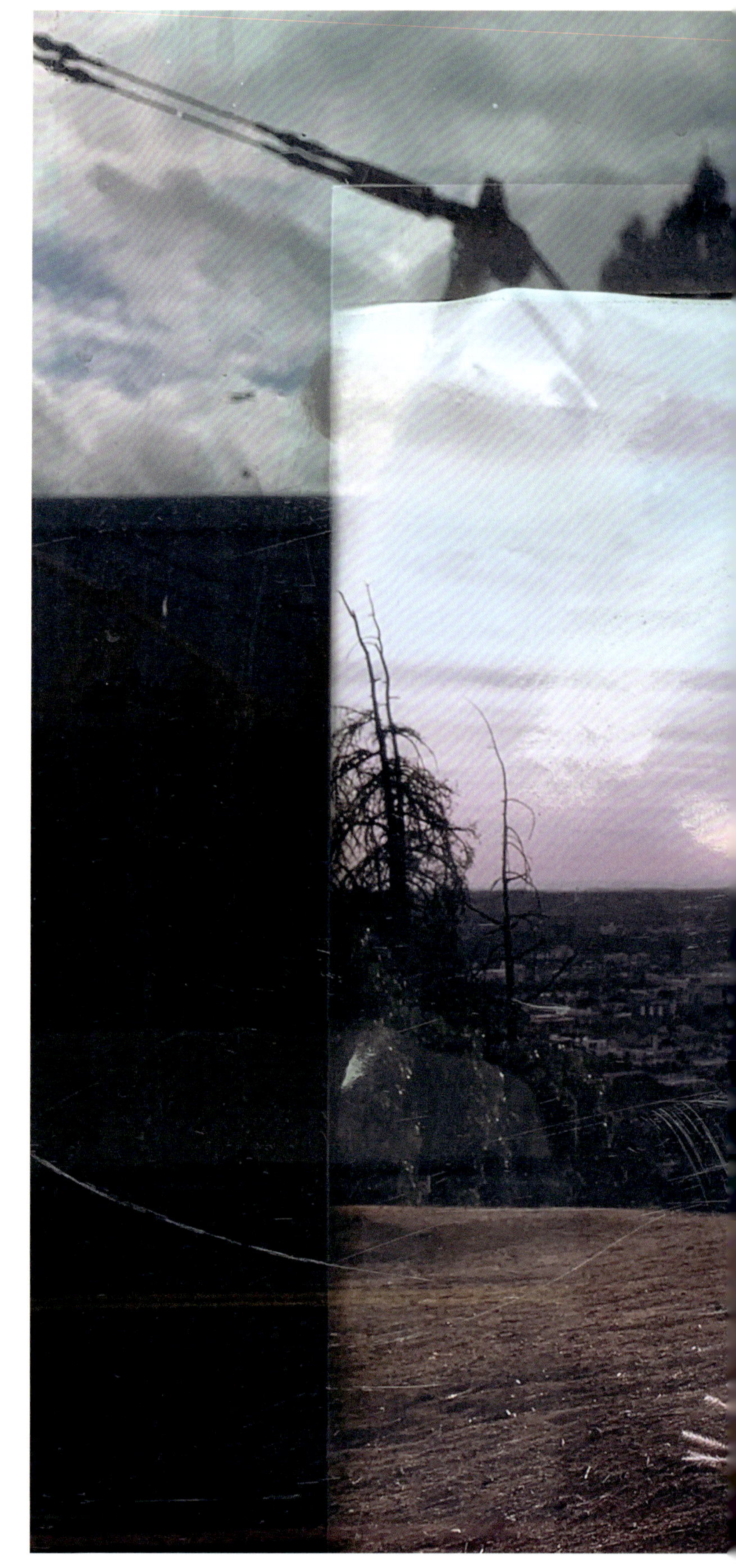

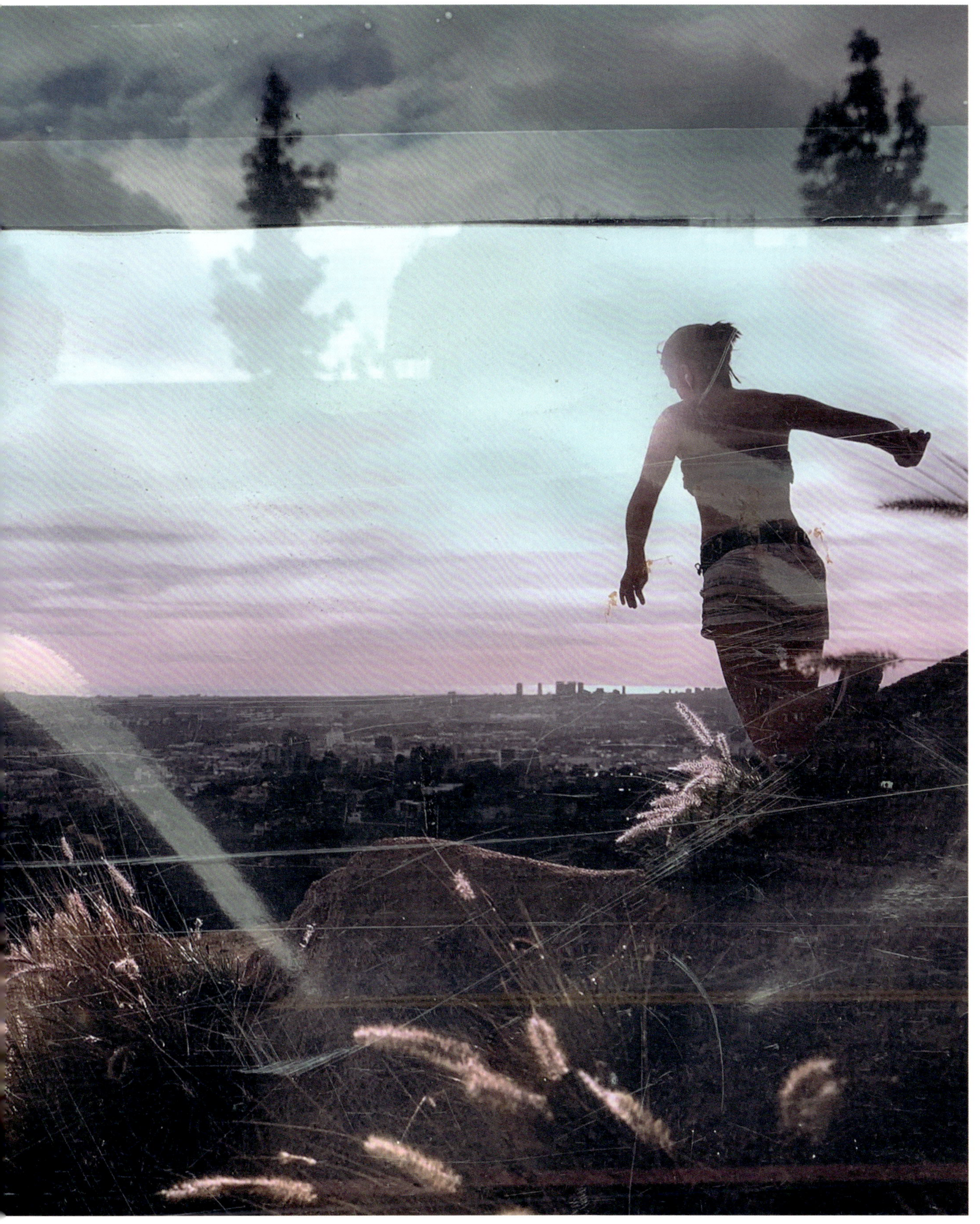

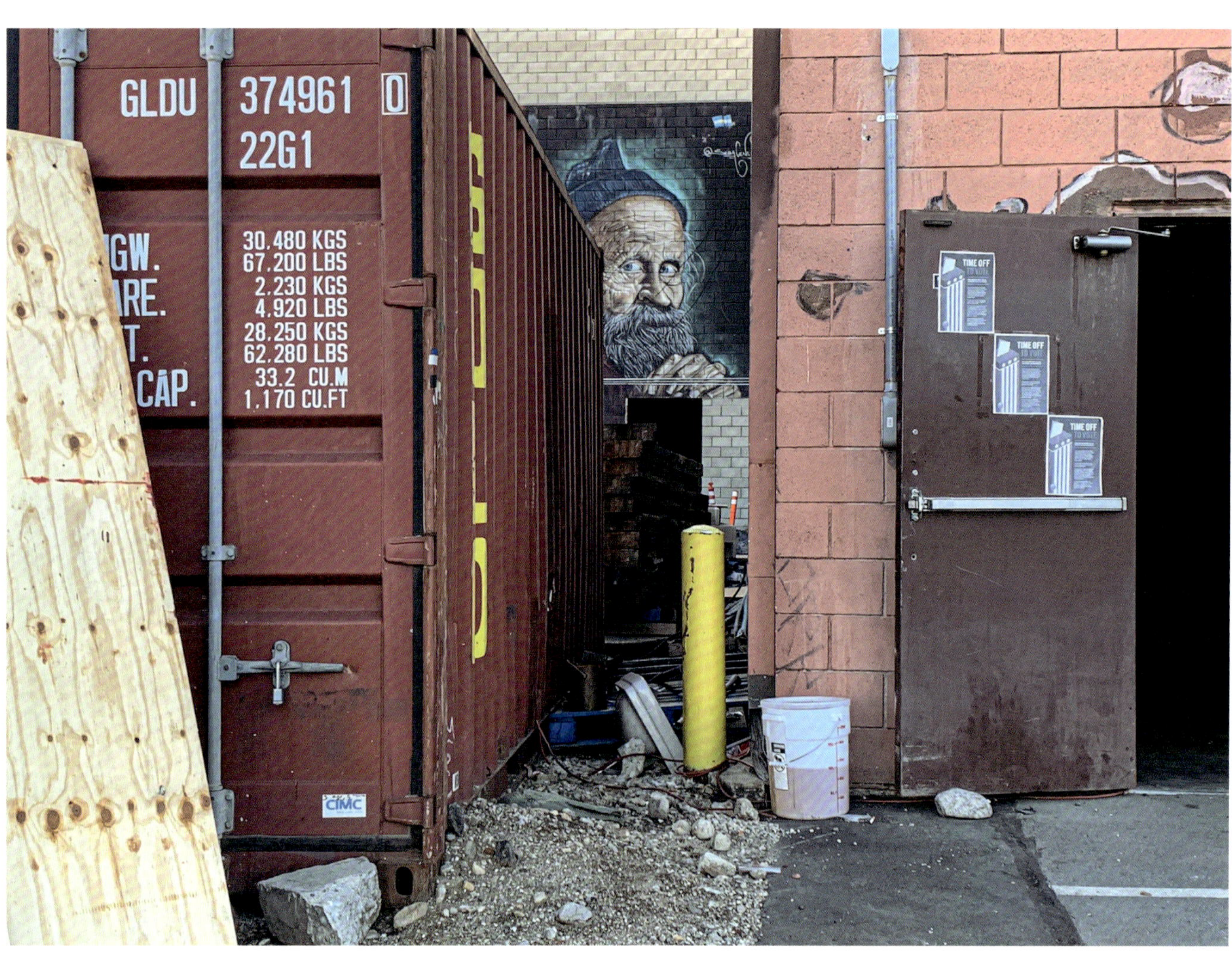
GLDU 374961 0
22G1
30.480 KGS
67.200 LBS
2.230 KGS
4.920 LBS
28.250 KGS
62.280 LBS
CAP.
33.2 CU.M
1.170 CU.FT
CIMC
TIME OFF

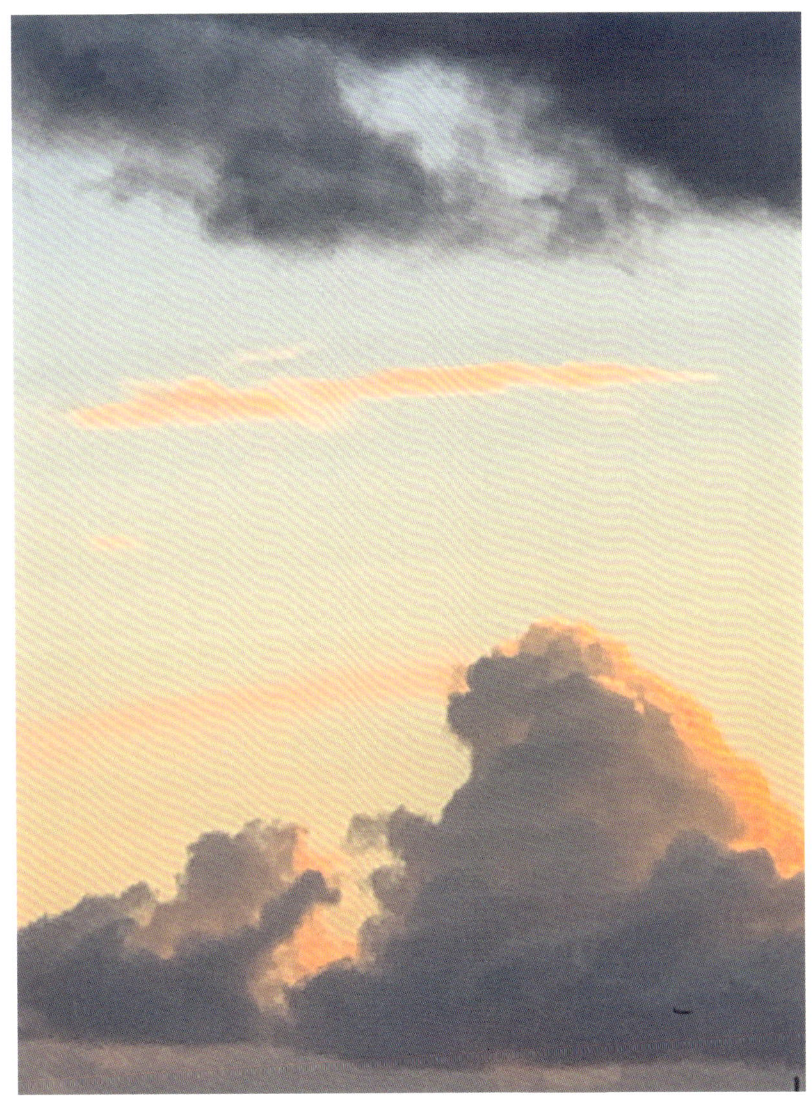

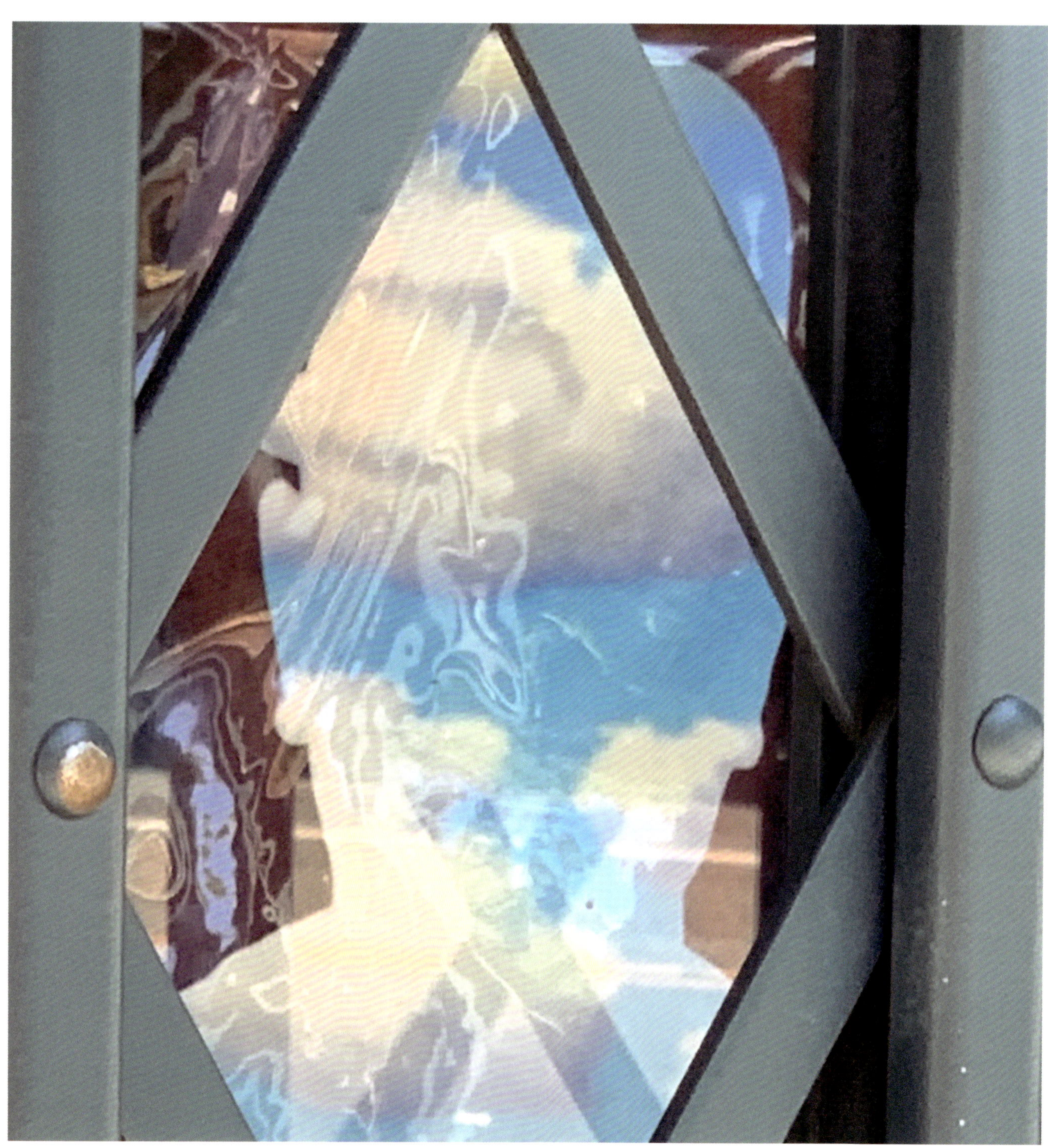

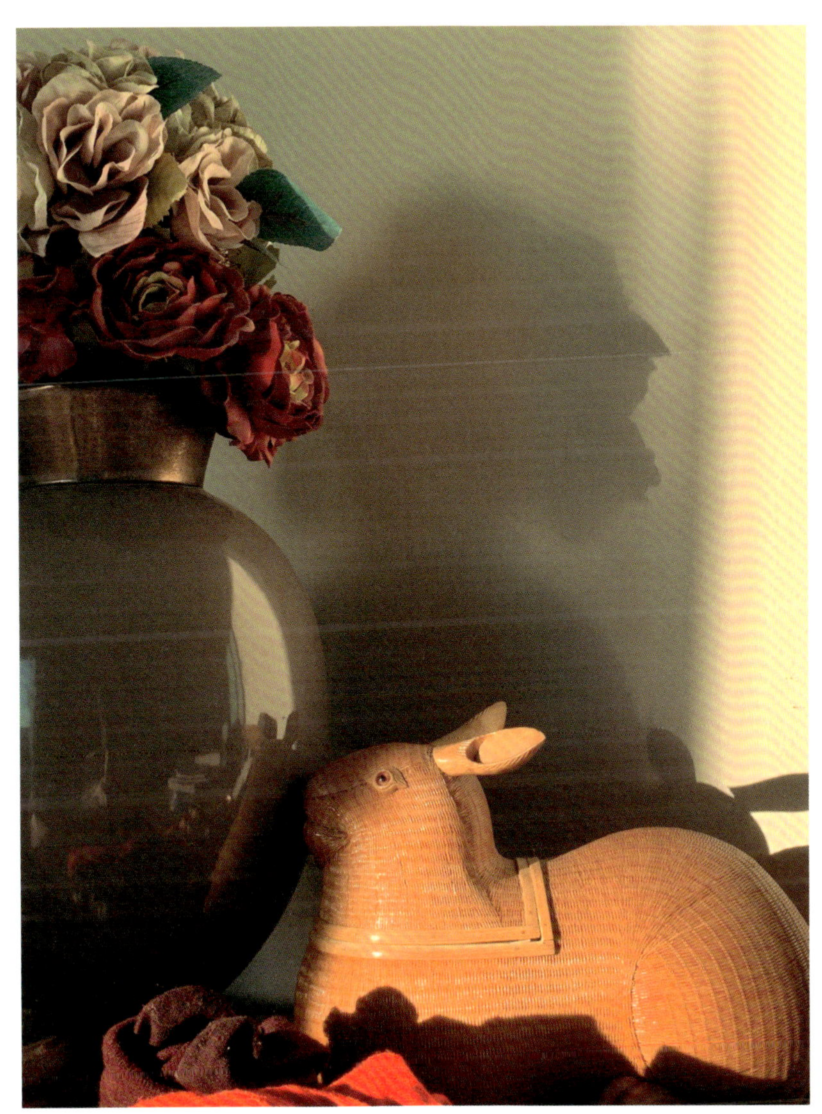

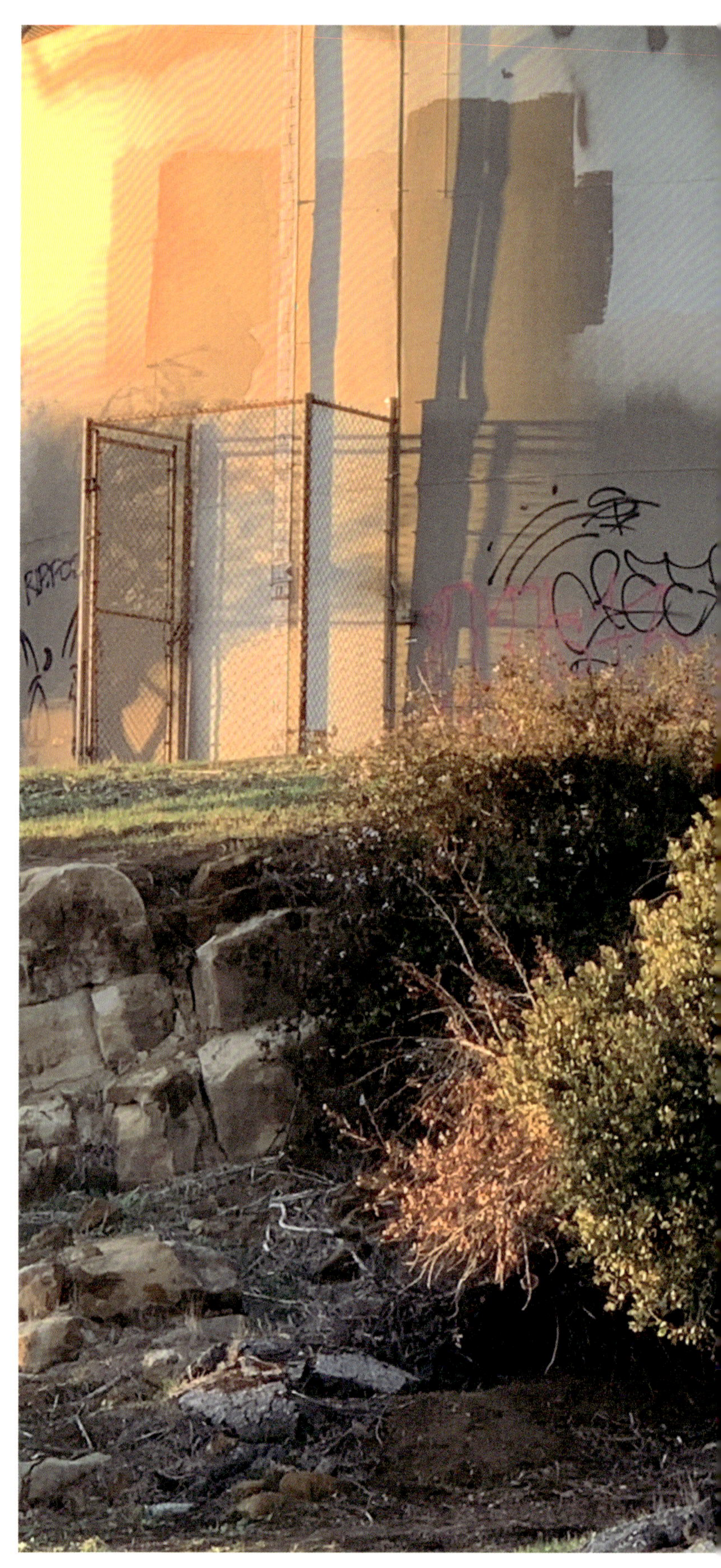

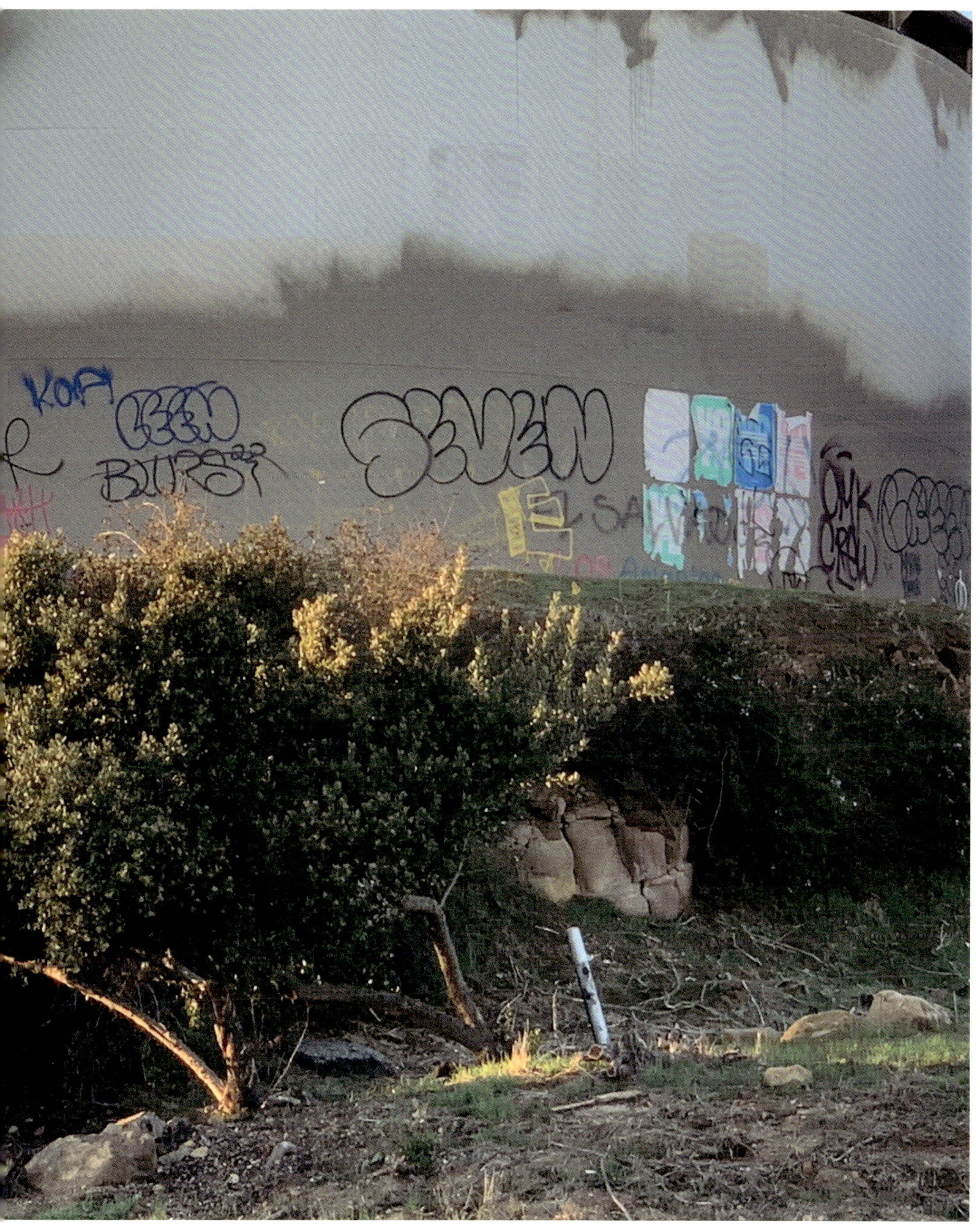

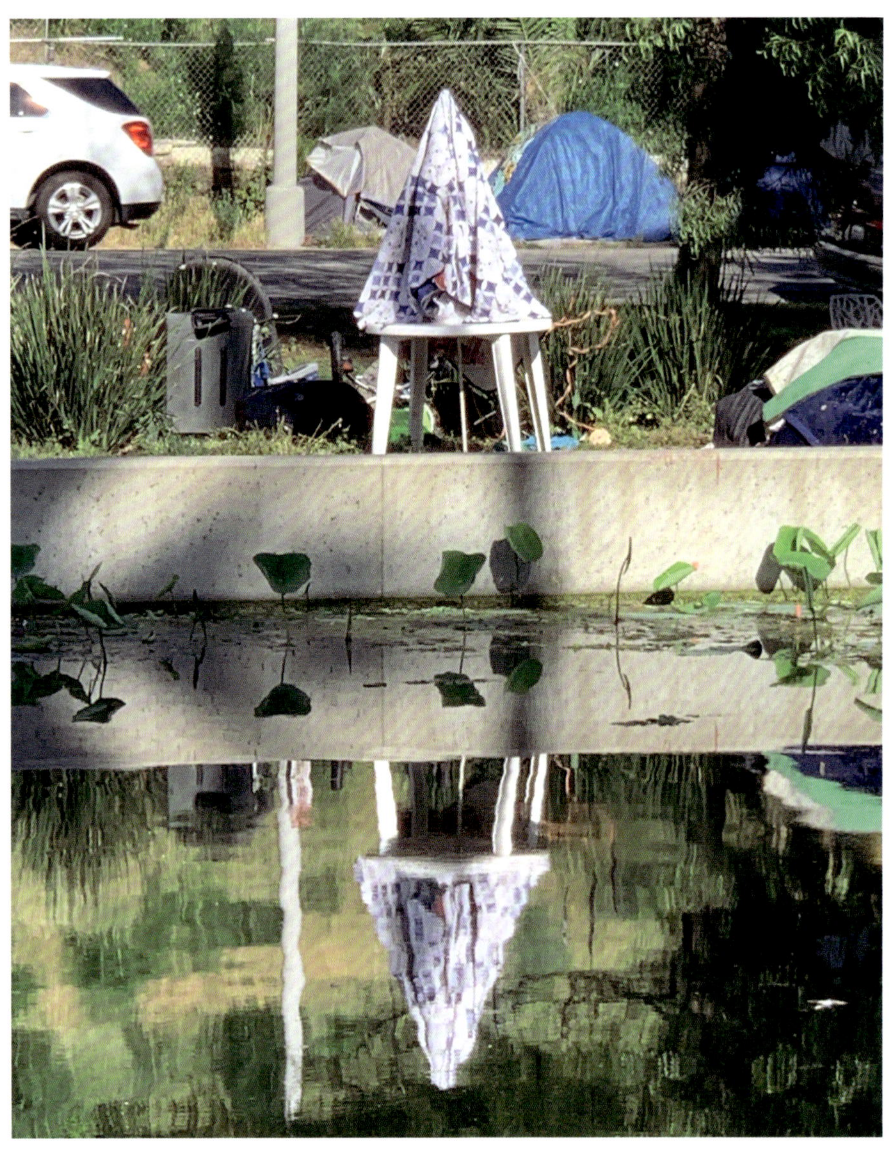

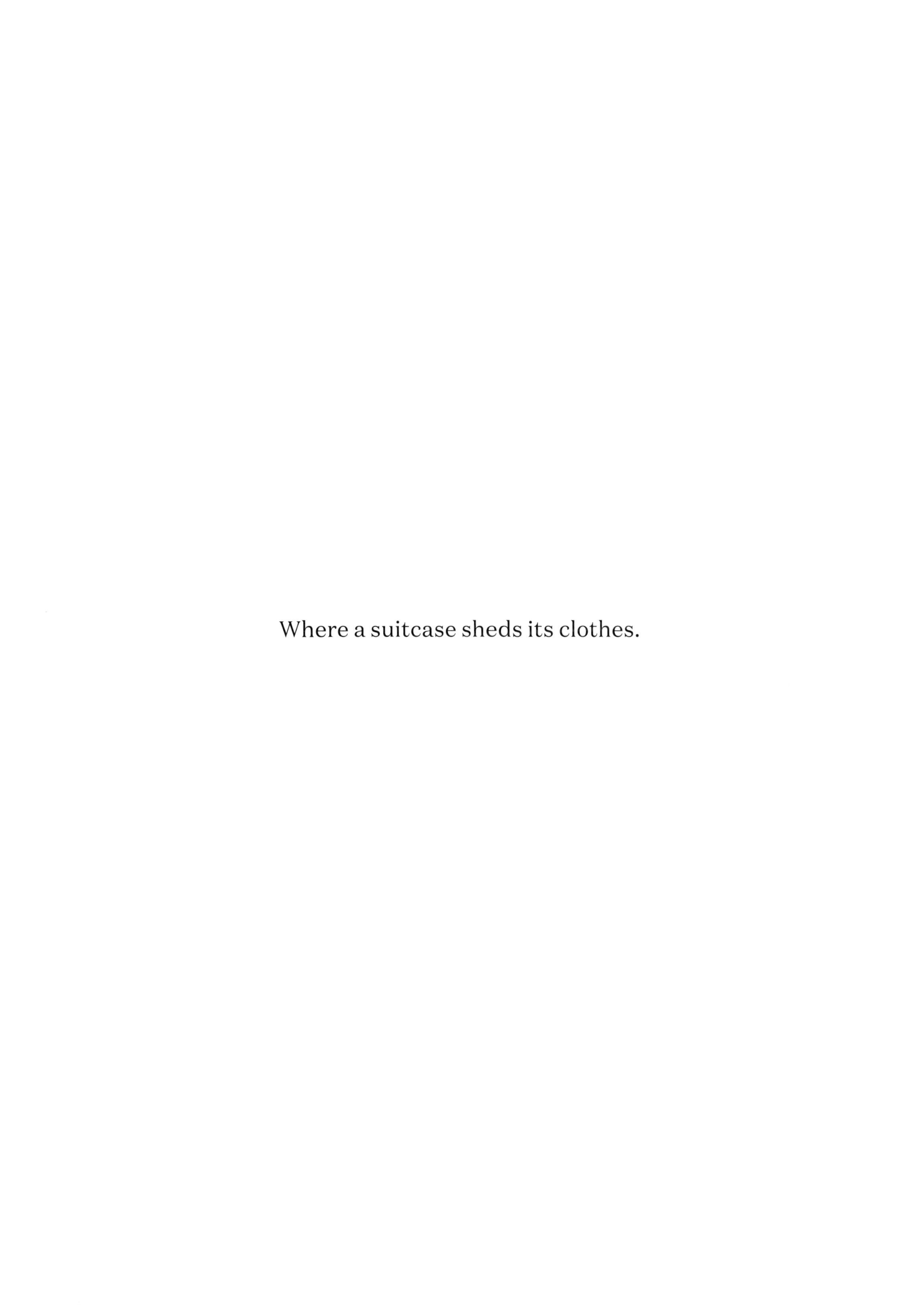
Where a suitcase sheds its clothes.

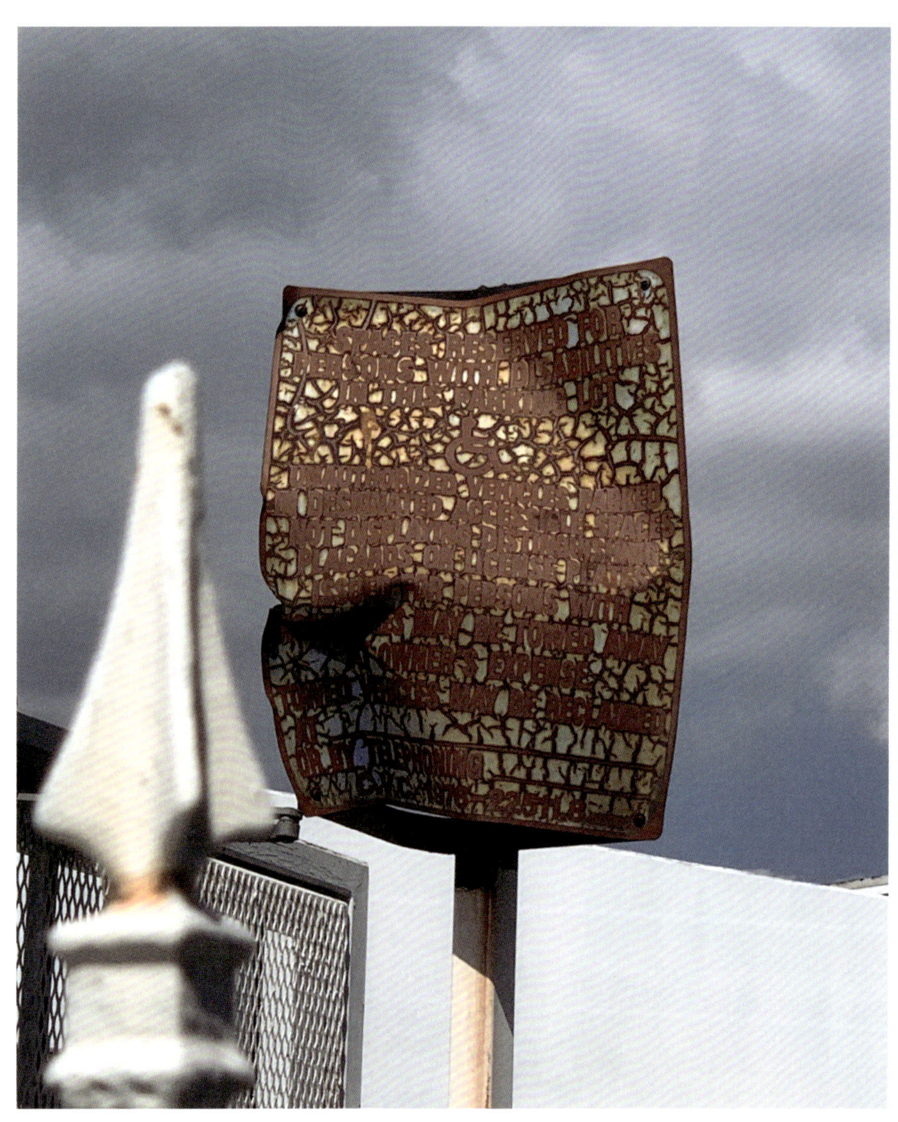

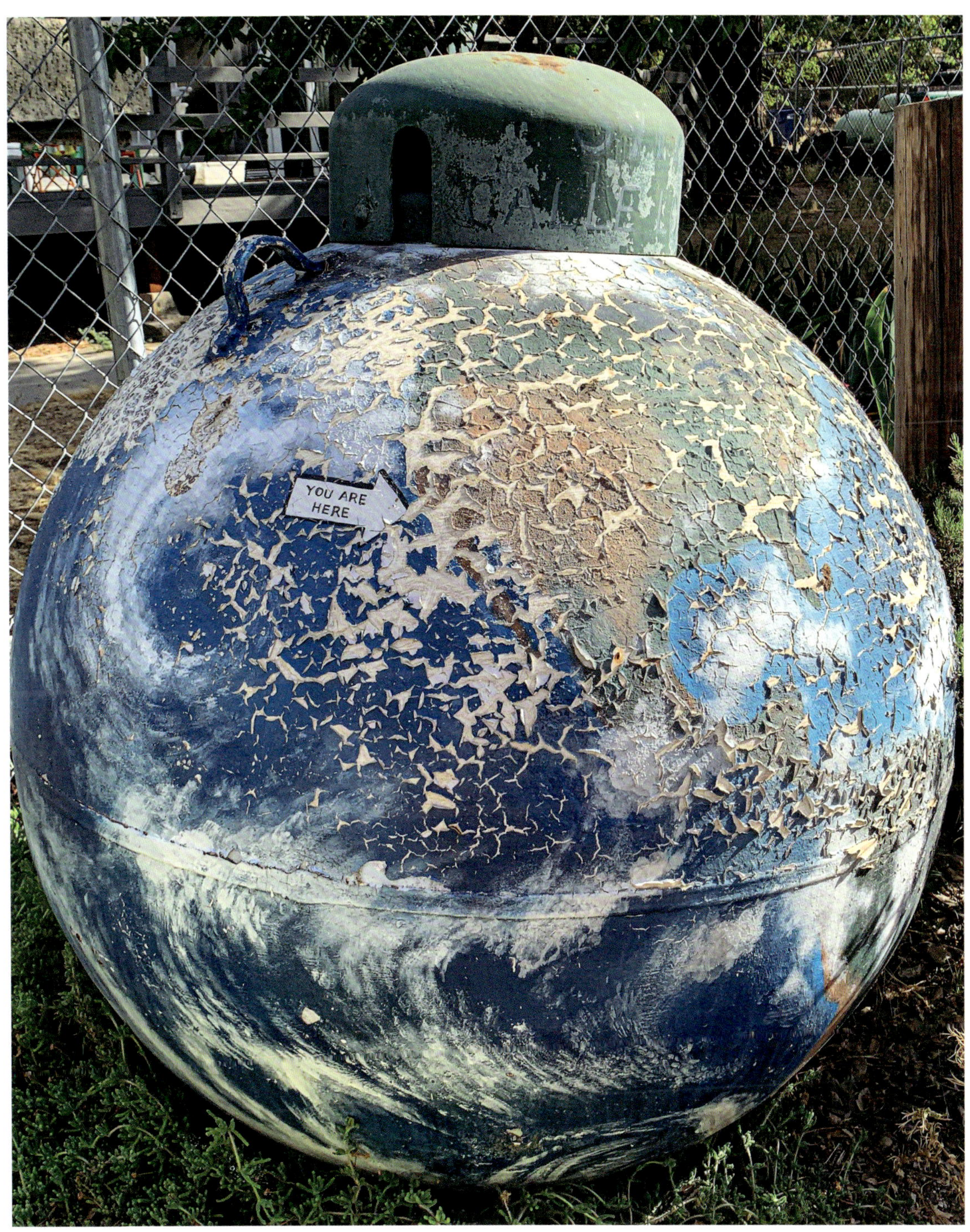
YOU ARE
HERE

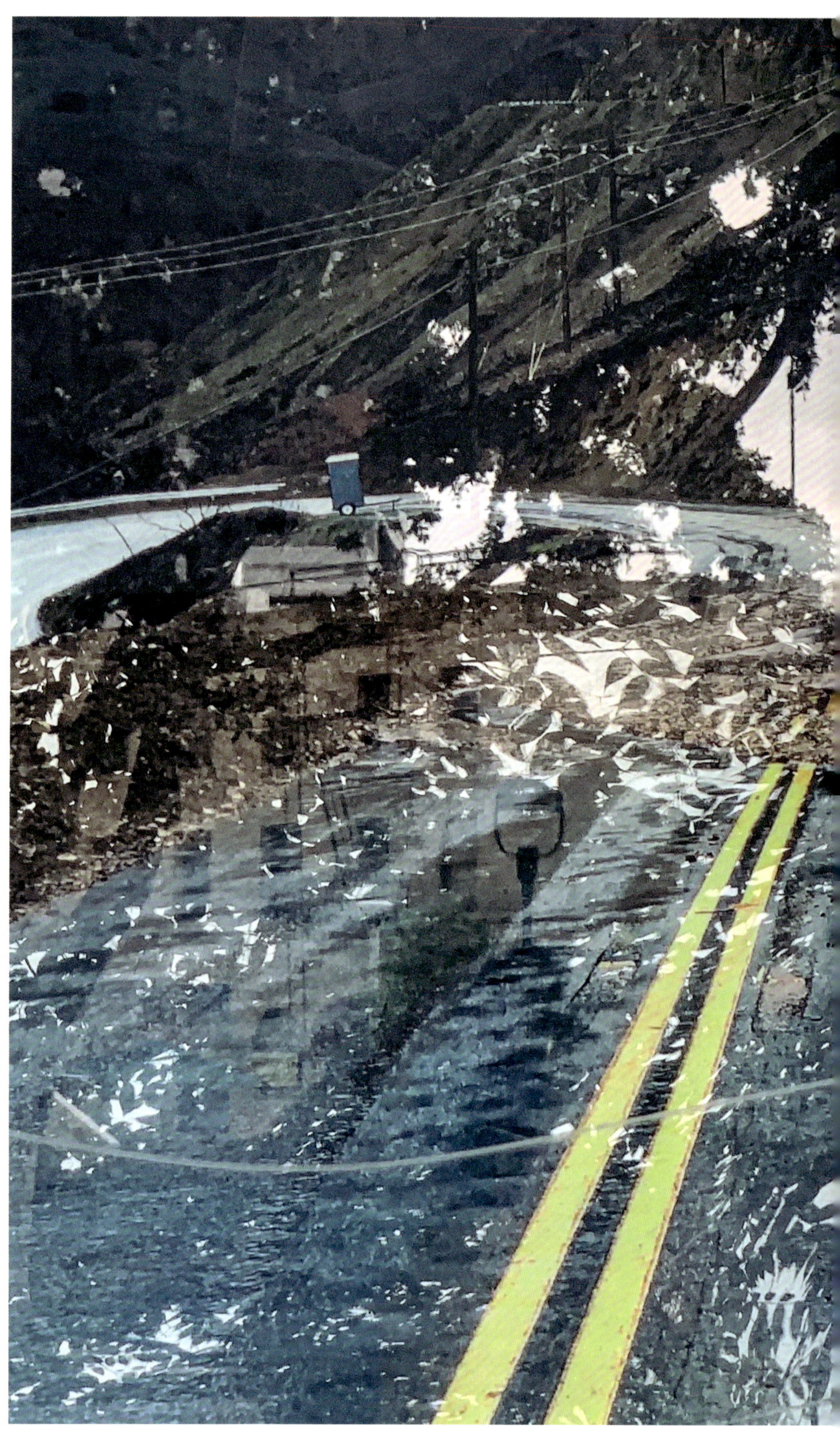

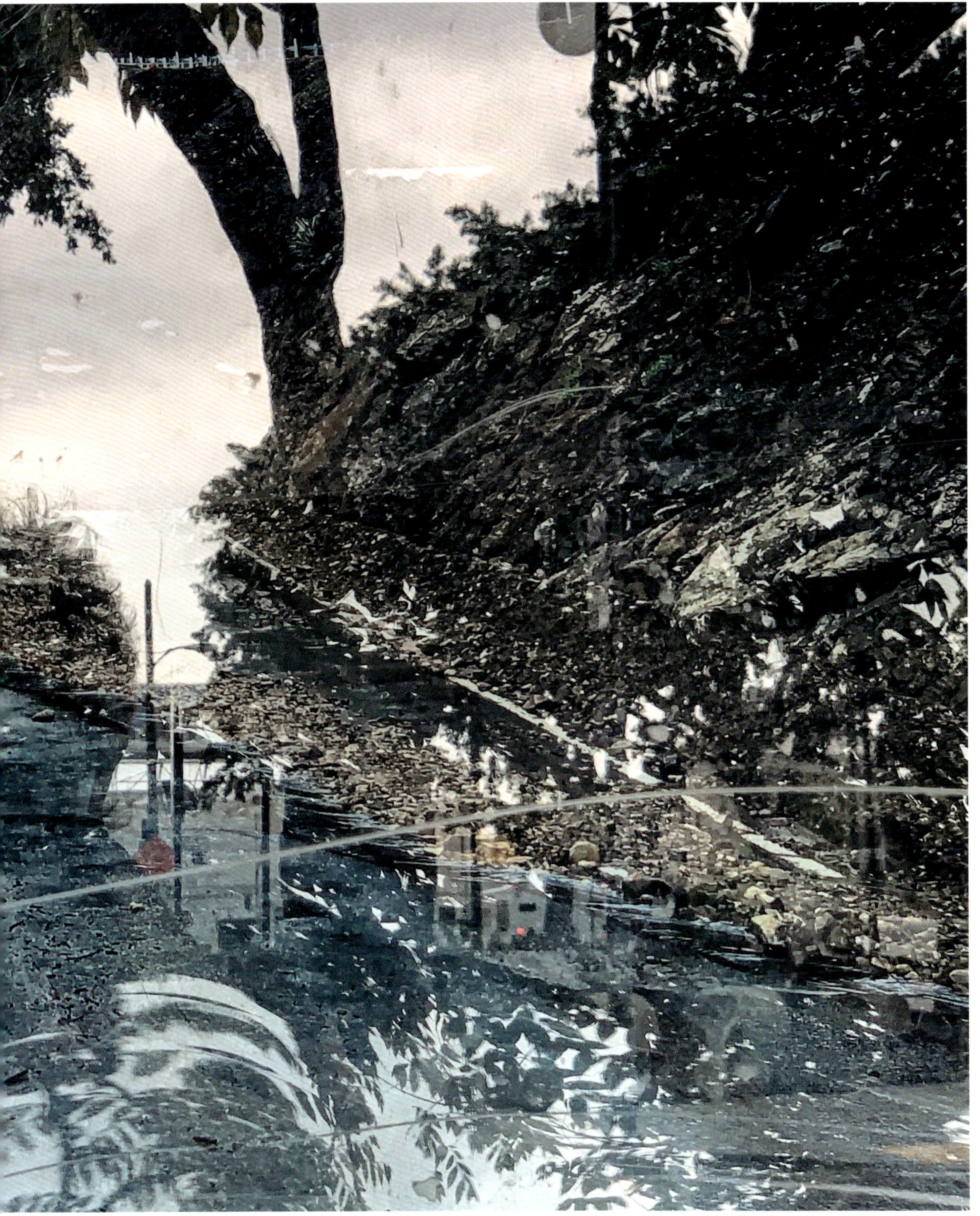

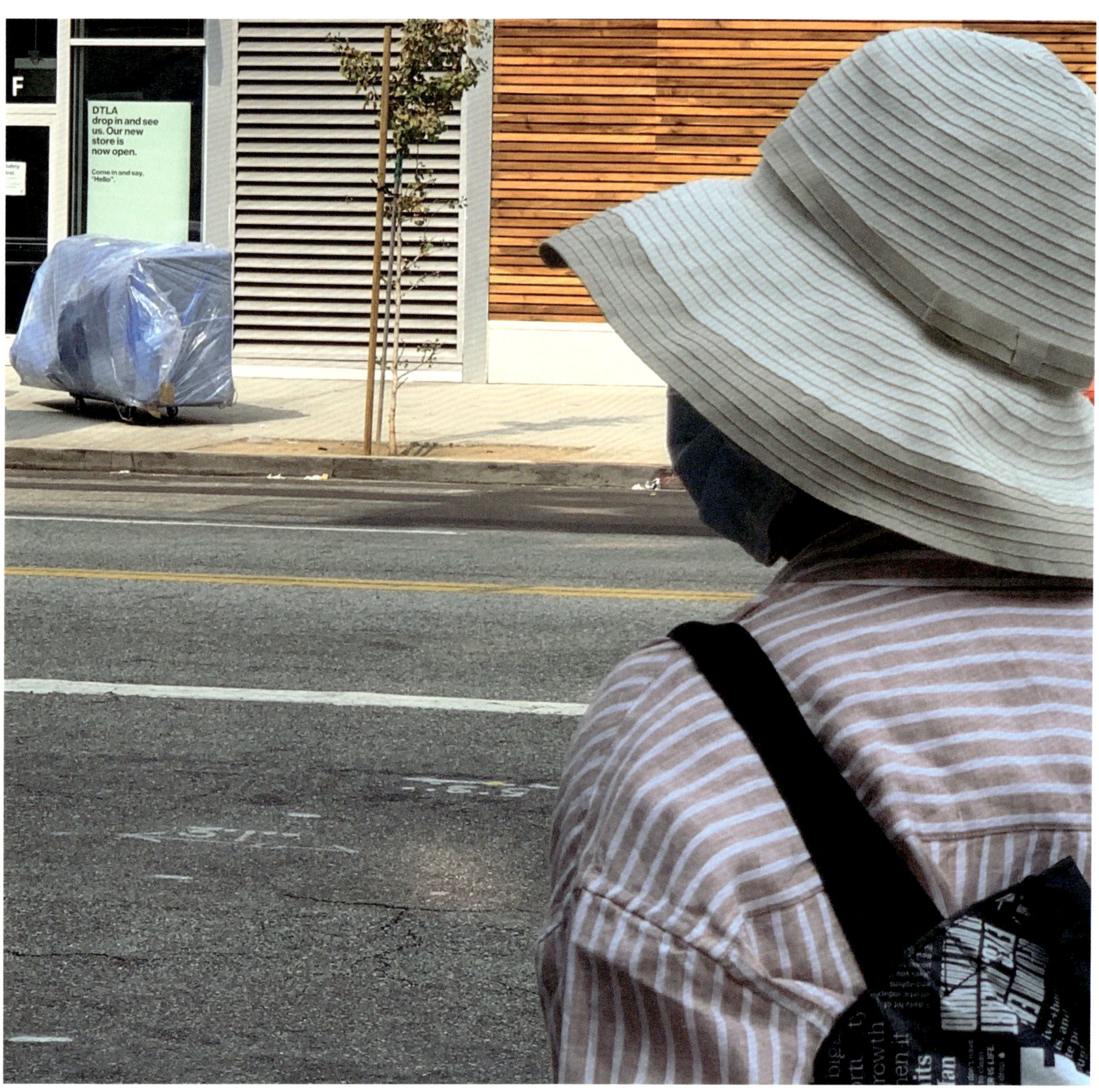
F
DTLA
drop in and see
us. Our new
store is
now open.
Come in and say,
"Hello".

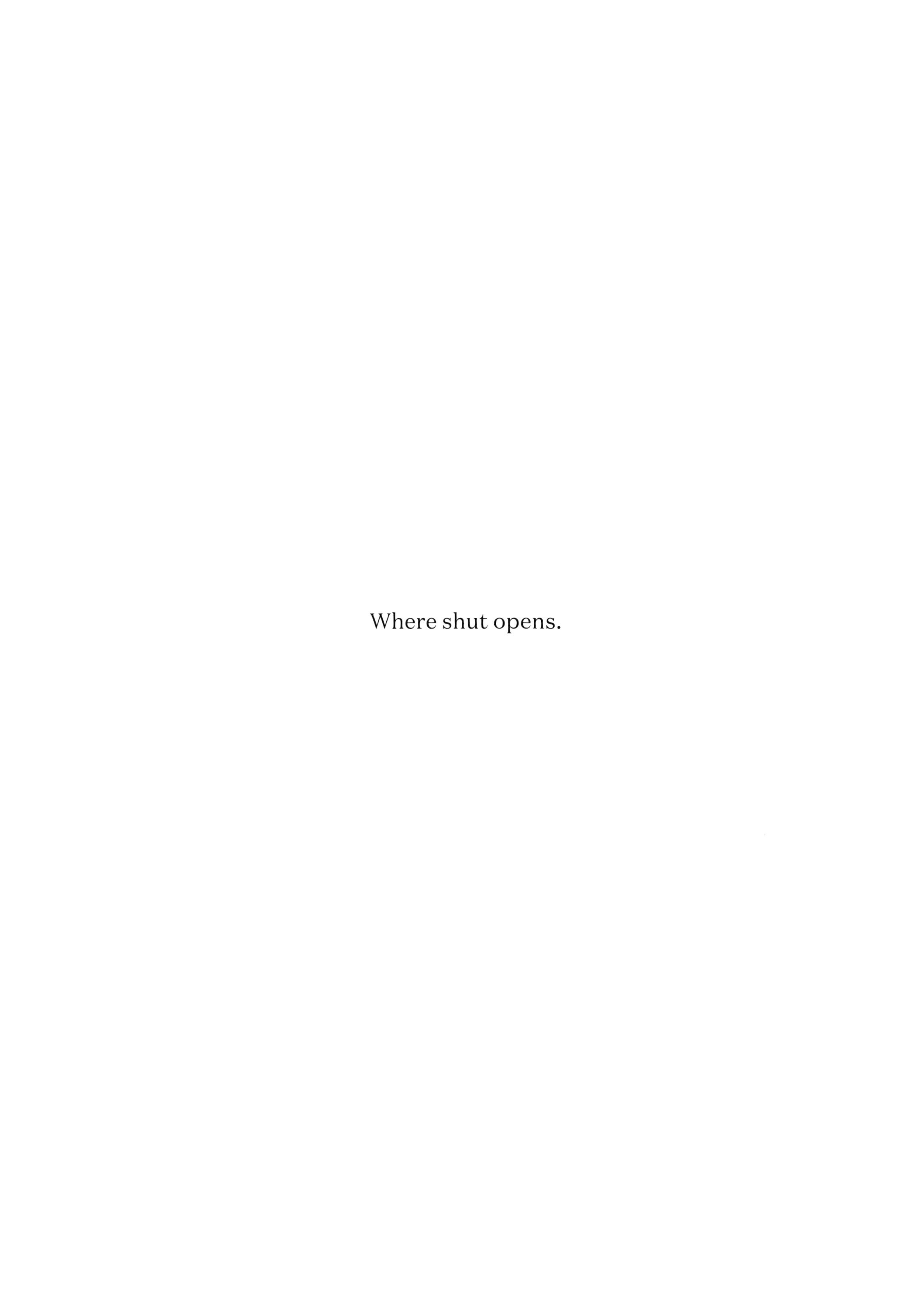
Where shut opens.

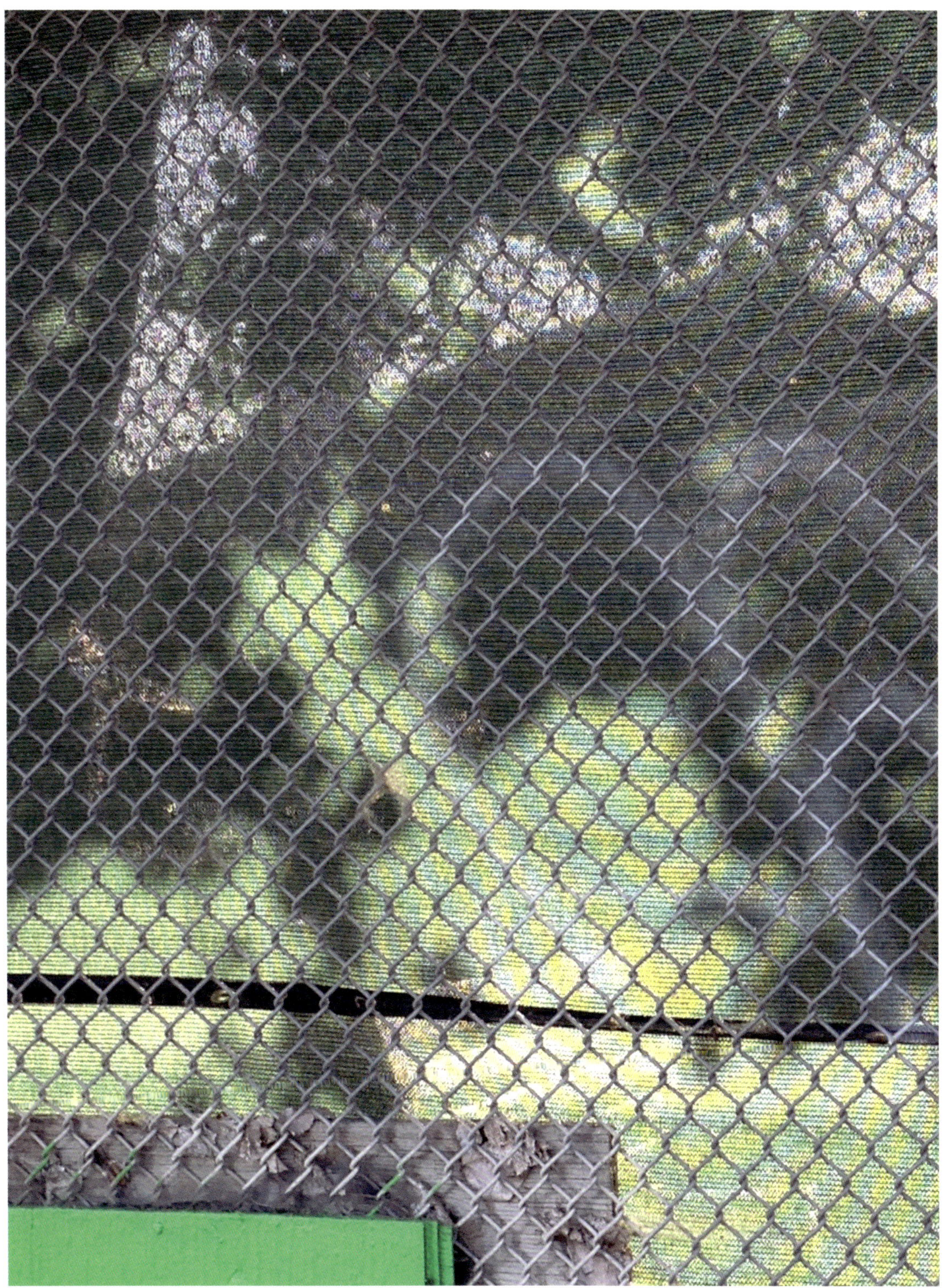

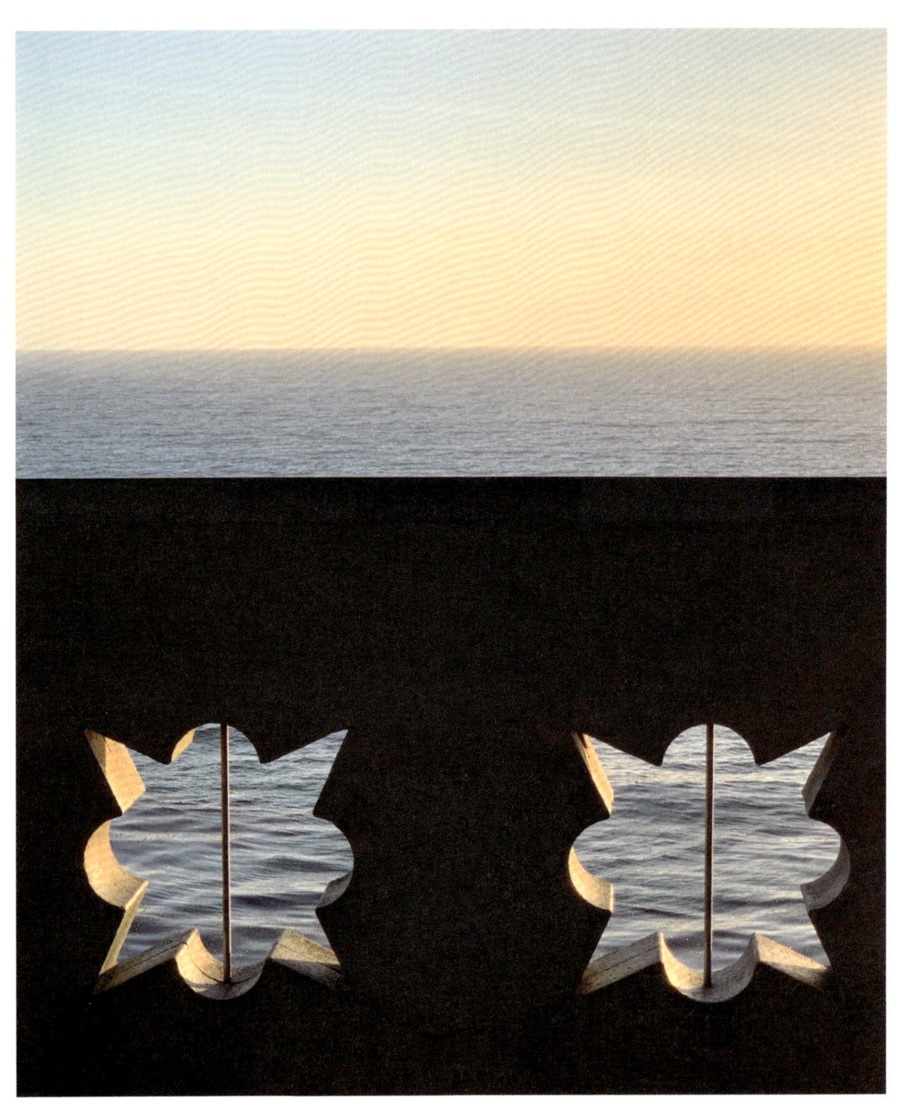

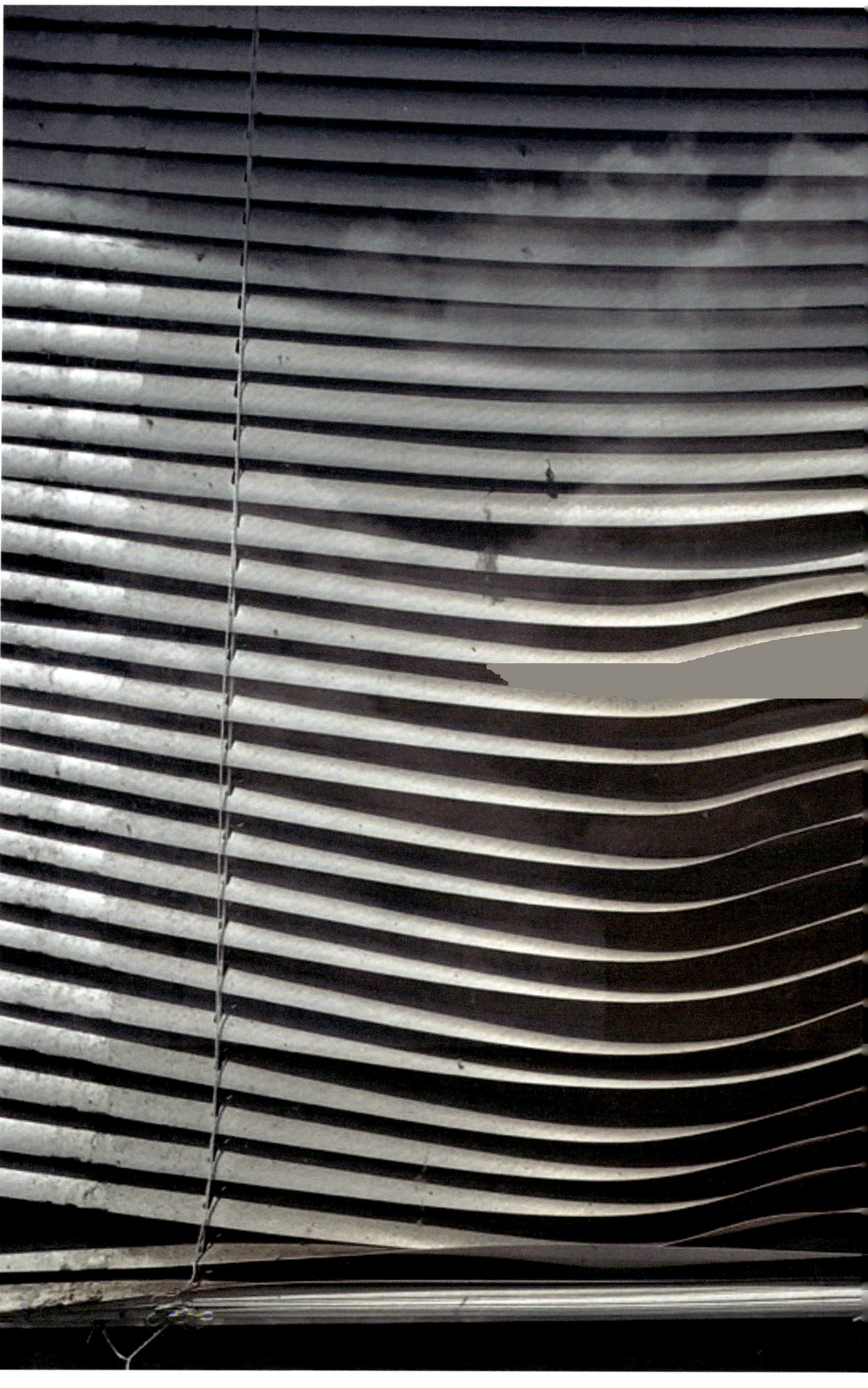

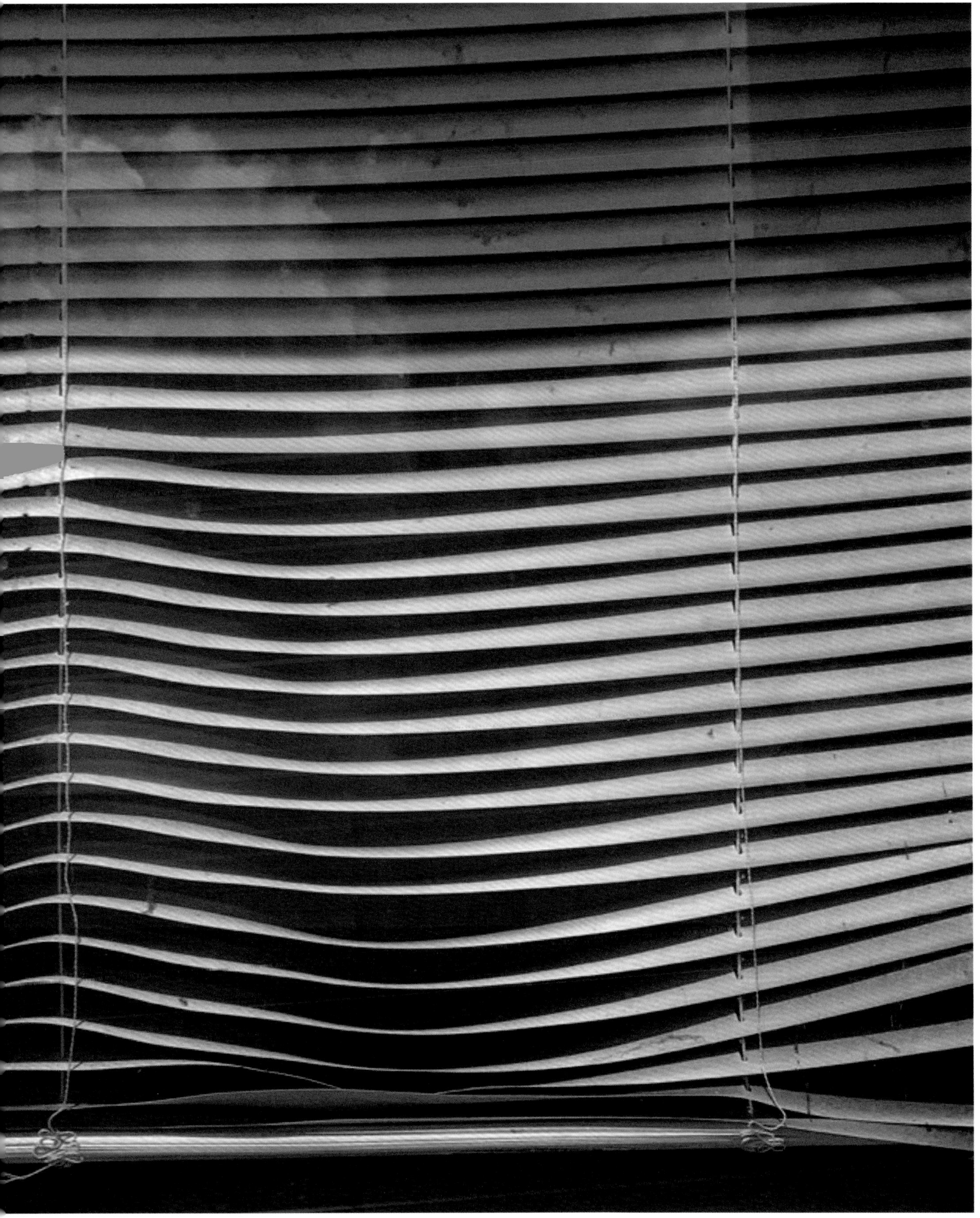

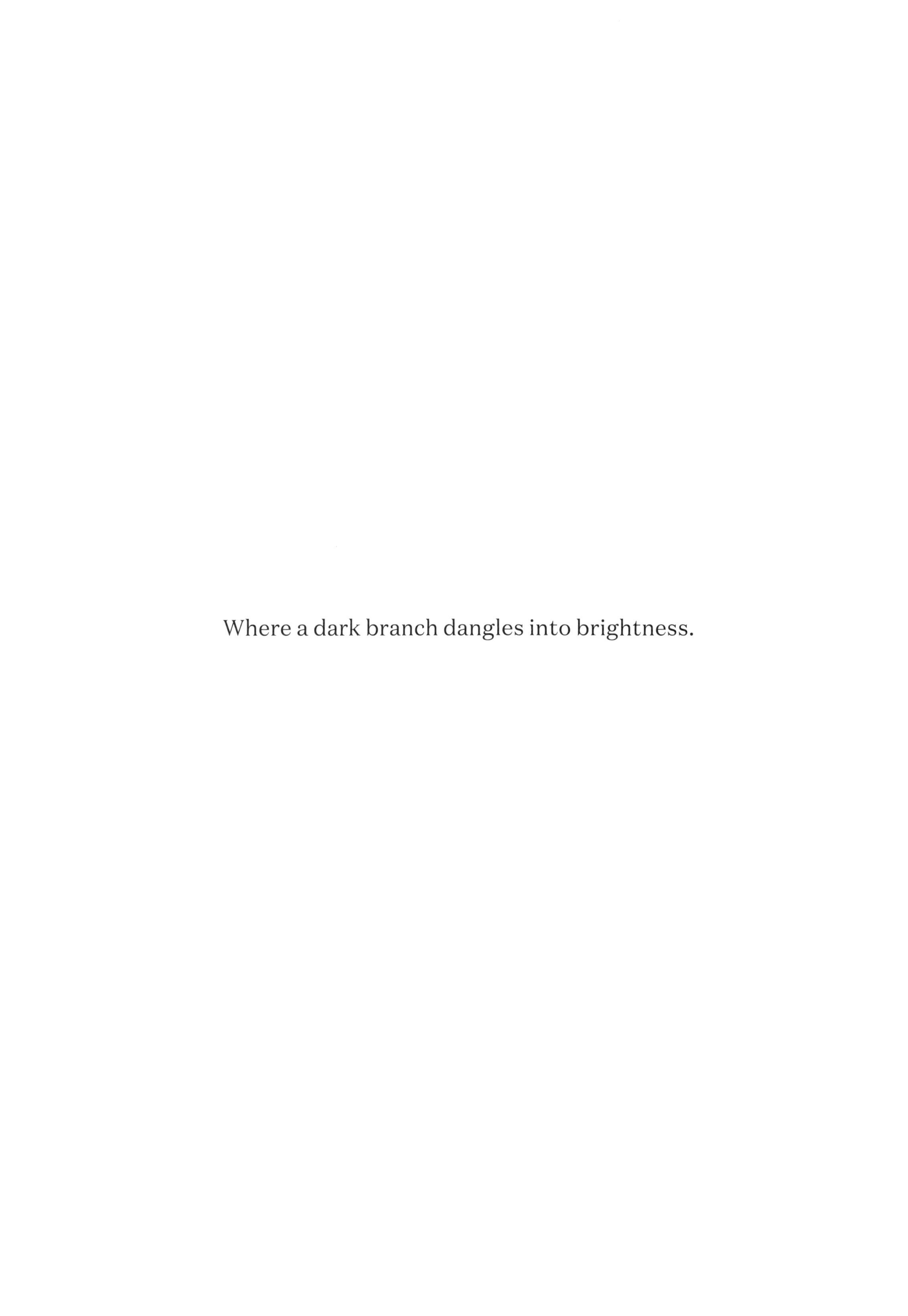

Where a dark branch dangles into brightness.

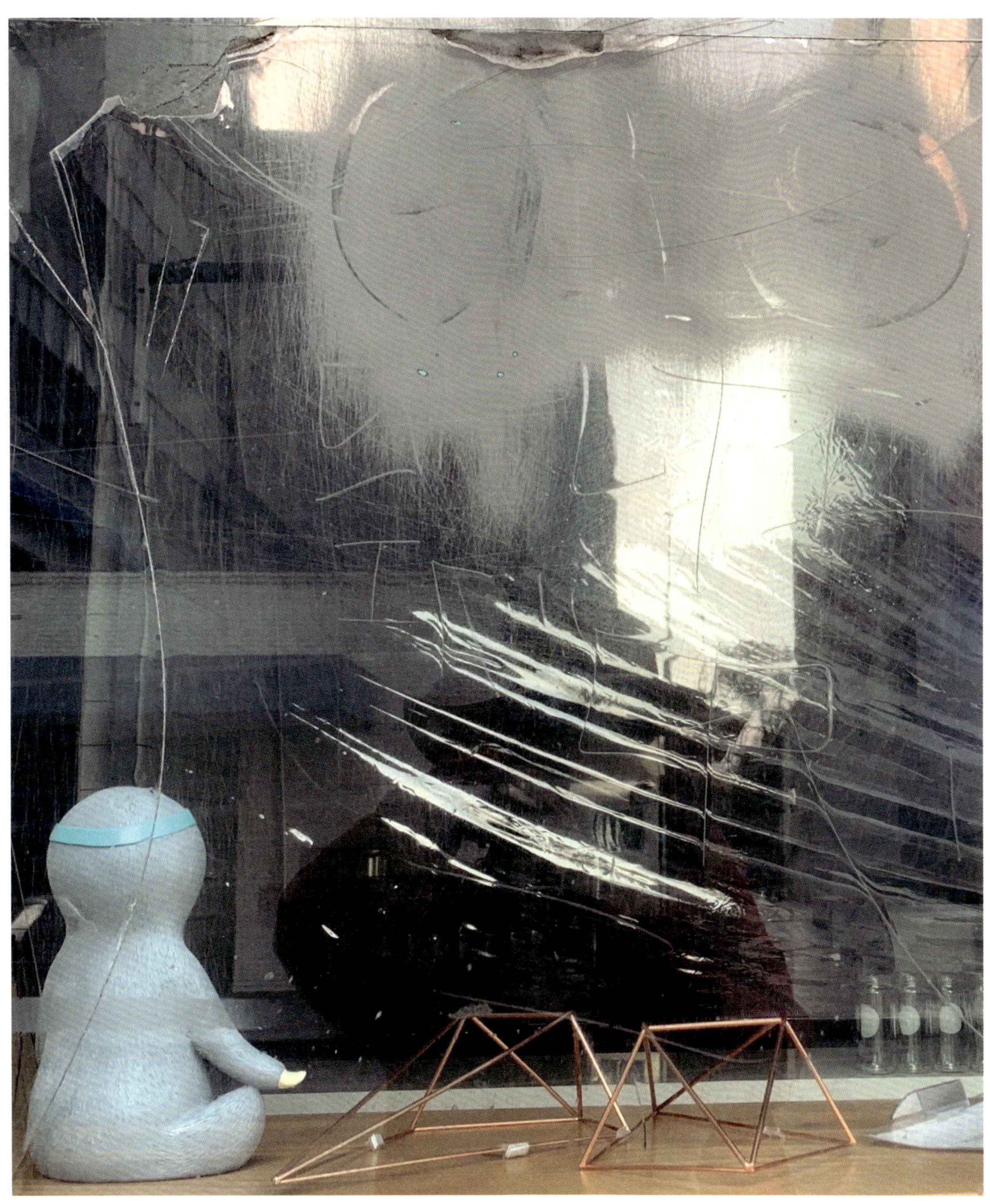

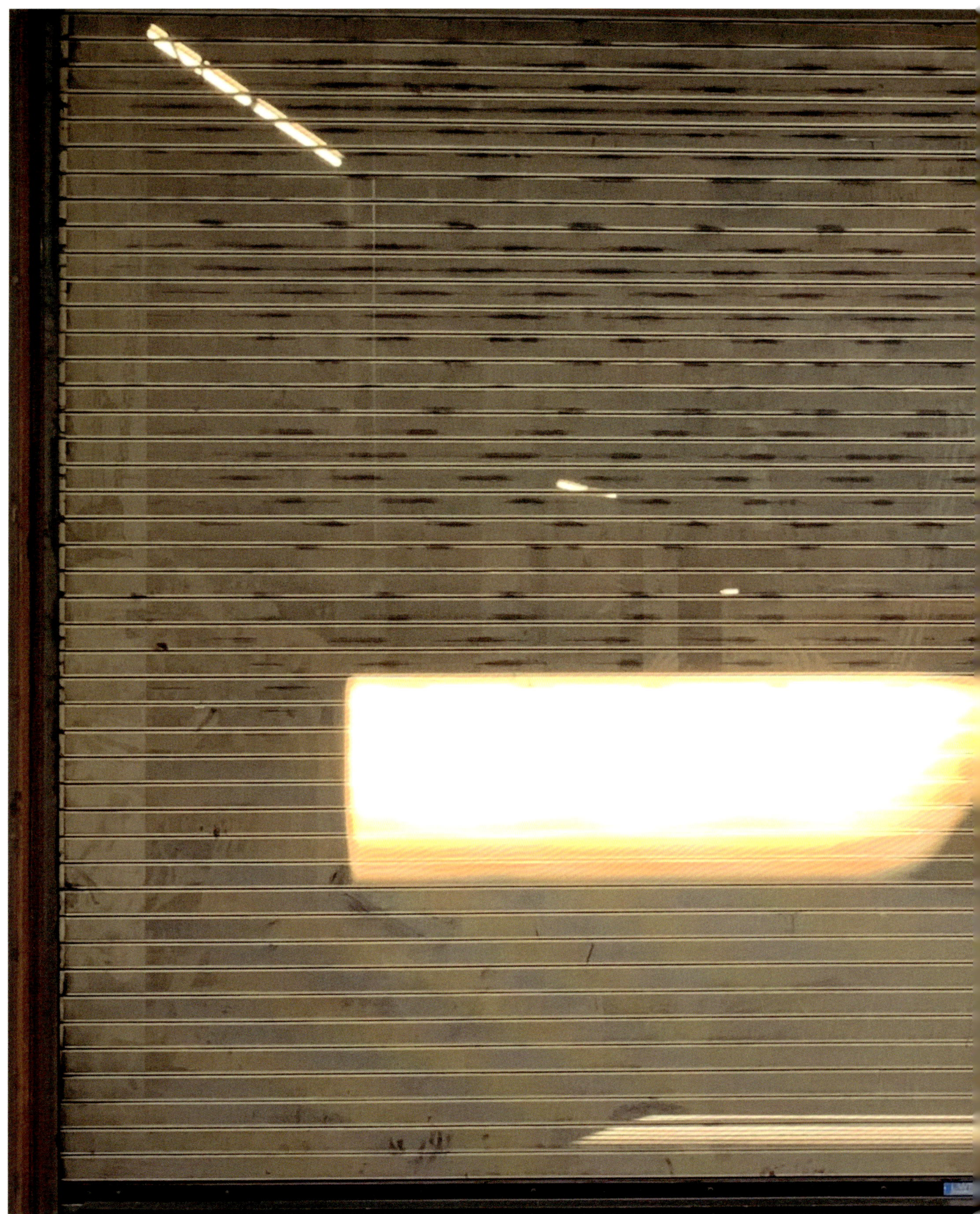

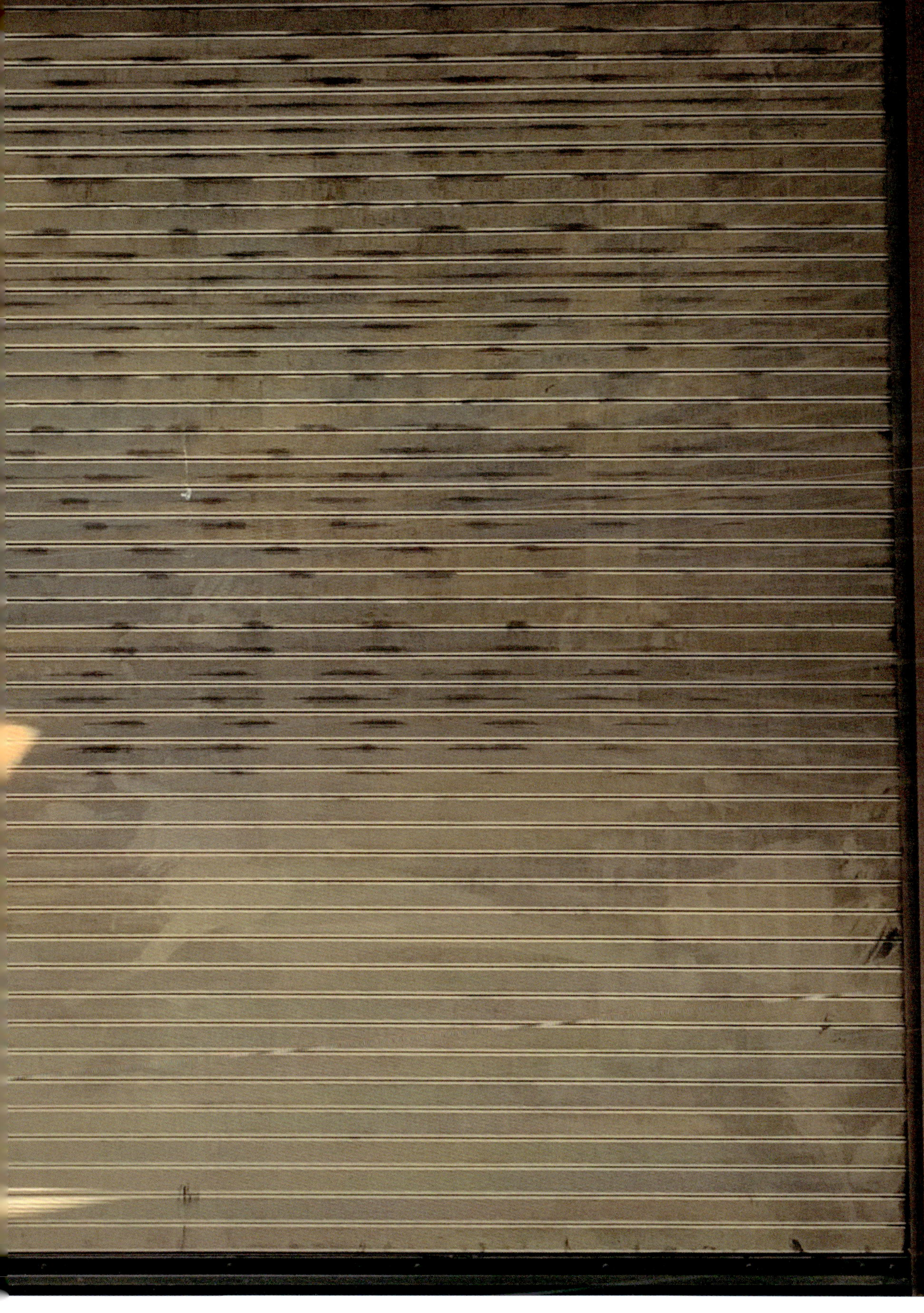

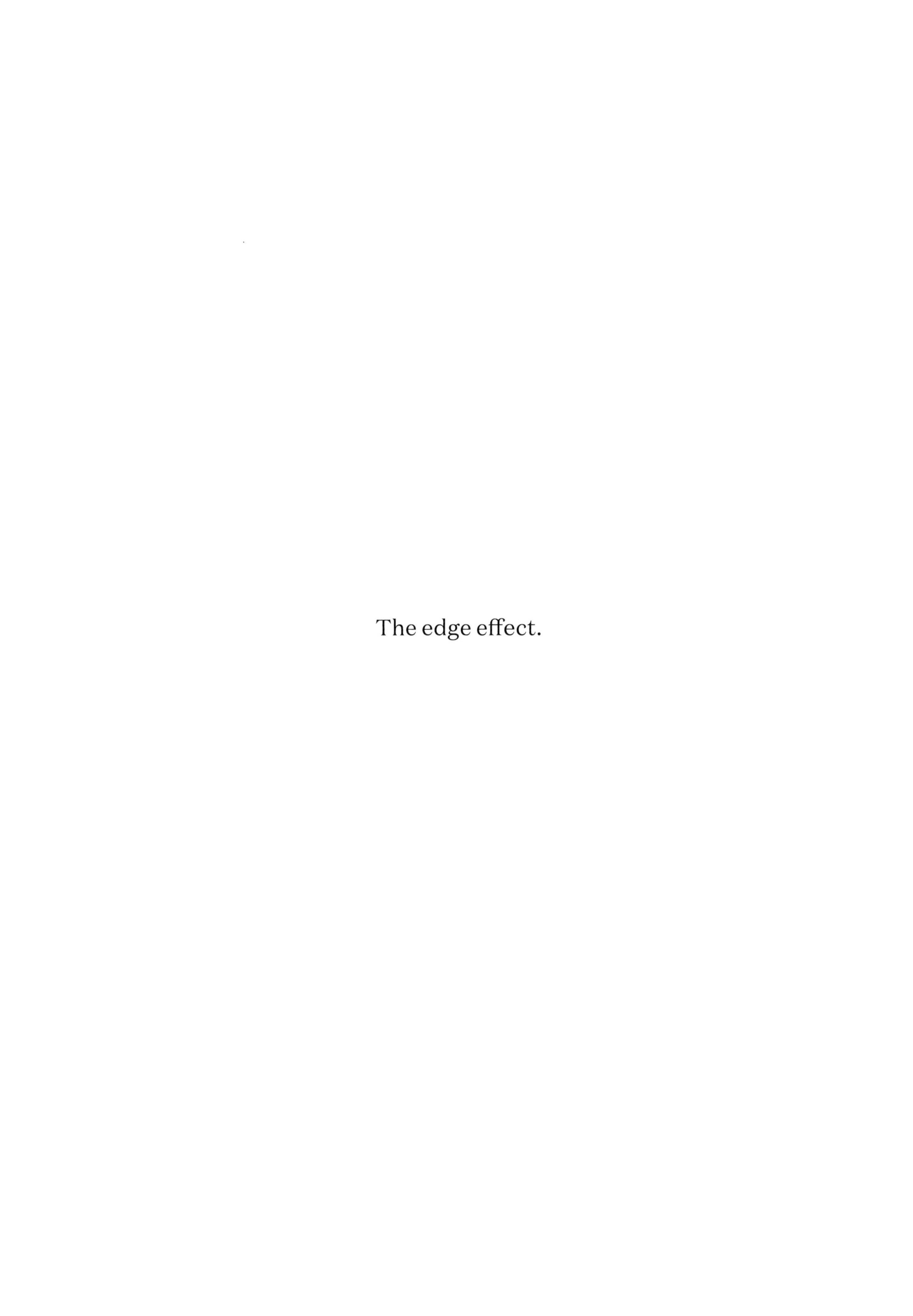

The edge effect.

You and I here.

Conversation, Janet Sternburg and Jane Bennett

Janet Sternburg (**JS**) with Jane Bennett (**JB**), philosopher and political theorist whose books include *The Enchantment of Modern Life* (Princeton University Press, 2001), *Vibrant Matter: A Political Ecology of Things* (Duke University Press, 2010), and *influx & efflux: Writing Up with Walt Whitman* (Duke University Press, 2020).

JB: I want to talk about the paragraph in your essay at the beginning of this book, where you write, "In a way that is new to me, these photographs are impersonal in the sense that they feel as though they have been given to me, appearing and accepted without my judgement." Could you say more about how you inhabit, in this book, being an impersonal thing in a gigantic world? In your other work, in both photography and writing, you're a person who has experiences that emerged out of a specific time and place, experiences that make up who you are. What is this new sense of impersonality that coursed through you?

JS: I'm using "impersonal" in my own particular way. I'm *not* using it to make distinctions between subjective and objective, not even between personal and impersonal, because I've always wanted to broaden the idea of personal to include history and science and politics and speculation.

JB: I don't see any of your work, whether in photography or writing, as being autobiographical in the traditional sense of that word. There's always a sense your being a body, a thing among other things.

JS: That's very interesting. I haven't thought about myself in those terms. Now I will. But to answer your question more directly, I want to talk about impersonal through the difference between seeing and seeking. In the past when I was taking photographs, I was looking for something that would become part of something larger. When I first started working in photography— twenty or so years ago—I became fascinated with disposable cameras because their limitations gave me images that raised philosophical questions for me. The camera allowed me to make use of reflection in such a way that everything appeared on a single plane. What was behind me and what was in front of me intermingled and interpenetrated, until you couldn't tell what was inside or outside, solid or fluid. I became so interested in that idea and the images it sparked that I went out in the world looking to take photographs of that kind.

Here's an example of what I mean by seeking: I was on a plane reading a guide-book to where I was going, an archipelago off the coast of Norway. I came across a photograph of a Dan Graham installation that really interested me. It seemed to say, "This is for me." I ended up seeing it at two in the morning during June, one of the months of white nights. It's a kind of pavilion on a promontory whose walls were made up of surfaces with an interplay between clear reflection and opacity. I used those surfaces as I'd been using windows.

None of that was in my mind when I went out this past year with my camera. I had no idea of what I'd find. I wasn't seeking. I was seeing. So "impersonal" means, I think, that intention had disappeared, and in its place came totally unexpected encounters.

JB: I first knew that you and I were on a similar wavelength when I saw that Wim Wenders had written on your work. In an early book of mine, I used a long quotation from a scene in his film *Wings of Desire*, where an angel comes across a man about to die on the street after a motorcycle crash. To comfort him, the angel begins listing the things about life that this man has loved: "the potato in the ashes, the Wild West, a white tablecloth, hopping...." It was just a list, but I think there's something about what Wenders does there, how he identifies discrete things, each packed with resonating forces, that you also do with your photographs.

JS: Yes. When I was out walking for this book, I felt as though I were seeing things in their habitats and they were speaking to me.

JB: The other thing I was thinking about your photographs was the way lines operate in them. In *Point Fermin* (p. 19), the lines behave in so many distinctive ways; it's like they're playing games with one another, having fun. I'm picturing a game where a bunch of kids are running around in an impromptu way, touching each other, and then escaping and running back and copying each other.

JS: Hearing you say that is very satisfying for me, because I tend to see my images as melancholy. I don't take photographs from that perspective, but afterward I often see them that way. I look at the *Point Fermin* image and I see a chair that suggests someone looking outward to the ocean--but the chair is uninhabited. Then, there's a spiral stairway that's connects the chair to an iron fence below, a guard rail of metal lines that arch backward, inward toward the house. I saw the image as ominous. You've added a completely other dimension for me.

JB: I want to talk about some of other photographs that I've singled out. *Branches & Stakes* (p. 48), for instance, is so simple and complex at the same time. There's foreground and background, there's a shadow, and then there's the blur of the shadow. There's also the sidewalk grid combined with the organic branching. There are all these co-presences.

JS: It took me a while to figure out what it was after I took it, because lines that are close together are straight and not straight. Then I saw that the straight lines are actually stakes holding up the tree. This is right outside the apartment building where I live. It's a very urban picture.

JB: My next choice, *Half Mile Ahead* (p. 42), is very different. In this photograph, there are so many time-scales superimposed on one another. It's like the super-slow time scale of a lichen, a gradual but relentless accretion over time. Super-slow, like a plant, sort of like a stone. That crusty stuff on the surface resembles and repeats lichen. Then you've got the speed of the highway. There's a curve ahead, and the sign suggests to me that it's dangerous. So, for me, this photograph moves at multiple speeds, different ones made of different materials. What do you see?

JS: I also see an intimation of danger and a question about those headlights that are from trucks coming to the rescue: will they arrive on time? That's a pretty literal question. I took this photograph at the CalTrans building in Downtown Los Angeles, where there's an exterior wall with recessed niches that contain old faded photographs of disasters with CalTrans coming to the rescue, which it does, from emergencies with animals to large-scale natural disasters. This past year, I stood in front of this wall many times, choosing a detail from each photograph and letting what was behind me also enter the picture. Of course there's no answer to my question. Like so much of this past year, time is suspended.

JB: In another one, *Vent* (p. 20), time is stilled. The composition couldn't be more perfect. Even that one little gap in the fence, that little space is perfect.

JS: I took this one from the passenger seat of a car. Passenger seats are my thing. I find I can see things on the move that I might not see if I were standing in front of them. You know, If someone said to me, "Do you like pipes and fences? And some kind of strange mirror?" I wouldn't know what to say. There's so much mystery...

There's one that I want to single out, *Toy District* (p. 63), which I took when I had recovered from my year of injuries and was able to go out into the world again. One of the things I love about this image is what's on the upper left. I'm not sure what it is, but I think it's a piece of wood with a circular hole at one end, perhaps for a dowel to go through. Another photographer might have cut that out, but to me it makes the picture. It roots the photograph in the world, so that it's not only an abstraction.

JB: What do you think about abstraction? I'm teaching a class on Dada and Surrealism this semester, and I'm just learning about it myself. I'm trying to get an education on what abstraction does, what work it performs. Adam Pendleton, speaking about Black. Dada, says that "abstraction is another word for freedom." Do you have thoughts about the abstract?

JS: That's an interesting formulation that I need to think about. But for now I can say that pure abstraction doesn't interest me. Certainly there are some abstract paintings that I appreciate, but what interests me more is that the world is full of abstraction that co-exists with the rootedness of the everyday. In my photographs, I want both the companionship of abstraction and the material fabric of the world.

JB: Another one of my favorites is *Fertile Confusion* (p. 50). I didn't even see the door for a long time, because I was just seeing the shapes and the contrast with the grid. I like those photographs where there's the geometrical and then the organic. With this one, it's like I'm sucked in down a wormhole.

JS: Let's call it a "wherehole," because in this image you really don't know where you are. Which I like. What I feel in this picture, and in a lot of my photographs, is that the everyday also contains something more. At one point I wanted to call my work "street photography as spiritual practice," but I thought that's a bit over-much, and "spiritual" can be such a cliché. So I don't call it that anymore. But I can say it to you, without fear of being over-much, because you know about being in the world this way, about something that alerts one to a presence larger than itself.

JB: I can't shake the idea that the world goes round by shimmering resemblances and connections. A focus on chasms between bodies, between things and places and people, this focus on the disconnect is just at one level of existence, which is, let's call it the political level or the social-structure level. I think that's a very small percentage of our existence. There's a level you could call the cosmic level. And also the kind of limbus level, you know, where things meld over and fold over at the edges, as you talked about in your exhibition of the same name at the USC Fisher Museum. Then there's the level of the everyday, the one you can't sense fully. It's on the edge of your perception. It's constantly there, haunting, not in a bad sense, always swirling around on the peripheries. And that's a really important part of our experience even though we don't focus on it that much. That brings me to one photograph I really wanted to get to, *Barbs & Stripes* (p. 67).

JS: This may seem weird, but I'm very fond of the inside of those cuffs—the shapes they make.

JB: Yes, those inside spaces of the cuffs are part of what makes the image dangerous because we're talking about something that's impaled on barbed wire. But that's not the essence of that picture. I didn't even notice those razor blades at first, but now I do and that makes the photograph even better.

JS: it's the left-behind, the abandoned, the trace. I gravitate to that. And again, I do not know why. But I find it moving in that sense of an object having agency.

JB: There are almost no people in your work. Why is that?

JS: I don't know. Years ago, I read something about objects to the effect that the poet speak for objects that cannot speak. It just hit me: yes objects do speak. And they interest me more.

JB: Although *Barbs & Stripes* is a still photograph, I can't convince my eyes that it's not in motion. The objects—the shirt: it's like a dancer, full of movement.

JS: I think we're both attracted to what's not fixed, to what doesn't stay in one place, to the state of becoming. I really like what you write about in *influx & efflux*: "the hover-time of transformation, during which the otherwise that entered makes a difference and is made different." That's like the edge effect that I write about in this book: the threshold, the adjacency, and abutting of habitats that create change. I know I'll change again in my work, and with whatever that change brings it will incorporate everything I've done before. There's a line that resonates with me, which I'll have to paraphrase because I read it so long ago. I often return to it. It's what the filmmaker Jean Vigo once said when he was asked why he made his films: "I had an itch that wouldn't let go of me. I had to scratch it." For Vigo, the scratching is the film. For me, the itch is the personal that happened to me, then lodged inside and I couldn't let it go. The scratch is the impersonal, a means in this book of letting go. That said, we're amalgams of everything, aren't we?

JB: Do you think it would be good if I were to write a short piece on your work, maybe only one page? Or would you prefer to just craft this conversation for the book?

JS: If I were to do tell the truth—and it's a greedy truth—the answer is both.

JB: Yes. I think I do want to write something short. On Sunday morning, I'll sit down with my coffee and I'll try to write something.

****

JS: And so it became an afterword.

Walking the Line

Jane Bennett

"Where have you been? How have you come to be here?"

"I've been walking," replies Janet Sternburg, and she shows me her photographs.

Before either of us can say more, the lines in the pictures pipe up—
"We've been walking too!"

How can lines walk? Paul Klee explains: they are the perambulations of points. The line, he says, is the effect of the "primordial movement" of a point, "a point that sets itself in motion (genesis of form)."

A point ignites and goads itself onward as line: "It goes out for a walk, so to speak, aimlessly for the sake of the walk."

A line strides outward, forward, backward, sideways, laying down paths of different speeds and shapes: languid tendril, intense curlicue, billowy fringe, serpentine arch, fractal branch, recursive fold, diffuse swarm, restless zigzag, straight or detouring arrow. A lineal (because not always linear) creature "About to take a trip":

More Klee: "Things on earth are obstructed in their movement; they require an impetus." The primordial movement, the agent, is a point that goes for a stroll.

In each of Sternburg's absorbent and absorbing photographs, we are shown the active lines that met her on her walks around L.A.:

deviant lines of mini-blinds
bronchial lines of weeds in pavement crack
smooth bend of chair arm
arched arrows of fence tops
ragged zag of plastic tarp
angular redirections of roof lines
circular blur of leaf-shadows
bounce-lines of clouds
plump lunge of a graffiti W
grid-lines of bathroom tile
delicate skateboard-curve
elegant, violent swoosh of razor wire

These lines, like the photographer herself, form what Gerald Raunig describes (in *Dividuum: Machinic Capitalism and Molecular Revolution*) as a "rhythmic pulse on its way elsewhere."

Sternburg's photographs display these active lines and their "lyrical force." Lyrical force is Roger Caillois's name (in his 1935 "The Praying Mantis: From Biology to Psychoanalysis") for the power of an object or a body or an image or a shape or a text to “act directly on the emotions to an exceptional degree,” to, that is, make an impress/impression that did not need to have first passed through the filter of consciousness.

In Sternburg’s meditative book of writings, *Phantom Limb*, there appears this beautiful and haunting “line”: “the pain of the human condition is death, the one condition we never get over. And it means we all lose parts of ourselves along the way. No one survives intact. No one is exempt. In that democracy of sorrow lies our consolation.” In *I’ve Been Walking*, Sternburg now gives us another site of consolation, that of the lively line which accompanies us wherever we go.

About the Artist

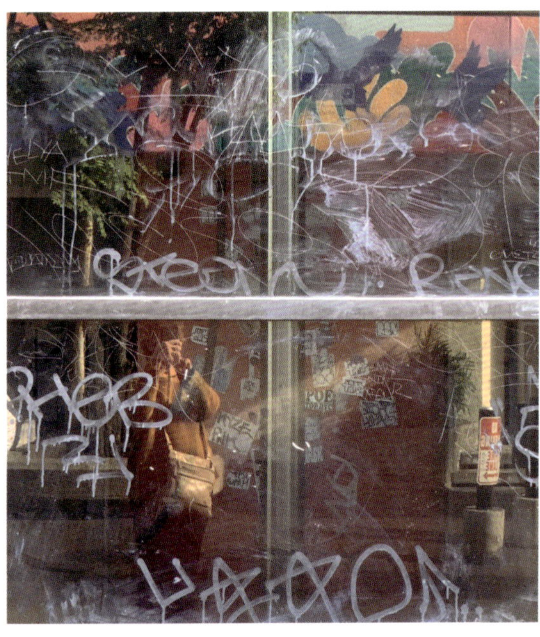

Janet Sternburg is a fine art photographer, a writer of literary books, a maker of theatre and films, and an educator.

Since 1998 when she began taking photographs, her work has appeared in *Aperture* (2002), that same year on the cover of *Art Journal,* and in 2003 in *The Utne Reader* ("A New Lens," 2003), in which she was selected as one of forty international artist and writers who "with depth, resonance, ideas and insights, challenge us to live more fully." A monograph of her photographs, *Overspilling World: The Photographs of Janet Sternburg,* was published in 2016–17 by Distanz Verlag with a Foreword by Wim Wenders in which he writes, "Photographers don't have eyes in the back of their heads. Janet Sternburg does."

Her photography has been exhibited in solo shows in New York, Los Angeles, Berlin, Milan, Munich, Mexico and Korea, where she received a commission for a full-building installation at Seoul Institute of the Arts. In 2018, the USC Fisher Museum of the Arts presented her solo show LIMBUS. She pioneered in the use of disposable cameras to create images in which elements interpenetrate, a visual world without borders.

Her literary books include the classic two volumes of *The Writer on Her Work,* (W.W. Norton, 1981 and 1991, called "landmarks" and "groundbreaking" by *Poets & Writers* magazine; her papers for that book are now archived at the Harry Ransom Center, University of Texas. Other critically praised books followed, among them *Phantom Limb* (University of Nebraska American Lives Series, 2002) and *White Matter* (Hawthorne Books, 2016), both using a hybrid form of memoir and essay to probe family, neurology, and history, as well as a collection of poetry, *Optic Nerve: Photopoems* (Red Hen Press, 2005).

Other creative work includes her film, *El Teatro Campesino,* a feature length documentary on the Chicano theatre troupe (1969) selected for the New York Film Festival at Lincoln Center; her film *Virginia Woolf The Moment Whole* (1971), broadcast on National Educational Television and winner of a Cine Golden Eagle, as well as her play, *The Fifth String* (2011–2014) about Arab and Jewish expulsions throughout history, produced in Berlin, New York, and Los Angeles.

Sternburg lives in Downtown Los Angeles' Little Tokyo, and San Miguel de Allende, Mexico. She has been the recipient of numerous grants, fellowships and artist residencies, among them from the National Endowment for the Humanities and The MacDowell Colony. She has taught in the Graduate Media Program at the New School University, and in the Critical Studies School at the California Institute of the Arts. In 2016 she was co-recipient of the REDCAT AWARD, given to "individuals who exemplify the creativity and talent that define and lead the evolution of contemporary culture. "

List of Works

Cover image:
Mother Courage

For the most part, the photographs in this book were taken in Los Angeles in 2020.